Canada on the Doorstep

Canada on the Doorstep
1939

William Rayner

DUNDURN
TORONTO

Editor: Nicole Chaplin
Design: Jesse Hooper
Printer: Webcom

Library and Archives Canada Cataloguing in Publication

Rayner, William, 1929-
    Canada on the doorstep : 1939 / by William Rayner.

Includes bibliographical references and index.
Also issued in electronic formats.
ISBN 978-1-55488-992-1

    1. Canada--History--1918-1939. I. Title.

FC580.R39 2011   971.063   C2011-903773-4

1   2   3   4   5   15   14   13   12   11

Conseil des Arts du Canada   Canada Council for the Arts   Canadä   ONTARIO ARTS COUNCIL CONSEIL DES ARTS DE L'ONTARIO

We acknowledge the support of the **Canada Council for the Arts** and the **Ontario Arts Council** for our publishing program. We also acknowledge the financial support of the **Government of Canada** through the **Canada Book Fund** and **Livres Canada Books**, and the **Government of Ontario** through the **Ontario Book Publishing Tax Credit** and the **Ontario Media Development Corporation**.

Care has been taken to trace the ownership of copyright material used in this book. The author and the publisher welcome any information enabling them to rectify any references or credits in subsequent editions.

J. Kirk Howard, President

Printed and bound in Canada.
www.dundurn.com

Dundurn
3 Church Street, Suite 500
Toronto, Ontario, Canada
M5E 1M2

Gazelle Book Services Limited
White Cross Mills
High Town, Lancaster, England
LA1 4XS

Dundurn
2250 Military Road
Tonawanda, NY
U.S.A. 14150

Dedicated to the memory of my Little Sunbeam, 1928–2009

Experience is the club with which an elder generation beats the young – but if no-one can truly say what happened, and why, in history, the experience of the outgoing elders is less relevant than they may care to think.

— EDMOND STILLMAN, 1969

Contents

Introduction

In the year of our lord 1939, Bobby Hull, Brian Mulroney, Margaret Atwood, and William Ian Corneil Binnie were born. A famous hockey player, a much-scorned politician, an award-winning author, and a noted jurist, all of these Canadians joined the scattered, querulous, hesitant, schizo Dominion during a year that would become a turning point in Canadian history.

Nineteen thirty-nine was not your typical year. Arriving at the tail end of the Great Depression, it was a year in which many Canadians wondered what it was all about and what the future held. We still saluted Great Britain's Union Jack and a respected member of the peerage occupied the governor general's mansion, but to some the British Empire was little more than a scattering of pretty pink blobs on a Mercator projection of the world. Squeezed between the alluring republicanism of America to the south and our restless, French-Canadian appendage on the other side of the Ottawa River, English-speaking Canada plodded into 1939 not quite sure where it was headed.

The Dominion would find out soon enough. For anyone planning an old-fashioned Hollywood epic about 1939, it had everything: drama, spectacle, suspense, even a touch of low comedy. There was a visit from the King and Queen of England; a world hockey championship won by a small-town team from British Columbia; and the first graceful steps of the Royal Winnipeg Ballet. On the other hand, there was the hostile reaction within political circles to the Mackenzie-Papineau Battalion's participation in the Spanish Civil War, and the official act of governmental anti-Semitism that denied asylum to a boatload of

Jewish refugees. This was also the year that saw the start of the Second World War. In itself, this did not constitute the watershed that would forever separate Canada from its beginnings, but the dramatic plunge into hostilities was a major factor.

To those living in the wireless, electronic, computerized, cellphone-infested world of the twenty-first century, Canada of 1939 was of another time and place. The population was rounded out to 11,267,000. The prime minister was William Lyon Mackenzie King and his Liberal government had a healthy majority in the House of Commons. At the beginning of the year, provincial governments were also Liberal, except in Quebec, where Maurice Duplessis's Union nationale machine held sway, and Alberta, where a bunch of monetary mavericks called the Social Credit League had ousted the United Farmers in 1935. (Manitoba's Liberals had a double-barrelled name — Liberal-Progressive.)

Canada had nine provinces in 1939; Newfoundland, which would join Confederation in 1949, was a failed Dominion under United Kingdom administration after going broke in 1934. Up north, along with the Yukon, there were three Northwest Territory districts named Franklin, Keewatin, and Mackenzie, and Inuit were still called Eskimos.

In the cities, mail was delivered twice a day, Monday to Friday, and once on Saturdays. Some daily newspapers cost three cents. Doctors made house calls. In department stores and office buildings, elevator operators would pilot you to the floor of your choice. Telephone exchanges still had such names as *PA*cific, *AD*elaide, *EL*gin, *UN*iversity, *JU*niper, and *MA*in, and many homes that could afford basic black phones attached to their walls were on party lines with two or more subscribers. When you recognized your own distinct ring, you picked up the receiver (or, as was the custom, listened in anyway). Those without a home connection either ran across the street to the neighbour's, or hunted down an old-fashioned telephone booth. A local call would set you back a nickel, as did a bottle of Coke, and the Saturday matinee at the neighbourhood movie theatre (double feature, cartoons, and a newsreel) could be enjoyed for a dime.

Hardly anybody just hopped into the car and drove to the super-market. In fact, there were no supermarkets as we know them in the today — and not that many cars. Family-run confectioneries and butcher shops serviced their neighbourhoods, although chains such as Safeway, Piggly Wiggly, A&P, and Red and White Stores were well-established on the urban landscape. The ubiquitous credit card was still several years in the future, but some customers were allowed to charge their purchases, with the expectation the bill would be settled at the end of the month (during the Great Depression, not an easy thing to do). Almost everything was delivered, usually by a lad gingerly balancing a cardboard box of goods on his bicycle's handlebars. "Cash and Carry" was also available. At these stores, you paid up front (thereby saving a few pennies) and carted your groceries home yourself, often in your son's Radio Flyer wagon. For the youngsters, there were candy counters in almost every corner grocery. For pennies, they gained possession of such delicacies as jawbreakers, sourballs, and licorice whips (my favourites were the red ones).

Trucks or horse-drawn wagons delivered the necessities: milk, bread, coal, ice. In the hot summer, the ice wagon's appearance was a welcome sight. Kids would wait for the driver to take up his huge tongs, clap them onto a block of ice, swing it onto his shoulder, and make his delivery. The kids would scoop up slivers of ice from the wooden floor of the wagon and pelt down the street, sucking on their prizes. Some cities also had retail icehouses, where cost-conscious consumers could save by sending a sturdy son and his wagon to collect the block of ice. In Winnipeg, for instance, there was an icehouse on Sargent Avenue near Sherbrooke Street, and anyone within a couple of miles would buy from there directly. The thing to do was put the block in your wagon, cover it with a piece of burlap, then drag the wagon pell-mell toward home as fast as you could so that only a minimum of ice melted.

The ice, of course, was for the ice box in the kitchen. Although refrigerators were available, they were not yet widely used. These could be bought at department stores, of which there was a considerable variety. Apart from the Hudson's Bay Company and Eaton's, both of which survived into this century, the shoppers' too-few dollars were sought after by the likes of Morgan's, Simpson's, Robinson's, Woodward's, R.H. Williams's, Ogilvy's, and Spencer's. Not to mention the five-and-dime stores S.S. Kresge and Woolworth's.

The big stores routinely chose the evening paper to advertise both the luxuries and necessities of life, since newspapers delivered in the late afternoon were in the majority in 1939. Paper boys would congregate at neighbourhood newspaper shacks in vacant lots around 4:30 p.m. and collect their bundles. Rain or shine or snow, six days a week, the lads would deposit a rolled-up or folded newspaper at somebody's front door — or toss it on the porch, on the lawn, or in the hedge, depending on their aim and dedication.

Many of these evening papers have fallen victim to that harsh mistress called the bottom line, or switched to morning circulation to avoid traffic problems that didn't exist in 1939. The *Toronto Telegram* is no longer with us, nor is the *Winnipeg Tribune*, the *Montreal Star* or the *Edmonton Bulletin*, to name just a few. The dominant newspaper proprietor was the Southam Company, with dailies in most major cities outside Toronto.

Because television was little more than a technological oddity in 1939, the daily paper was the primary link between the merchant and the consumer. Stores and advertisers strained to corral every stubborn Depression dollar. A refurbished electric washing machine could be had for $29.50, and a forty-ounce bottle of White Horse scotch went for $4.80. The one-cent sale had been born by this time (buy one item for the regular price and get another for an additional cent). On weekends, drugstores might run an eight-cent sale. Buyers could get such esoterica as an ounce of aromatic cascara or two ounces of distilled extract of witch hazel for that bargain price.

While there was no TV for the masses, they had their radios. Programs ranged from soap operas, westerns, crime, and adventure serials to gospel broadcasts and both classical and popular music. Most papers ran daily schedules for the four U.S. networks — NBC Red and Blue, Mutual, and Columbia — as well as the CBC, local programming, and shortwave stations. Gossip, features, and occasional tips on shortwave reception rounded out the package.

In 1939, ordinary Canadians were only dimly aware of the metric system. They talked of inches and feet and miles, of pounds, ounces, and tonnes with only one *n*. When somebody said it was twenty below outside, they meant Fahrenheit. Nobody had to translate it into or out of Celsius.

Trains were a big part of everyday life. Trans-Canada Air Lines was in its infancy and steam ruled the transportation scene. Pulled by locomotives that ranged from small, utilitarian, and often decrepit to powerful, streamlined giants, passenger trains took people almost everywhere. The faster, more important ones had names like Dominion, Continental Limited, Washingtonian, International Limited, Chicago Express, Ambassador, and Mountaineer. Both the Canadian Pacific Railway (CPR) and Canadian National Railways (CNR) crisscrossed the country from coast to coast. You could also catch a fast express train to such exotic American destinations as Boston, New York, Detroit, Washington, Chicago, and even Minneapolis.

The local, bread-and-butter stops weren't forgotten, either, because the CPR and CNR weren't just in the people-moving business. They also transported goods, farm products, and raw materials — the freight that kept commerce functioning. Both railways had routes fanning out to every point of the compass from the hub cities: Montreal, Toronto, Winnipeg, Calgary, and Edmonton. From one of these stations, you could catch a train or ship to such stops as South Stukely, Zorra, or Old Wives Lake; Winnipegosis, Moosonee, or Carrot River. A lot of these plodding trains were "mixed," their consists a blend of passenger and freight cars.

The Great Depression exacted a measurable toll on the railway business. By 1939, some timetables had been cut back or eliminated. Weeds grew on more than a few branch lines. And a noticeable reduction in traffic forced the two transportation giants to reluctantly pool their passenger trains between Toronto and both Ottawa and Montreal.

After almost a decade of hard times, jobs were still scarce. Stock markets were functioning, profits were being made and the commodities future looked a little brighter, but your average Canadian couldn't help wonder now and then what good it did being a member of something called the British Empire (or British Commonwealth, in some circles). That was Canada, more or less, in 1939, presided over by George VI, King of England and all her Dominions.

Ah, the king. Pale-faced, delicate, shy. They called King George VI "Bertie" before he was thrust onto the throne by the abdication of his elder brother, Edward, three years earlier. King George VI and Queen Elizabeth's railroad journey from sea to sea in the spring of 1939, with the ominous clouds of war barely visible on the horizon, endeared the Royal Couple not only to moms, dads, and schoolchildren of every age, but also the weary farmer, the sullen jobless, and the top-hatted captains

A bandaged right hand is cheerfully displayed by His Majesty after catching his fingers in a door on the Royal Train.

of industry alike. When it was over, Canadians were — somehow — more united, more aware of the Empire they were part of, and Bertie had emerged from his shell to become a people's king.

The warm regard and fuzzy sentiments engendered by the Royal Visit were still evident when war began in September 1939. However, Canada being Canada, and Mackenzie King being Mackenzie King, we did not immediately gallop into the fray with sabres flashing. Instead, it took the Dominion seven days to join Great Britain in the fight against Nazi Germany.

Reluctant combatants, perhaps (at least at the political level), but Canada was nevertheless firmly wedded to the Empire. As at the start of the Great War in 1914, old scores were left unsettled, the haughty Colonial Office mindset of the Westminster mandarins went ignored, and the chatter about Canada going it alone were replaced by patriotic fervour. No more insidious isolationism championed by powerful voices in the United States and Quebec. No more talk of breaking up the con-federation and repudiating the mother country.

The pain of the Great Depression had forced Canadians to question their very self-worth and their raison d'être. There was a sense that the country was drifting, with no clear destination on the horizon. A new trade agreement between Ottawa and Washington had made it a little easier to live next door to those pushy neighbours across the border, and the European connection became increasingly more tenuous. But when 1939 came to a close — amid dogged preparations for war — any doubts had been laid to rest by the unquestioned acceptance of our British heritage and by memories of a smiling, approachable Bertie and his beautiful consort.

January

Out on the Swiftsure Bank, at the entrance to the Strait of Juan de Fuca, crewmen aboard the wildly tossing lightship logged the wind strength as Force 10 and made sure their oilskins were securely fastened. Torrential rain was sheeting in from the southwest and the seas were getting steeper by the hour.

The year 1939 was roaring in like a lion, riding a Pacific Ocean storm that brought death, destruction, and millions of tons of rain to the west coast of British Columbia. The storm swept over Victoria, flooding some sections of the city, ripping pleasure boats away from their moorings in the Inner Harbour, and uprooting trees in Beacon Hill Park. Then it bore down on the inner coast of Vancouver Island, pummelling the Island Highway north from Nanaimo with washouts and mudslides. A provincial works employee was electrocuted at the height of the storm on New Year's Day when a power pole toppled and a high-tension wire was whipped across the highway.

On the outer coast, several vessels were reported in distress. A fishboat went missing in the raging seas, never to be seen again. The British-registered freighter SS *Boulderpool* had to return to Victoria after her load of prime British Columbian lumber was washed away at the entrance to the Strait.

Rain plagued the Lower Mainland. A Vancouver newspaper estimated that thirteen million tons had fallen on the city during the holiday weekend. In the Fraser Valley, some farmers had to use rowboats to get from their houses to their barns. Inland, both the Canadian Pacific and Canadian National rail links were severed for several hours by washouts, mudslides, and a derailment near North Bend.

The storm had passed by the time Richard Bedford Bennett began stirring up a wee tempest of his own. The former prime minister, who was emigrating to Great Britain, launched his farewell tour of Canada by warning a Vancouver audience that the dark forces of discord were threatening the fabric of the Dominion. A staunch defender of all things Imperial, the Conservative Party's elder statesman was disturbed by evidence that internal conflicts over the country's role in the British Empire had led many Depression-weary Canadians to ponder American-style isolationism.

He had a point. Canada's honeymoon with the mother country had actually begun to unravel scarcely thirty-five years earlier when Great Britain colluded with the United States in the matter of the Alaska Panhandle. The year was 1903, and six "impartial jurists of repute" — who were not impartial at all — awarded Washington almost every inch of territory it demanded in its dispute with Canada over the Alaska– British Columbia boundary.

Prime Minister Sir Wilfrid Laurier retaliated four years later when he declined to support a plan calling for every Dominion in the Empire to supply the Royal Navy with battleships. Sir Wilfrid eventually lost an election over reciprocity with the United States. However, the lesson of 1903 had not been forgotten, although the jingoism of the Great War would keep patriotic hearts beating for a while.

Heightening the sense of abandonment was the cruel reality of the Great Depression. By the end of 1938, many Prairie dwellers were demoralized. Disillusioned by the apparent failure of existing institutions and accepted values, their mood was anti-immigrant, anti-refugee, and anti-Semitic. Farmers had gone deeply in debt early in the decade, expecting that grain prices would remain high. When wheat sank to thirty-four cents a bushel and the banks started foreclosing, many Canadians were convinced the system was broken. Despite Imperial Preference, which ostensibly gave the Dominions a break when trading with Britain, the erection of high tariff walls in every civilized country left the farmer in the field and the worker on the shop floor — if he had a job at all — with little to live on. Surely, many thought, a continental "Fortress America" liaison with the United States could do no worse.

"Whither?" R.B. Bennett asked a luncheon audience of 1,250 in the Crystal Ballroom of the Hotel Vancouver (soon to be replaced by a newer version two blocks to the west). "Where are we going in Canada?" He pointed out that there were 120 million people living south of the border and only eleven million in Canada, but this didn't mean the Dominion should succumb.

"We are a small nation occupying the northern half of this continent," he said. "The unconscious pull of the tremendous nation to the south, the unconscious influence of the radio, transportation, speech, ideals are all at work in Canada.... Eleven million people can't stand up to that sort of thing alone. We must belong to some economic group."

That group, he said, was the British Empire.

Internal differences also contributed to the perception that Canada was coming apart, the former prime minister said. "Take for instance the proposition that one of our provinces threatens that it may secede. Do not take these things seriously; they are evidences of democracy itself. But I am not unmindful of the fact that the creation of prejudices between east and west contributes to these things."

In conclusion, Bennett said, "we must decide whether we will remain in the British Empire or cast in our economic lot with our great neighbours. But our young men must decide now their answers to the question: 'Whither shall we go?'" Indeed. As Bennett continued his farewell tour eastward, "Whither Canada?" was a question lurking in Ottawa's nooks and crannies when Members and Senators assembled for the fourth session of the eighteenth Parliament.

Lord Tweedsmuir, the governor general, read the Speech from the Throne in the red and gold Senate Chamber on January 12, 1939. The recitation of the Liberal government's intentions was the usual confection of high-flown phrases, but did contain a few interesting nuggets. Prime Minister William Lyon Mackenzie King, when drafting the speech, had sensed that 1939 would be an extraordinary year — there was the Royal Visit of Their Majesties in the spring; the vexatious unemployment situation; a trade deal with the United States to be ratified; the refugee

problem; and the ominous news from Europe — so he took extra care.
In fact, the prime minister was still rewriting the speech the day before
it was to be presented. That afternoon, King had shown the final draft
to Lord Tweedsmuir at Government House. Tweedsmuir, who was the
novelist John Buchan when in civilian dress, noted that it was a bit long,
but "very good. The best of speeches so far."

Lord Tweedsmuir was the governor general of Canada until his untimely death in early 1940.

"My ministers have found it necessary to give anxious and continuous consideration to developments in the international situation and their effects upon Canada," the governor general told the Chamber the next day. Therefore, he said, "the government have considered that the uncertainties of the future and the conditions of modern warfare make it imperative Canada's defences be materially strengthened." To this end, the government will "vigorously" pursue a program of modernization and expansion, with particular emphasis on air defence.

"Legislation will be introduced to establish a defence purchasing board, with power to purchase equipment for the defence services and to ensure that, where private manufacture is necessary, profits in connection with such are fair and reasonable, and the public interest is protected."

This last, unexpected reference was obviously Prime Minister King's attempt to defuse the Bren Gun Scandal, which had been simmering for several months. In September 1938, George Drew, a Conservative politician in Ontario, had accused the governments of Canada and Great Britain of making a secret sweetheart deal with

The controversial Bren gun plant in Toronto, subject of much debate in Janaury, was in full swing in December 1939.

Library and Archives Canada, e00760063

a Toronto businessman to manufacture Bren light-machine guns. A Royal Commission, chaired by Justice H.H. Davis, considered Drew's charges for two months. His report, which had reached Prime Minister King's desk on December 30, made one solid recommendation: place the purchase of munitions and armaments into the hands of competent business men rather than those of the defence department.

The throne speech also promised an expanded program of public works, emphasizing aid to municipalities. As an alternative to direct relief, this aid was coupled with grants-in-aid to provinces "to assist in the care of those suffering from unemployment and agricultural distress."

Noting that "the problem of unemployment has been aggravated in recent years, by recurrent crop failures in the western provinces," the speech announced that the Prairie farm rehabilitation plan would be continued, and that legislation would be introduced to regulate grain exchanges.

The Bren Gun Report was tabled in the House during the first two days of the session. It was little more than a recitation of evidence, but Justice Davis cleared anyone connected with the government of any wrongdoing. Drew's article in *Maclean's* (for which he was paid $750) claimed that a Toronto businessman named James Hahn had resurrected the James Inglis Company, a bankrupt boiler manufacturer, through a court order. Hahn had then conspired, Drew said, with Defence Minister Ian Mackenzie and British officials to secretly set up the Bren gun facility, clearly implying that the deal bordered on patronage and corruption. Not only that, he wrote, "for good or evil, the stage is now set for the private manufacture in Canada of primary implements of war."

Justice Davis refused to rule on whether it was proper for a government to make private arrangements for the production of war materiel, claiming that the question fell into the realm of government policy and was therefore not one of his terms of reference. To the *Vancouver Daily Province*, this was simple evasion and not good enough.

"Mr. Justice Davis leaves it to government and Parliament to say whether the Bren gun contracts were properly and responsibly given out by a government department to be performed," said an editorial.

The strong implication of the evidence is that they were let to a man who was a friend of friends of the government party, and that he was recommended to the British government by a department of the Canadian government, on no apparent better justification than that he was a very good party friend. And it is a fact that he got the contracts by way of private negotiation, and did not have to win them in competition with anyone else.... The unctuous assumption that there was nothing to justify investigation at all, is a little too much.

The Toronto contract was in fact Prime Minister King's attempt to have his cake and eat it, too. On one hand, producing arms for both Canada and Great Britain would create jobs and also be a step toward bolstering the Dominion's woeful defence posture. On the other hand, however, an open alliance with the British on arms procurement would signal that Canada was too closely allied to the Empire's war machine. The answer was two — not one — contracts quietly negotiated with a private firm. Mackenzie King's insertion of the defence purchasing board proposal into the throne speech was an optimistic attempt to minimize flak from the Opposition benches.

That parliamentary session was the first for Robert James Manion, the new Opposition leader. When Manion was selected at the July 1938 Conservative Convention, Mackenzie King sniffed that he was the most distasteful of the candidates to replace R.B. Bennett. "The Tory party likes men of bitter tongue," he wrote in his diary, and the new leader seemed to be from the same mould. Although, Mackenzie King wrote, "he had a generous side to his nature."

The first skirmish on the House floor between the two leaders came during the reply to the throne speech. Manion had moved the obligatory amendment expressing regret that the government had failed to deal adequately with the economic crisis, but then made several references to the strained relationship between Mackenzie King and Mitchell Hepburn, the Liberal premier of Ontario. The outspoken, erratic Hepburn had feuded with the prime minister for years over their differing versions of Liberalism, and was being particularly obstreperous that winter.

For his part, Prime Minister King took issue with several of Manion's arguments. He accused the Tory leader of attempting to create animosity between Canada and the United States by criticizing Washington's foreign policies. The exchange between the two was restrained, though, and lacked the accumulated bitterness of Prime Minister King's relationship with Bennett.

January 1939 also witnessed the repudiation of one political movement and the quiet death of another. On January 2, as the West Coast was being buffeted by Mother Nature, voters in Toronto turned out in record numbers to deny Communist Party of Canada leader Tim Buck a seat on the city's board of control. Some 146,424 citizens — 20,000 more than ever before — responded to what was essentially a Red Scare orchestrated by the press, the Roman Catholic Church, and a coalition of industrial, business, and veterans groups to hand Buck his fourth straight defeat in municipal elections.

The voters also ousted both a Communist alderman and a school trustee, leaving just one alderman to carry the party banner. Buck attracted more than 45,000 votes, but still finished sixth in a nine-man race for the four-seat board of control (which, along with Mayor Ralph C. Day, essentially ran the city's business).

The campaign against Buck's "reformist pretensions" reached its climax on the day before the vote when Father Charles Lanphier, a Roman Catholic priest, claimed in his Sunday radio sermon that a Buck victory would lead to Canadian Christians being "butchered by the millions and made [the] pitiable, miserable, heart-rending spectacles that Russia and Spain have offered to a horrified world."

The result stunned both Buck and the CPC, who had made success at the municipal level a priority (with the ultimate goal being a Communist ensconced as mayor of a major Canadian city). Buck had steadily increased his support in every Toronto election since 1936 and the party hierarchy felt this was the year his message of popular reform would carry the day. It didn't. Tim Buck never won an election at any level of government.

On January 19, at its Calgary convention, the United Farmers of Alberta decided to abandon the political sphere it had entered exactly twenty years earlier. Like similar organizations in Ontario and Manitoba, the UFA had become disillusioned with traditional politics following the First World War, and voted to do something about established, big-city parties indifferent to rural Canada. "We as farmers are downtrodden by every other class," declared H.W. Wood, UFA leader in 1919. "We have grovelled and been ground into the dirt; we are determined that this shall not be. We will organize for our protection; we will nourish ourselves and gain strength, and then we shall strike out in our might and overthrow our enemies."

Overthrow them they did. In the 1921 provincial election, the United Farmers swept away the Liberal incumbents and formed the government. They would stay in office for fourteen years. United Farmers in Ontario and Manitoba had similar success. In Ontario, the UFO won the largest number of seats in the 1919 provincial election and formed a coalition government with the Independent Labour Party. In 1922, the UFM won the Manitoba provincial election.

On the federal level, the United Farmers of Alberta managed to send eleven Members of Parliament to the House of Commons in 1926. The number shrank to nine in 1930 when Bennett's Conservatives took office. Prime Minister King's Liberal juggernaut of 1935 gobbled up those nine MPs, despite the UFA's liaison with the newly-formed Co-operative Commonwealth Federation (CCF). In 1932, many UFA members had become disenchanted with the Alberta government's answer to the Great Depression: curtailling spending and raising taxes. What was needed, the parent group said, was a broad program stressing economic changes to relieve Canadians from poverty. At a meeting in Calgary that August, representatives from several organizations agreed to unite with the UFA under the banner of the CCF. Three years later, the UFA lost the provincial election to William Aberhart and his Social Credit League. By 1939, membership in the UFA had shrunk to approximately 7,000 — from a peak of 37,721 in 1921. The lone United Farmer in the House of Commons came from Ontario.

Originally conceived as a farm lobby group, the UFA's 1939 decision at the Calgary convention ended all affiliations and political activities, and redirected its efforts to the educational and economic action fields.

In a nation's capital, one does not live by debates alone. There are social engagements, discreet tête-à-têtes, official functions, and all manner of distractions competing for the attention of the political class. One of the more glittering events of January 1939 was the formal ball marking the opening of the new French Legation in Ottawa. Situated on a bluff overlooking Rideau Falls, the three-storey building was designed as both an embassy and the residence of Comte Robert de Dampierre, the French Ambassador to Canada. Mackenzie King himself laid the cornerstone of the edifice on Bastille Day 1936, and was on hand that January evening along with Lord and Lady Tweedsmuir and 700 other guests.

Press reports gushed about the seventeenth-century Gobelin tapestry lining one wall of the huge ballroom, the floor-to-ceiling windows banded in brass, opalescent folding doors, wide mirrors, and the *petit salon*, where "bowls of lilies were effectively used against the blue satin hangings." Prime Minister King, however, was not impressed.

"Personally, I am greatly disappointed in the new legation," he wrote in his diary. "It is an attempt to be modern in design, decoration, etc., with the result that the whole business is, to me, almost a nightmare. The rooms are like great boxes, the halls overdone with descriptive scenes, some of them none to pleasant to look at. It really made me a little sad to see France, once so truly represented by artistic beauty, being represented at this time by what seems to be a distinct deterioration in architecture and other forms of art."

Among the visitors to Prime Minister King's office during January was Premier Thomas Dufferin Pattullo of British Columbia, along with his finance minister, John Hart. Duff Pattullo was one of the nagging provincial thorns in the federal government's hide, along with William Aberhart of Alberta, Mitchell Hepburn of Ontario, and Maurice Duplessis of Quebec. Each one regularly sought the most favoured province status, in the form of budget grants, increased autonomy, or — in the case of Aberhart — unconstitutional legislation. Both Pattullo and Hart had made earlier trips to Ottawa in an attempt to cajole Bennett and then Mackenzie King into loosening the federal purse strings. Pattullo had won an election in 1933 with the slogan, "Work and Wages," which smacked of socialism to the prime minister. Privately, Mackenzie King wondered if the Liberal premier would become a liability to the party.

"He entertains absurd ideas about the extent to which public monies should be spent at this time," Mackenzie King confided to his diary after a 1936 confrontation with Pattullo. This latest visit, however, had more to do with the Asiatic hordes across the Pacific than with economic packages. Pattullo and Hart were pitching one of their favourite projects: the Alaska Highway.

Pattullo had been pushing for the British Columbia-Alaska link ever since American President Franklin Roosevelt's visit to Victoria in 1937. The two hit it off right away. Roosevelt had become concerned with Japan's military adventures in Asia and thought a highway to Alaska would help defend the northernmost American territory should Tokyo cast its eyes eastward. Pattullo thought FDR's Alaska project was a splendid idea. He made a special trip to the American capital in 1938 and came away with a pledge for $14 million in financing. Roosevelt's generous commitment to North American defence did not impress Prime Minister King. At the January meeting with Pattullo, the prime minister suggested the federal government would not look with favour upon such a "financial penetration" by the United States.

Prime Minister King also offered no support for a British Columbian initiative to control Japanese immigration. The federal Exclusion Act of 1923 had virtually halted Chinese immigration and Pattullo wanted it extended to Japan as well. Mackenzie King pointed out that such a ban would be sure to trigger serious demonstrations in Tokyo, as well as serve as an embarrassment to Great Britain. The cabinet also decided not to pursue Pattullo's further suggestion that all Japanese people in British Columbia be registered.

As the month drew to a close, Prime Minister King felt it necessary to reinforce Canada's policy on immigration. During a heated debate on the refugee question, the prime minister hinted broadly that the door was still closed. Abraham Heaps, a Jewish MP from Winnipeg, had criticized Secretary of State Fernand Rinfret for declaring in a Montreal speech that, "despite all sentiments of humanity," refugees would be kept away until the jobless problem was solved. Heaps made a strong plea that Canada give asylum to some of the persecuted Jews in Europe. Prime Minister King, in defending Rinfret's remarks, said that "the thing he referred to as not being possible was the open door, which is a very different thing from giving consideration to a situation and meeting it in the best way possible short of an open door."

That door had been firmly closed for decades, and Prime Minister King, while often expressing sympathy for the plight of the Jews, was still a politician above everything else. As he wrote in his diary in November 1938, he had decided to fight for the admission of some refugees because it was "right and just and Christian," although it would be "difficult politically."

Difficult, indeed. There is no evidence the prime minister fought overly hard to change immigration policy, and his statement on January 30 blandly reinforced the status quo. Prime Minister King was well aware, along with the cabinet and many other politicians, that anti-Semitism was prevalent throughout English-speaking Canada, as well as Quebec. Any large-scale effort to admit European Jews, Prime Minister King feared, might very well disrupt the Dominion's unity. He knew that reaction in Quebec would be particularly violent and that riots were not out of the question. "My own feeling is that nothing is to be gained by creating an internal problem in an effort to meet an international one," Mackenzie King wrong in his diary. The prime minister also knew that there were no votes to be gained by admitting Jews — and who knew how many would be lost?

Mackenzie King seemed truly torn during the months of the refugee crisis, at one point fearing that Canada would play the role of "the dog in the manger ... with our great open spaces and small population." He also wrote about "the brotherhood of man," and expressing "the conscience of the nation" on the one hand, while remarking in other diary entries that "we must … seek to keep this part of the Continent free from unrest and from too great an intermixture of foreign strains of blood," and that "one has to look at realities and meet these situations in the light of conditions and not theories."

Mackenzie King was also conflicted by his relationship with Adolf Hitler. A meeting with the Nazi dictator in 1937 had left Prime Minister King full of admiration; in a 1938 diary entry he commented that Hitler "might come to be thought of as one of the saviours of the world." (In contrast, Mackenzie King wrote during King George VI and Queen Elizabeth's Royal Visit that Winston Churchill "is one of the most dangerous men I have ever known.")

On January 25, 1939 the cost of Canada doing business was tentatively pegged at $457,241,215. This was by no means a final figure for the fiscal year beginning April 1, because Finance Minister Charles Dunning's estimates, which were tabled in the House, had some notable omissions. Not included were the Canadian National Railways deficit, grants-in-aid to the provinces, or public works projects intended to ease unemployment. In 1938, the special supplements for these items totalled an additional $95 million.

A big chunk of the 1939 estimates was earmarked for defence. The total — $63,447,175 — was almost 75 percent higher than that of 1938. Of this, air services were pencilled in for more than $23 million, which was a huge increase over 1938's $11.6 million. The militia got some $20 million and the navy, $8.5 million. A one-time item was the $425,000 tabled for the Royal Visit. Transportation expenses (such as the Royal Train) were estimated at $350,000, with "general expenses in connection with the visit to Canada of Their Majesties, the king and queen, $75,000." (The prime minister's preliminary estimate was $50,000, "hesitating to go to $100,000.")

Some assorted esoterica: advertising in countries outside the Dominion, $620,000; government motion picture bureau, $150,000; penitentiaries, $2,999,780; Canadian Council on Nutrition, $14,000.

Dunning's estimates were tabled two days after Labour Minister Norman Rogers outlined the government's employment policy for 1939.

Ottawa would increase its share of the cost of direct relief to 40 percent from the previous 30 and 35 percent. Provinces would contribute 40 percent and the municipalities, 20 percent. The federal government would also pay half the direct labour cost of any new civic improvement program, if the provinces paid the other half. In addition, the Dominion would go 50/50 with the provinces in meeting the relief needs of transients. Other initiatives included expansion of the youth-training plan, forest conservation, and "continued attention" to such projects as tourist roads, national park improvements, mining roads, development of historic sites, and the elimination of level crossings.

Rogers claimed a reduction of 30 percent from November 1936 to November 1938 in the number of persons receiving relief. All regions showed an improvement, except the Prairies where persons on relief rose by 12.5 percent. (There were an estimated 522,000 jobless people in Canada in November 1938.)

Dunning called on employers in private industry to do their share by increasing staff levels, even at some risk to themselves: "I believe that, given the kind of co-operation, the kind of enterprise and initiative that exists in this country, at least potentially, it is not beyond the powers of government and good citizens to make progress towards the solution of this problem of unemployment."

However, a darker canvas was being painted in Toronto, where Eric Cross, the minister of welfare and municipal affairs for Ontario, predicted the province's relief bill for 1939 would be at least $1 million higher than the $21.5 million total for 1938. By the end of January, he said, approximately 283,000 Ontario citizens would be receiving direct aid, compared with 254,000 in January 1938. Cross criticized the federal government for its miserly contribution to the cost of relief. Nearly half the cost, or 46.13 percent of it, was borne by Ontario in 1938, Cross said, with only 25.96 percent coming from Ottawa:

> It is worth noting that in 1934, the Dominion paid 36.53 percent of unemployment relief in the province. Last year, their contribution ... dropped to 25.96 percent. Year after year, it appears that Ottawa is placing

more of the relief burden upon the province and the time must come soon when our taxpayers will obtain a greater measure of assistance from the federal powers.

Events from abroad competed for Canada's attention as January dwindled down to its final few days. In Chile, a severe earthquake rattled the southern section of the country; the cities of Conception and Chillan were virtually wiped out. Initial reports suggested 10,000 people had been killed, but later estimates ranged from 28,000 to 50,000 dead. The magnitude of the earthquake was pegged at 8.3 on the seismic scale. "Light, power, water, and drainage are gone," said one early dispatch from the stricken area, which was based on "fragmentary reports gathered by amateur operators at a hundred battery sets."

Across the Atlantic, General Francisco Franco's khaki-clad Nationalist troops marched triumphantly down the palm-lined boulevards of Barcelona on January 26, effectively ending the Spanish Civil War. The situation was of some concern to Prime Minister King. "The whole business is perfectly appalling," he wrote in his diary. A visiting British marquess, Lord Lothian, felt the same way. He suggested that were England and France to confront an alliance of Fascist Spain, Nazi Germany, Italy, and Japan it would be "like a man with two arms fighting a man with three arms." (Lord Lothian became British Ambassador to the United States in August 1939 and served as the principal intermediary between FDR and Winston Churchill.) Prime Minister King noted that war could break out "in the Mediterranean area or on the Atlantic or in the near East … I don't trust Japan. I think there is some subterfuge here. I am sure all three have had an understanding from the beginning."

That daunting prospect hadn't yet swum into the prime minister's ken when he decided that it was time to prepare Canadians for the prospect of war. However, he botched the job by repeating a statement made by Sir Wilfrid Laurier in 1910 to illustrate why the possibility should not be ignored: "If Britain is at war, we are at war and liable to attack." Laurier's words in Mackenzie King's mouth stirred up waves of protest. Montreal newspaper, *Le Devoir*, unleashed a stinging article under the headline QUEBEC LIBERALS LISTEN IN STUPEFACTION TO THE PRIME MINISTER'S DECLARATION IN OTTAWA. Angry correspondents wanted to know whether Mackenzie King thought Canada was still a British colony. The cabinet grumbled. Justice Minister Ernest Lapointe, Prime Minister King's Quebec lieutenant, argued that his words were contrary to the precepts of the Statute of Westminster (which granted Canada the right to decide its own foreign policy) and threatened to resign.

The somewhat perplexed prime minister responded to his colleagues: "The circumstances abroad at the present time were the threat to freedom the world over which we could not possibly hope to escape ... whatever views we might hold or obligations arising out of Imperial connections."

Adolf Hitler muddied the tense European scene nicely on January 30, delivering a major speech that was relatively benign. In a two-hour oration to the Greater German Reichstag in Berlin's Kroli Opera House, Hitler fulminated against the "apostles of war" who attack Nazi policies, but his harangue lacked the usual militaristic overtones. In fact, Hitler managed to put in a good word for almost all nations, including Britain, America, and France. He declared Germany's next objective as the return of her former colonies, and, along with Italy and Japan, the redistribution of the world's riches among nations in proportion "to their number, their courage, and their worth."

The inclusion of conciliatory passages and the lack of any plans for further Nazi expansion in Europe brought sighs of cautious relief in the world capitals. British Prime Minister Neville Chamberlain went to work on a major conciliatory address of his own, while Canada's Prime Minister King caught part of Hitler's speech on the radio and concluded that the German chancellor spoke in "a very moderate way," while sounding much older and less excitable. "I gather it was much milder than expected and did not contain any threats," Mackenzie King wrote in his diary, "beyond indications Germany would support Italy if she found it necessary to fight."

Also on January 30, the resignation of R.B. Bennett as a Member of Parliament was announced in the Commons. Bennett had posted his letter of resignation in Halifax before sailing for Britain on the liner *Montclare*. In his farewell speech, the former prime minister stuck to his theme of Canadian unity and pleaded for an intelligent democracy. Good riddance, was Prime Minister King's reaction. "I think everybody on the whole is pleased that he is out of Parliament," he wrote in his diary. "Quite clearly, he has cut all his bridges.... I imagine, however, he will be bitterly disappointed once he settles down in the old world and discovers that having ceased to be a Canadian, he has lost a large part of whatever power he may formerly have had."

The Way Things Were

LORD'S DAY ACT

In 1939, it was pretty hard to have any fun or conduct any business in most of Canada on Sundays. The Lord's Day Act, which came into force on March 3, 1907, essentially banned all forms of entertainment, commercial activity, and even some leisure pursuits. You couldn't watch a professional hockey or baseball game, take in a movie, go shopping, or buy a newspaper. Even hunting, fishing, and shooting were illegal. Quebec was the exception, though; its Members of Parliament forced the inclusion of a clause giving provinces the right to opt out. Quebec did so a week before the act became law. Enforcement by the other provinces was not exactly uniform, but there wasn't much happening on a Sunday in the rest of Canada. There wasn't that much going on during the rest of the week, either. Some department stores closed Wednesday afternoons, and no retail enterprise dreamed of staying open to 9:00 p.m. "Banker's Hours" usually meant 10:00 a.m. to 3:00 p.m., Monday to Friday, and woe betide anyone who ran out of cash on the weekend because there was no such thing as an ATM. The sale of spirits by the glass was also largely prohibited (with the exception, again, of Quebec), so people drank draft beer in smelly, noisy beer parlours. Although some jurisdictions made provision for mixed drinking in public, women usually stayed home. The Lord's Day Act was declared unconstitutional by the Supreme Court of Canada in 1984.

Robert Marvin Hull. He was born January 3 in Pointe Anne, Ontario, to Robert Edward Hull, a cement-company foreman, and Lena Cook Hull. The elder son in a family of eleven children, Bobby worked as a labourer before embarking on a meteoric career as a hockey superstar. He played in the National Hockey League and the World Hockey Association from 1957 to 1979. Hull is a member of the Hockey Hall of Fame, scoring 1,018 goals in 1,653 regular season and playoff games.

Memories. The Hudson's Bay Company in Winnipeg offered a $100 bonus to the best description of an early "trading incident" with the company by a long-time customer. "Did you trade with us in Old Fort Garry?" it asked. "Did you shop in the old Hudson's Bay Store down on Main Street?" The best letter would receive "Bay's $100 Good Will Bonus." Judges were the editor of the *Winnipeg Tribune*, the managing editor of the *Winnipeg Free Press*, and the editor of *The Beaver* magazine.

Show Time. *Angels With Dirty Faces*, starring James Cagney and Pat O'Brien, opened in Canadian theatres. ONCE UPON A TIME HE HAD A HEART! said the newspaper ads about Cagney's character.

February

Partisan sniping from the Opposition trenches provoked Canada's minister of national defence into a snarling counter-attack early in the month when the government tried to shove the Bren gun business under the carpet. Fireworks sparked to life after notice was given on February 2 that the matter be sent to the public accounts committee for study, including Justice Davis's report and the contract itself.

It's hard not to imagine the chuckles in the Liberal cabinet room when this stratagem was devised. The public accounts committee was a ponderous entity, consisting of fifty members. It hadn't been asked to do anything since 1926. Months would pass before anything would be decided. What could go wrong?

Well, nothing, really, although the Opposition still had to have its say. Serious attacks would be launched within a week, but the barbs began almost immediately. Conservative MP A.J. Anderson called for repudiation of the deal. "If it goes further than this," he said, "the Imperial authorities will feel Canadians are not worthy of trust in matters so important as the purchase of munitions." And, despite Justice Davis's findings that no government member was involved, Anderson linked two of Toronto Liberal MP Hugh Plaxton's brothers to the Inglis group. "In the old days, we called this nepotism," Anderson said.

A few days later, the Opposition Leader Robert J. Manion rolled in. Others would chip in from both the Conservative Party and the Co-operative Commonwealth Federation, but Manion did the heavy work. In the first of two speeches, he took an opening shot at Defence Minister Ian McKenzie by noting that the legislation setting up the proposed war materiel purchasing board bypassed McKenzie's department entirely. It was a clear case of recognizing the minister's incompetence.

Manion also said forty out of fifty pages of Davis's report were a "devastating condemnation" of the government. "It is true no corruption has been established, and I do not charge any, but the judge has painted many subtle vignettes to hang on the wall."

In his second speech on February 9 — Prime Minister King described it as "about as exciting as any day I have known" — Manion demanded that the fate of the report be decided in open Parliament rather than behind the closed doors of a committee room. He claimed there were five other companies in Canada better equipped than Inglis to take on the job, and the contract stood as a "shameful" example of patronage. "Not that I criticize a certain amount of patronage," he added, "but I object to one man in all this country being chosen while other industrial people are ignored." Manion said that Mackenzie had forfeited the confidence of the country and had no right to spend this year's defence appropriations.

Speakers on the Liberal benches — including C.D. Howe, the minister of transportation, and James Gardiner, the minister of agriculture — responded with practical, precise defences of the contract. They emphasized that no definite charges had been made: not by Drew in his original magazine article, not by the Davis Commission report, and not by the Opposition.

That was in the afternoon.

In the evening and fuelled by a liquid dinner, Defence Minister Ian Mackenzie rose to speak. Almost immediately, the House was thrown into an uproar as Mackenzie shouted his defiance at the Opposition, at one point threatening to "knock their heads off." He accused one Conservative of having a "Prussian mentality" and called another member "a dirty liar." He branded the attacks on himself and the contract "a sustained campaign of political calumny," and implied that fascists and communists were working together to destroy the morale of "the great department of national defence." He also claimed there was a "sinister alliance" between the Tories and the CCF and accused them of undermining the confidence of the country. He said that George Drew didn't have the manhood to lay specific charges and claimed that the joint Anglo-Canadian contract with Inglis had saved taxpayers $1.3 million.

The prime minister was not impressed. "While [Mackenzie] was under a great deal of emotional strain," King wrote, "I think he did both himself and the cause harm ... simply because he had sought to fortify himself in advance by taking a stimulant — a drink. Had he spoken in the afternoon, as I pressed him to do, when he was calm, he would have avoided some extreme and provocative statements ... Several of his remarks were wholly unparliamentary and diverted sympathy from him where he might easily have gained considerable sympathy."

Mackenzie was, in fact, a weak minister and an inexperienced administrator who was severely ill-informed about the Inglis contract details. He also had a drinking problem, of which Prime Minister King was well aware. Later, the prime minister wondered whether Mackenzie "had not aroused an antagonism which will pursue him relentlessly and possibly down him in the end. I feel extremely sorry for him but if he is undone it has been his own undoing from the kind of habits that have been contracted through associations that are not too good."

"There was a time when I really believed that he might succeed to the leadership of the Party," Prime Minister King wrote in his diary, "but that time has disappeared." Later in the year, Mackenzie would be relieved of his defence portfolio.

As the fog of debate about weapons of war hung over Parliament Hill, the "Pope of Peace" died in Rome. With "peace" as his final word, Pope Pius XI slipped away in the pre-dawn hours of February 10. He was eighty-one. The Pope, who succumbed in his private quarters on St. Peter's Square, was moved to the Sistine Chapel, as church bells tolled. The mournful procession was led by the Swiss Guards and included both lay and ecclesiastical dignitaries.

As the body lay beneath the famous Michelangelo ceiling, only the diplomatic corps and Vatican state officials were permitted to approach the bier. The next day, a solemn crowd of approximately 40,000 to 50,000 people waited as the Pope's body was transferred to the Chapel of the Blessed Sacrament in St. Peter's Basilica, the mother church of the Roman Catholic world. Only then was the public allowed to view the remains.

Ambrogio Damiano Achille Ratti, the son of a silk manufacturer in the Lombardy district of the Austrian Empire, became Pope on February 6, 1922, amidst the global tensions following the Great War when the adrenaline of battle hadn't entirely dissipated. He chose the name Pius — Piety — and adopted "Christ's peace in Christ's kingdom" as the motto of his papacy. His *Pax Christiana* was a crusade to bring peace to the world based on Christian notions of love and brotherhood.

Pope Pius believed in the concordat — an agreement between the Church and a sovereign state on religious matters — as a means to maintain the influence of the Church, and concluded several of them. One was with Adolf Hitler's Nazi Germany, which Hitler promptly ignored and continued persecuting Roman Catholics with almost the same vigour as he did the Jews.

Pope Pius was a scholar open to science and research, but he was also strong-willed and dogmatic. He doubled the number of missionaries and sent them to vigorously spread the message of Catholicism abroad, especially in Southeast Asia. He feared the godlessness of communism, and accepted fascism as the means of maintaining order in a secular state. He soon soured on the concept, though, because of Hitler's excesses in Nazi Germany

Pope Pius had been ill for some time when he suffered two heart attacks in November 1938. Complicated by serious respiratory problems, his health deteriorated early in 1939, and he suffered a third and fatal heart attack at 5:31 a.m. on February 10. His final, whispered words were, "My soul parts from you all in peace." He was buried in the crypt of St. Peter's Basilica, in the main chapel, close to the tomb of St. Peter.

While Pope Pius XI sought peace, Peter the Purger Verigin sought only power. Verigin, who died in Saskatoon, Saskatchewan, one day after the pontiff, was the leader of Canada's 6,000 Doukhobors. The Doukhobors are a stubborn, devout, and mostly peaceful sect who fled religious persecution in Czarist Russia near the turn of the twentieth century and settled in what is now Manitoba and Saskatchewan. They believe that man is a vessel of God and that nothing should intrude between the soul and divinity. They resist any external authority's right to control their actions, which has led to conflicts with various levels of government over schooling and land claims. The sect moved to the mountainous Kootenay region of southeastern British Columbia between 1908 and 1914.

The Doukhobors were led westward by Peter the Lordly Verigin, who was murdered in 1924 when someone blew up the railroad car in which he was riding. He was succeeded by his son, who earned the title of Peter the Purger because of his obsession with personal power and his harsh attitude toward an arson-prone breakaway group called the Sons of Freedom.

Peter the Purger's secular life was rather untidy. In 1931, he sued a fellow Doukhobor called Chutskoff in Yorkton, Saskatchewan, for $1,000 he claimed he was owed on a land transaction. Verigin lost the case and a subsequent appeal, then attempted to have Chutskoff charged with perjury. Instead, Verigin was convicted of perjury and spent several months in prison. He narrowly avoided deportation and was later convicted of assault. A drunken brawl in a Nelson, British Columbia, beer parlour in 1934 resulted in another conviction. In 1935, Peter the Purger Verigin fell ill with cancer and died in a Saskatoon hospital on February 11. He was fifty-eight.

On February 5, 1939, a bitterly cold night in Toronto, more than 10,000 people thronged Union Station to welcome 272 Mac-Paps returning from the Spanish Civil War. The tumultuous greeting lasted for three hours before the crowd calmed down enough for the speeches to begin. No one from the government said anything, though, because the only federal representatives there were the Royal Canadian Mounted Police. They stayed in the background, taking pictures and making notes. There were more crowds across Canada — in Halifax, Montreal, Winnipeg, and Vancouver, where a crowd of 2,500 braved a rare, six-inch snowfall — as the veterans of the Mackenzie-Papineau Battalion wended their way homeward.

All this excitement was in vivid contrast to their departure in 1937. Then, there was secrecy, deception, doubletalk, and no crowds at all; the government had declared fighting on the Republican side in Spain illegal and that anyone who did so was a criminal. And a Communist to boot.

The war began in July 1936 when elements of the army based in Spanish Morocco rose up against the left-wing Republican government in Madrid. They were led by General Francisco Franco, and the bitter confrontation quickly engulfed the whole country. Nazi Germany and Fascist Italy quickly pitched in to help Franco's Nationalist forces. The Soviet Union went to the aid of the Republicans, ordering Communist Party groups around the world to assist in the formation of International Brigades.

By September of that year, the Republican side was in bad shape and appealed to the League of Nations for arms. The League, which by that

Members of the Mackenzie-Papineau Battalion arrive in Montreal after returning from the Spanish Civil War.

time had become largely irrelevant and lacked the power to enforce any of its dictates, refused. Instead, in February 1937, the League decided to ban the use of foreign volunteers by the Spanish combatants. This fit in well with the Canadian government's paranoia about socialist states. It had already drafted a Foreign Enlistment Act (as had Great Britain and America.), making it a crime to leave Canada to join the fighting.

The "Act respecting foreign enlistment" was passed by Parliament on February 19, 1937, and proclaimed via cabinet order-in-council on April 4. Its relevant passages read in part:

> 3. Any person who, being a Canadian national within or outside Canada, voluntarily accepts or agrees to accept any commission or engagement in the armed forces of any foreign state at war ... or, whether a Canadian national or not, within Canada, induces any other person to accept or agree to accept any commission or engagement in any such armed forces is guilty of an offence.
>
> 4. Any person who, being a Canadian national, leaves or goes on board any conveyance with a view of leaving Canada with intent to accept any commission or engagement in the armed forces of any foreign state at war ... or ... induces any other person to leave or go on board any conveyance with a view to leaving Canada, with a like intent, is guilty of an offence.

The legislation was aimed squarely at the Communist Party of Canada, which had hovered between illegality and barely tolerated legality since its inception in 1922. The Communist Party kept a very low profile as it began recruiting volunteers from all over the Dominion. These recruits were either outright Party members or fellow travellers. There were some CCF supporters in the mix and even a few Liberals. They were all working-class adults, shoved to the left of the political spectrum by the Great Depression.

The volunteers would slip in and out of Toronto via the Party's staging headquarters at the corner of Queen and Spadina Streets.

Because the government refused to issue passports to anyone they suspected of going to war, applicants would lie and insist they were off to Europe — France, usually — on a pleasure jaunt. The volunteers would then travel to New York, sometimes Montreal, and catch a "conveyance." The Party would pay all their expenses. Actually getting to Albacete, their Spanish destination, often involved trekking over the Pyrenees Mountains from France, usually in their street shoes (and clothes).

Estimates of the number of Canadians volunteers vary from 1,400 to almost 1,700. Michael Petrou, in his book *Renegades: Canadians in The Spanish Civil War*, lists 1,673 volunteers. They range, alphabetically, from George Abocheski (missing in action) to Kornil Zygarowicz (killed in action). More than 60 percent of the names are of European extraction. Dr. Norman Bethune, who achieved heroic status for his work with the wounded, is on the list, which includes two women.

In July 1937, the Mackenzie-Papineau Battalion was formed; the name honoured William Lyon Mackenzie and Louis-Joseph Papineau, who led the 1837 rebellions in Upper Canada and Quebec. After minimal training in Albacete, the Canadians were thrown into the fray. In 1937, they fought in the battles of Jarama and Brunete. Three more major clashes followed in 1938: the Aragon Offensive, the Battle of Teruel, and the Battle of the Ebro.

The Canadians fought with bravery and enthusiasm, but socialist idealism was no match for the modern weaponry supplied by the Nationalists' Fascist pals. Casualties were very high. An estimated 721 Mac-Paps were killed. Finally, on September 21, 1938, Republican Prime Minister Juan Negrin relieved the battered International Brigades of any more duty and they were withdrawn.

For the Mac-Paps, the way home seemed as arduous as getting to Spain. For a long time, the Canadian government refused to let them return. France, surprised by all these foreigners coming back over the mountains, was getting shirty. At one point, it demanded $10,000 before allowing the Canadians to continue on to England for passage home. The group's leaders contacted many people in their efforts to raise the money, including Matthew Halton, the *Toronto Daily Star's* correspondent in London. The paper got a major scoop out of the deal: the Canadian volunteers' imminent departure for Canada.

The Mac-Paps' sacrifices in the fight against fascism were never officially acknowledged in Ottawa. The veterans received no benefits, and some were even denied enlistment in the Second World War because of "political unreliability." Belatedly, a monument inscribed with 1,546 names was unveiled in Ottawa in 2001. There is also a monument to the Mac-Paps in Victoria, British Columbia.

The state of the Canadian railway business was always good for an argument in the House of Commons. February's throne speech debate was no exception.

Back in 1918, the government created Canadian National Railways in response to citizens' concerns about unreliable transportation. During the next five years, the organization acquired such bankrupt and failing railways as the Canadian Northern Railway, Canadian Government Railways, Grant Trunk Pacific Railway, and the Grand Trunk Railway. When the Liberals inherited the Canadian National Railways after regaining power in 1935, the sprawling system was in poor shape. It wasn't much better in 1939.

Various federal railway ministers (including Dunning under an earlier Liberal administration) had tried to make the unwieldy collection of trunk and branch lines work, with little success. In 1935, Clarence Decatur Howe, an MP from the blue-collar riding of Port Arthur, took over as Liberal transportation minister. Massachusetts-born, Howe had moved to the Lakehead to make his fortune in the grain elevator business. His first move was to dump the board of trustees the Conservatives had set up to run the railway and replace it with a streamlined, more efficient board of directors. All were solid businessmen, including Samuel J. Hungerford, a seasoned railway executive, as chairman and president. Hungerford breathed life into the lethargic corporation, cutting expenses and welcoming input from his managers. Meanwhile, Howe went to work on the CNR's "stupid" accounting practices. However, the CNR's huge debt load remained, as it would for several years.

The topic of who had made a bigger mess, the present government or the Conservatives, arose on the House floor that February day when a Liberal backbencher from Winnipeg charged that the CNR was "systematically sabotaged" during R.J. Manion's tenure as minister of railways. Manion, who had swapped that job for one as Opposition leader, flung out a sweeping denial, declaring that anyone who would sabotage the national railway "wouldn't be fit to bear the name, 'Canadian.'"

"I am prouder of the work I did for the Canadian National Railways between 1930 and 1935 than anything else I have done during the twenty years I have been in public life," he said. Manion admitted that he had to effect some economies because of the Great Depression, but that the CNR's expenses were reduced from $199 million in 1931 to $180 million in 1937: a saving of $19 million. "We started it and our honourable friends are carrying it on," he said. "We were not saboteurs but friends of the railway."

Charles Dunning, the finance minister, opted for reason. "There is no subject on which we all — and I include myself — require more heart-searching than our great, publicly-owned utility," he said, but he acknowledged that mistakes can be made. Furthermore, he asked, what railwayman in Canada, what business executive, what cabinet minister, what member of this House, foresaw what was coming in the fall of 1929?

Manion put to rest the lingering question of amalgamating with the Canadian Pacific Railway. Quoting the R.J. Bennett policy of "amalgamation never, co-operation ever," Manion emphasized that the Conservatives were still thoroughly opposed to any merger with the privately-owned CPR. In response to his taunts — that no one on the government benches seemed to care — both the prime minister and the transport minister went on record as opposing unification.

Amalgamating Canada's two great rail networks had been Sir Edward Beatty's goal, as president of the CPR, for years. An arrangement to pool passenger traffic between Quebec City, Montreal, Ottawa, and Toronto had been in effect for some time, but for economic reasons only. A full merger was simply not in the cards, falling victim to politicians' enlightened self-interest. In the words of author and CNR chronicler Donald

MacKay, "CN autonomy won the day, if for no other reason than that unification would mean politically hazardous layoffs, tearing up tracks and abandoning communities."

How much was the CNR in the red? A written answer provided the day following Manion's statement reported that total indebtedness to the public at the end of 1937 was $1,221,997,399, bearing an annual interest of $48,888,546. The national CNR debt, as of March 31, 1938, was also tabled at $3,540,277,814. The net debt — liabilities less actual assets — amounted to $3,101,567,570.

Other answers among the pile of documents dumped on the clerks' table between the two members' benches included the number of cattle on Canadian farms as of June 1, 1838 (8,511,200) and the cost of printing two of the prime minister's speeches ($328.85). Also, during the first nine months of the 1938 fiscal year, 1,162,800 radio licences were sold in Canada for $2,679,216. Some 1,410 individuals were convicted of failing to obtain licences.

Out west, the deadbeat Social Credit government in Edmonton quietly admitted that the feds had agreed to renew $4.478 million in treasury bills held as security for unemployment-relief advances. The bills were due February 2.

This was yet another stumble in the Social Credit League's search for economic bliss. The basic theory of social credit was postulated by W.O. Douglas, a British engineer, in the 1920s. Although larded with economics, philosophy, Christianity, and even a dash of physics, Douglas's premise was that as production exists for the benefit of the consumer, so the consumer should share the profits, which could be accomplished by such instruments as a "National Dividend" and a "Compensated Price." Thus, production would serve the little guy, not the other way around.

Douglas's theories attracted widespread attention between the wars. Among those buying in was school principal and evangelist William "Bible Bill" Aberhart, who had decided to get into politics. His newly-minted Social Credit League rode the promise of shared prosperity to a surprising victory in the 1935 election, winning fifty-six of sixty-three seats.

The new government inherited a provincial economy that was distressingly weak. In 1936, public and private indebtedness in Alberta was $395 million. The annual cost of carrying this debt was $40 million. Theories about creating new purchasing power, thereby strengthening the bottom line, were as ineffective against that sort of burden as any other, more conventional approach. At one point, the government issued Douglas-inspired "Prosperity Certificates." Quickly dubbed "funny money," they were almost worthless. The problem, of course, was that it was darned hard getting money to flow down as easily as it flowed up.

In early 1936, the Bank of Canada refused to loan Alberta $3.25 million to meet a bond issue due on April 1. Alberta defaulted, sending its credit rating into a nose dive. After another loan was refused in October of that year, the province defaulted on another bond issue, this time for $1.25 million. In 1937, there were three more bond defaults within three months.

As Aberhart's frustration grew, he began lashing out at the establishment. He hated the central financial institutions, most notably the banks, which he held responsible for Alberta's economic hardship. He introduced several acts limiting the influence of these institutions, but they were all disallowed. Aberhart's nemesis was Lieutenant-Governor John Campbell Bowen. Instead of giving routine Royal Assent, Bowen reserved all of the province's major acts for Ottawa's approval — and eventually the Supreme Court of Canada. In 1937, this included the Accurate News and Information Act, Aberhart's attempt to muzzle the critical daily press.

The relationship between Aberhart and Bowen became strained and remained so for a number of years. During the Royal Visit to Alberta in June 1939, this animosity would result in a few tense moments.

Over in British Columbia, a small city in the West Kootenays didn't have much truck with fancy economic theories. Hunched down on the banks of the Columbia River, in the shadow of the huge Consolidated Mining & Smelting Company smelter, Trail was a place for working men. Like C.D. Howe's Port Arthur, strictly blue-collar. If you worked up the hill, you got pretty dirty every day before collecting your paycheque every week. If you had been laid off by Cominco during the hard times, well, you hung in there.

On February 12, the no-nonsense work ethic paid off big-time. The Trail Smoke Eaters, a men's hockey team, won the world championship. The previous spring, the Smokies had captured the 1938 Allan Cup, emblematic of Canada's senior championship, by defeating the Cornwall Flyers, three games to one, after surviving a hard-fought series of elimination rounds. This made them eligible for the world championship in Switzerland.

Beginning in December 1938, and with only thirteen players, the gritty Canadian champs played fifty-five exhibition and tournament games in Europe. Between bouts with frantic autograph-seekers, they won fifty-three, tied one, and lost one. Instead of the traditional white uniforms worn by touring Canadian teams, they wore their colourful home jerseys emblazoned with the smoke-belching stacks of Cominco's smelter. In the championship tournament, played in Basel and Zurich, the Canadians defeated the Netherlands 8–0, Britain 4–0, Germany 9–0, Czechoslovakia 4–1, and Switzerland 7–0, before shutting out the United States in the final 4–0. During a period still dominated by the Great Depression, the hard-working boys from the depths of British Columbia gave Canadians something to be proud of.

In Vancouver, meanwhile, Premier T.D. Pattullo had a few words to say about national unity. In a speech to the Board of Trade, Pattullo told "eastern protagonists of disunioin and disturbance" that British Columbia would co-operate fully with the Dominion. "But we are not willing to be bullied, bulldozed or coerced," he warned. Pattullo claimed a movement was under way to centralize authority, even to the extent of abolishing provincial legislatures. "The *Globe and Mail* of Toronto has been strong in its advocacy of centralization," he said, "so strong in fact that its language has become very intemperate and all who disagree with it are self-interested and unpatriotic."

He said that alarm over an Alaska Highway from the American border through British Columbia and the Yukon was misplaced. A military road would be invaluable if war came to the Pacific, he claimed, "and all the more reason to build it. If the United States is in a war to test its strength, Canada will certainly be in it with her."

Back east, Camillien Houde, the bombastic, hugely popular mayor of Montreal, had a loud mouth. First, he threatened to secede — not from Canada but from Quebec. Houde was aroused by a suggestion that a provincial controller supervise both revenue and expenses in the city. He promised that any attempt to control Montreal from the "outside" would be enough to trigger the move. The Quebec premier, Maurice Duplessis, was more interested in the province's relations with Ottawa and paid little attention.

Later in the month, Houde's posturing became more ominous. In a speech at a local YMCA, he suggested that French-Canadians were more sympathetic toward Italy than England:

> If war comes and Italy is on one side and England on the other, the sympathy of the French-Canadians in Quebec would be on the side of Italy. Remember that the great majority of French-Canadians are Roman Catholics and that the Pope is in Rome. We French-Canadians are Normans, not Latins, but we have become Latinized over a long period of years. The French-Canadians are Fascist by blood but not by name. The Latins have always been in favour of dictators.

Houde's remarkable disclosure aroused the ire of the prime minister. Mackenzie King called it a demagogic appeal with a religious motive and placed Quebec "in a deplorable light before other parts of Canada and the world." Such an extreme message, he said, "from the chief magistrate of the largest city in Canada to Germany and Italy, at a time like the present, might throw the scales in the direction of war."

Houde maintained his anti-British stance after war began, and, on August 2, 1940, publicly urged the males of Quebec to ignore the National Registration Act. Three days later, he was arrested, charged with sedition, and interned until 1944.

On the last day of February, Great Britain announced that it would spend £536,606,861 on the Royal Navy in a new building program. This worked out to $708,333,405 in 1939 Canadian dollars. The naval estimates were part of Britain's total defence spending bill of £680 million. The estimates covered 173 vessels and were expected to give the economy a major boost. "I am informed that ... far from alarming financial circles in this country [my statement] has been very well received," Sir John Simon, chancellor of the exchequer, told the House of Commons. "It has in fact operated as an encouragement to British trade and finance." Two battleships, an aircraft carrier, four cruisers, sixteen destroyers, and four submarines were among the craft to be built.

The Way Things Were

AT THE MOVIES

Despite the Great Depression, the motion picture industry was alive and well in 1939. Downtown, the movie theatres, which were constructed in the 1920s to look like fancy opera houses, offered patrons a glittering night out. Elaborate staircases, ornate balconies, high ceilings, and private boxes were all part of the décor. The numerous neighbourhood theatres were much smaller, much less ornate, and less expensive. Some of them offered a complete Saturday program for only ten cents. The motion picture palaces and their more modest brethren had lots to offer, because Hollywood produced a magical crop of movies in 1939. The parade of blockbusters (to use a phrase coined many years later) made it probably the best year ever for feature films. The stars, of course, had lots to do with this success: Clark Gable, Cary Grant, Errol Flynn, and James Stewart; Greta Garbo, Judy Garland, Bette Davis, and Shirley Temple. The movies themselves ranged from drama and adventure to romance and farce.

Biggest of them all was the epic romantic drama of the Deep South, *Gone With The Wind*, which won a host of Academy Awards. Other dramas included *Wuthering Heights*, *Dark Victory*, and *Goodbye Mr. Chips*. The reclusive Greta Garbo starred in *Ninotchka* and Jimmy Stewart appeared in *Mr. Smith Goes to Washington*. *Gunga Din* had Cary Grant and *The Wizard of Oz* had Judy Garland. The Marx Brothers offered *At The Circus*, while there were adventures such as *Beau Geste* and *Drums Along The Mohawk*. Charles Laughton stole the show in *The Hunchback of Notre Dame*. Two top Westerns were *Destry Rides Again* and *Stage Coach*. There were also *Intermezzo*, *Of Mice and Men*, and *The Roaring Twenties*.

Bren Gun Shares. The majority of the shares in the John Inglis Company, which had been awarded the controversial Bren gun contract, were held in escrow by the Bank of Montreal, as Ontario Attorney-General Gordon Conant revealed in St. Thomas: "Obviously, those 184,000 shares are an ample guarantee that the control of the company will never pass to any foreign interests," despite whistle-blower George Drew's "very bad and extravagant" claims of impropriety.

Mighty *Bismarck*. The pride of the German fleet, the 45,000-ton battleship *Bismarck*, was launched at the Hamburg naval shipyard on February 14. She had 833 days to live.

Baby Masks. An order was placed by the British government for 1.2 million gas masks for infants. Already, forty million adult masks had been distributed.

Show Time. *Moonlight Sonata*, with Paderewski "in his first and only motion picture!" the ads blared.

March

The concept of a comfy North America aloof from the rest of the planet got a boost on March 9 when the House of Commons ratified a three-way trade agreement with Great Britain and the United States. The House's decision was a solid indication that Canada was backing away from its trade embrace with the Old Country and edging closer to a more meaningful relationship closer to home. Painfully negotiated during the latter months of 1938, the complex deal (which addressed such minutiae as the length of Douglas Fir exports from British Columbia compared with that of Baltic timber) saw Ottawa relinquish some of its Imperial Preference status to enlarge its footprint south of the border.

Imperial Preference was concocted by Joseph Chamberlain, Great Britain's secretary of state for the colonies at the turn of the twentieth century, as a way to stop the Dominions from thinking too much about independence. They were, as a French economist put it, "like fruits which cling to the tree only until they ripen."* Chamberlain's plan was to erect a tariff wall around the Empire, inside of which the former colonies would get preferential treatment. A proposed duty of a shilling per ton on foreign corn (what Britons called wheat) to help pay for the Boer War was the starting point. Chamberlain fought to get corn grown within the Empire exempt from the duty, thus laying down the first brick of his Imperial Preference wall. Although bitterly opposed by government free-trade proponents, the scheme had become generally accepted by the 1920s.

---

* Robert K. Massie, *Dreadnought* (New York: Random House, 1991), 325.

There was some cost to getting cozy with the Americans: Canada did reduce its own duties on a healthy range of products. But British Columbia, for instance, liked the deal because it enlarged the market for wood products. The Prairies welcomed the lower costs for American manufactured goods, and in the East, the lowering of the tariff wall benefitted a wide range of products.

For the isolationist camp, this was good stuff: an interdependent North America meant estrangement from the Continent and its messy entanglements. One strong voice in Ottawa, that of Oscar Douglas Skelton, the undersecretary of state for external affairs, had Prime Minister King's ear, while across the line, the famous aviator Charles A. Lindbergh made no secret of his desire that America avoid any foreign adventures. There were others, of course: French-Canadian nationalists, who scorned any involvement with Britain, as well as the neutralist pacifism of J.S. Woodsworth and the Co-operative Commonwealth Federation, which had gained a foothold on the Prairies. In contrast to Lindbergh, who became increasingly more strident as the months passed, Skelton stated his views quietly.

In the 1920s, when Prime Minister King began loosening the apron strings constraining any independent foreign policy, he recruited Skelton, a brilliant academic at Queen's University with strong views about Canada's role as a Dominion within the British Empire. Skelton's belief that "each part of the Empire has its own foreign affairs and must substantially have its own foreign policy in dealing with those affairs" struck a chord with Mackenzie King, who wrote in his diary in 1922 that Skelton's views "would make an excellent foundation for Canadian policy on external affairs and Skelton himself would make an excellent man for that department."

Skelton was Prime Minister King's adviser at the 1923 Imperial Conference in London, and became undersecretary for external affairs in 1925 (the prime minister acted as his own secretary of state). Skelton was a gifted, hard-working administrator with a quick grasp of the complexities of international politics, as well as a strong and committed isolationist. He became Prime Minister King's right-hand man, despite his views about separating Canada from the European morass (propagating the assumption that Mackenzie King himself was an isolationist. He was not). When the Liberals lost the 1930 election to R.B. Bennett's Conservatives, Skelton stayed on in external affairs; he was there waiting in 1935 when Mackenzie King assumed power once more.

The prime minister's right-hand man in the external affairs department, O.D. Skelton was a committed isolationist.

Skelton's refrain of neutrality and Canadian self-interest hadn't changed. He had no deep affection for Mother England, unlike Prime Minister King, who was a loyalist despite being named after a famous Canadian rebel. Skelton firmly believed that the crafty colonial masters in Westminster were still trying to manipulate the Dominion in the name of Empire solidarity. Moreover, despite characterizing Benito Mussolini and Adolf Hitler as two paranoiacs loose in Europe, "with their hands on the levers of war, one imagining that he was a Roman Caesar and the other that he was an Aryan God," he didn't believe that Germany's ambitions in Eastern Europe were a real threat to Canadian security.

"The convention that if Germany gets control of the Danube she will next gobble up Canada might frighten children in Canada," Skelton wrote in a memo to Mackenzie King in September, 1938, "even children in Europe would laugh at it. We are the safest country in the world — so long as we mind our own business."

The prime minister finally decided, however, that events on the Danube might very well be Canada's business after all. In a speech to the House on March 20, 1939, Prime Minister King publicly rejected isolationism: "If there were a prospect of an aggressor launching an attack on Britain, with bombers raining death on London, I have no doubt what the decision of the Canadian people and Parliament would be." Prime Minister King still insisted, as he would continue to do, that Canadian Parliament would ultimately decide on a course of action, but he left no doubt about his government's position: "We would regard [an attack on Britain] as an act of aggression menacing freedom in all parts of the British Commonwealth."

"My mind was fully made up," Prime Minister King wrote in his diary:

> Public opinion has mounted very quickly and strongly in all parts of Canada. People have sensed the menace to freedom, and Chamberlain's speech of Friday has caused them to feel — and I think rightly — that there must be world assertion of the power of free countries against Germany if she is to be subjected.... I feel tonight I

have made a strong and bold stroke for freedom today, and feel perfectly sure that the course taken has been the right one.

The cabinet supported Prime Minister King's decision, but, as Ernest Lapointe predicted, there was hell to pay. The Quebec press saw this as Mackenzie King openly declaring his intention to back Britain, and muttered ominously about French-Canadians withdrawing their support from a government so ready to participate in a European war. In the rest of Canada, the press mostly agreed that Prime Minister King should have been more forthright. Some editorialists pointed out that Canada had neglected to announce its support of Britain's policies before blindly deciding to go to war in her defence. The *Globe and Mail* described the speech as "far from the rallying cry for the Empire and other democracies."

The *Toronto Daily Star* was somewhat more positive. After noting that Australia had unequivocally informed London that it would not be found wanting in a crisis, *The Star* remarked that Prime Minister King's declaration "may not have contained these assurances in so many words because of the premier's oft-reported pledge that Parliament would determine Canada's policy in any emergency ... it is a right assumption that his declaration had that meaning."

Ontario Premier Hepburn's legislature unanimously passed a resolution urging that "the wealth and man-power of Canada shall be mobilized by proclamation ... for the duration of the war in defence of our institutions."

While Skelton was vainly pushing as many isolationist buttons as he could, Lindbergh returned to America after an extended period abroad. He immediately began voicing his creed of non-intervention, having left Europe with definite ideas about who was going to win and who was going to lose.

In 1938, Lindbergh had been involved in discussions about building warplanes in Canada for the French air force, using machine tools, parts, designs, and subassemblies shipped across the border from the United States. Called the Canadian Plan, it was dreamed up by the French and the British to circumvent America's Neutrality Act of 1935, which forbade the use of American war materiel by foreign belligerents after hostilities broke out. Lindbergh was brought on board because of his standing as an aviation expert and roving world ambassador, but he was the wrong American to ask.

First of all, he thought the Canadian Plan was a sneaky way to bypass the Neutrality Act. Secondly, regardless of where the aircraft came from, he felt Great Britain and France were doomed: the British Empire was a spent force, the English were lethargic, and the French inefficient and volatile. On the other hand, Lindbergh was greatly impressed by Germany's vitality and strength of purpose, but he was appalled by the fanaticism of the Third Reich. Although he saw the French and British position as hopeless without American support, Lindbergh's message to his fellow Americans was that Washington should mind its own business. If America adhered to its position of strength and neutrality, "at least one strong Western nation would remain to protect Western civilization," should the Europeans "prostrate themselves once again in internecine war."

There was also an ideological undercurrent to Lindbergh's campaign of non-intervention. Like many others (including a number of Parliament Hill occupants in Ottawa), he preferred fascism over communism. A strong, victorious Germany in Europe would act as a formidable bulwark against the ravaging Communist hordes of the Soviet Union.

For Prime Minister King, isolation had a byproduct, and that was national unity. It seemed, in those early months of 1939, that the fabric of the Dominion was about to tear at any moment. There was Quebec nationalism, there was Duff Pattullo in British Columbia more enthralled with a highway to Alaska than one linking the West to the East, there was Mitch Hepburn in Ontario snarling about Liberal policies — and there was wheat.

Tariff reduction was fine, but there was fresh grumbling out on the Prairies. Specifically, the price of wheat as related to the Canadian Wheat Board. Back in 1938, Agriculture Minister James Gardiner had optimistically promised the elimination of the board and a return to the open market. Now it was time to deliver. The Canadian Wheat Board had been established by the Conservative government in 1935 (not long before losing the federal election) as a means of controlling the marketing of wheat and other grains, thus ensuring that the Canadian farmer was not laid low by weak prices. The board would buy the wheat and resell it on the world market.

Prime Minister King wanted to dump the board as soon as it cleared its inventory, but production was high in the summer of 1938 and a steep decline in world prices was expected. The farmers, of course, wanted a fair return for their labours. So Prime Minister King reluctantly agreed to postpone the dismantling of the board "because of exceptional circumstances." As he wrote in his diary, it was "a very difficult problem, the choice being between retaining Wheat Board with prospect of Government purchasing and price-fixing becoming a permanent policy, and finding a way to get rid of the Board without completely prejudicing the position of the party."

The board bought the 1938 crop for eighty cents a bushel, taking a loss of $60 million when it was eventually peddled on the world market. Both Mackenzie King and Gardiner favoured the free market concept, but realized that the farmers had come to rely on guaranteed prices. The cabinet was sharply divided on how much the West should be subsidized at the cost of national unity, and Gardiner's revised plan in March 1939 didn't calm their concerns. It called for the virtual elimination of the board, barring any unexpected catastrophes, along with an insurance scheme guarding against crop failures.

The insurance element — the Prairie Farm Assistance Act — raised few eyebrows when it was introduced in the House. However, the companion legislation, the Wheat Board Amendment Act, calling for a floor price of sixty cents a bushel, kicked up a storm. Amid a deluge of angry petitions and telegrams from farmers denouncing the measure, cabinet ministers from the West told that the party stood to lose five seats on the Prairies if that floor price was maintained. The last thing the prime minister wanted was a showdown with a posse of tractor-riding vigilantes on Parliament Hill, so the old compromiser got everyone to agree on a floor price of seventy cents. The change was made for second reading in May, and the farmers' tractors stayed at home. Another threat to national unity had been dissolved, but the Canadian Wheat Board remained. It would stay in place for several more years.

On a colourful winter evening, a Lockheed airliner rose into the sky above Sea Island airport south of Vancouver. The date was March 1, 1939, a historic moment in Canadian aviation history as Trans-Canada Air Lines inaugurated a transcontinental airmail service. As the gleaming craft and its 795 tons of cargo took off, a *Vancouver Daily Province* reporter was duly impressed. The scene, he wrote, "was bathed in an orange glow, diffused by the white rays of a searchlight.... A purple sunset tinted the airfield, while the brilliant rays of cameramen's lamps showed the streamlined Lockheed airliner in a yellow light. A three-quarter moon pierced the clouds, as Canadian aviation took another step forward."

The first step for Trans-Canada Air Lines came on April 10, 1937, when the company was created by an act of Parliament. The act was part of Transport Minister C.D. Howe's thrust to create government-owned and controlled transportation on the ground, in the air, and on the sea. Its controlling agency would be the Canadian National Railways, "just as it was used as the means for operating such shipping as the government owned, and the means of operating other government transportation facilities." Howe advised TCA not to worry about losing money, to just serve the country. The brand new airline operated its first scheduled flight — Vancouver to Seattle — on September 1, 1937. The return fare was $14.20 and there were two passengers.

One must assume that the 100,000 pieces of mail bound for Ottawa, Montreal, and Toronto from Vancouver and Victoria were properly stamped, bringing revenue to the post office. Among the items was a bouquet of flowers from Mrs. E.W. Hamber, the British Columbia lieutenant-governor's wife, to Lady Tweedsmuir, Canada's governor general's wife.

One month after Canada's mail took flight, regular, transcontinental passenger service began. Some sample fares from across the country included Montreal-Vancouver for $144.65 ($255.10 return); Toronto-Vancouver, $130.90 ($228.50 return); Toronto-Winnipeg,

$67.30 ($121.15 return); Vancouver-Winnipeg, $70.15 ($126.25 return); Regina-Vancouver, $50.15 ($90.25 return); Montreal-Toronto, 20.15 ($36.25 return); and Edmonton-Calgary, $10.50 ($18.90 return). Heeding Howe's advice not to worry about the bottom line, TCA's net operating loss for 1939 was $236,269.71.

While Prime Minister King was appeasing Prairie voters and Canadians were opening letters mailed from the opposite end of the Dominion just the day before, events in Europe took on an ominous sheen. Noting some loud noises emanating from Adolf Hitler's Third Reich, President Roosevelt warned that America would give "no encouragement" to tyrants, and that it would not be passive and silent about persecution of religion in lands where democracy had been snuffed out. "The answer to that is 'No,'" Roosevelt said. "Just as the First Congress of the United States said, 'No'." Roosevelt affirmed that America would use every peaceful means to keep personal freedom alive.

Shortly after this speech, under pressure from Hitler, the Slovak Republic separated itself from its alliance with Czechia. German troops promptly invaded Bohemia and Monrovia-Silesia, the northernmost provinces of Czechoslovakia. Storm troopers romped through Prague, scooping up thousands of suspected subversives and sending them to prison camps. Great Britain recalled its ambassador from Berlin. The U.S. State Department branded the seizure of Prague as "wanton lawlessness" and a threat to the structure of modern civilization. Hitler (egged on by Lord Rothermere, the proprietor of London's *Daily Mail*) followed up by demanding concessions from Romania and pledging support for Italian Dictator Benito Mussolini's plans to grab some real estate for himself.

Mussolini's goal, apparently, was domination of the Mediterranean. During a speech in Costanza, he stressed that Italy was ready to stand up for its claims, including concessions regarding the Suez Canal. Pounding his fist on the stone-balcony railing of a government building, Mussolini told a cheering crowd that "Pacts or no diplomatic pacts, we will never resign ourselves to remaining prisoners in the Mediterranean." Before leaving Rome by train for the Calabria region, Mussolini ordered 250,000 men of the class of 1918 and two-thirds of the class of 1919 to report for army duty.

In a dramatic speech before a packed House on March 30, Prime Minister King appealed to the country to remain calm. He didn't say what Canada would do in a crunch, but again rejected neutrality and isolationism. Neutrality, he said, would give "aid and comfort to any country which might be inclined to aggressive action against the democratic peoples or against the United Kingdom specifically." He also made another carefully worded statement against conscription: "The present government believes that conscription of men for overseas service would not be a necessity or an effective step. Let me say that so long as this government may be in power, no such measure will be enacted." ("Present government" being the operative phrase; the crafty Mackenzie King was letting future Liberal governments off the hook should the conscription question arise again — which it did, once the war had started.)

Ernest Lapointe, in an incisive speech the following day, argued that Canada's participation as a member of the Empire in the war was in its own self-interest and asked neutralists "whether they seriously believed that this could be done without a civil war in Canada." He also declared that he would never support conscription. Then, he asked English Canada to try to understand the views of French Canada on the issue, concluding with this forceful rejection of isolationism:

> The ostrich policy of refusing to face dangers will not keep them away. Indeed, a deliberate policy of drift may involve a greater risk.... Much of the bloodshed and misery that history records has been the direct result of honest, idealistic, but impractical wishful thinking.... So I say this and I want my colleagues to understand me: if there is one chance in a thousand that what our experts say could happen may occur, I should be a traitor to Canada, to my own people, if I would not help to provide against it.

Lapointe's speech got good reviews, especially in Quebec, whereas the prime minister took it on the chin once again. The *Globe and Mail* repeated its familiar theme that Prime Minister King had not gone far enough in declaring Canada's intentions, while *Le Devoir* snapped editorially, "Since when is Canada a country of Europe?"

Mackenzie King was disappointed at some of the responses, but wrote in his diary that, "... as I look on Lapointe's speech and mine, I feel that between us, we have built a substantial support for the structure of Canadian unity." Later, he would admit, "I feel more and more that I have at this time made a mistake in letting myself be too controlled by the isolationist attitude of external affairs. Where I have made a mistake it is where I have not followed my own political judgment and yielded to that of others."

On the same day as Lapointe's speech, British Prime Minister Neville Chamberlain said that the United Kingdom would fight if the Nazis invaded Poland. This was an abrupt about-face from Britain's 1938 appeasement policy, and committed it to an apparent alliance with France, and perhaps even Soviet Russia. Although his government had no official confirmation of rumours about Germany's intentions, Chamberlain said that both Britain and France were prepared to stand up for Poland's independence. His government had been in consultation with Moscow on the matter.

Chamberlain's tough words elated the Polish government in Warsaw, which was nervously mobilizing after yet another threat from Hitler. Back in Canada, Prime Minister King was appalled. Yanking an ambassador home was one thing, no-nonsense talk of war was quite another — especially when the rest of the Empire hadn't been consulted. The crisis even seemed to impact the forthcoming Royal Tour of Canada. After Prime Minister King had referred in the Commons to "impending events of far greater importance than anything now before the House," rumours began to fly that the trip would be cancelled. The same jitters over the situation in Europe caused the stock exchanges in Toronto and New York to sink to lows for the year.

Meanwhile, Madrid surrendered to General Francisco Franco and his Nationalist troops without a shot being fired and the whole country celebrated the virtual end of the Spanish Civil War. Franco's forces had taken Barcelona in January. In February, Britain and France had extended diplomatic recognition, but the Nationalists ended it by marching into Madrid with the Fascist flag flying and the crowds cheering. (Formal unconditional surrender by the former Republican government came in April.)

Back in Ottawa, both Prime Minister King and Opposition Leader Manion again pledged that there would be no conscription of Canadians in the event of war. "Men's lives and men's will cannot be put on the same

Conservative Party leader R.J. Manion did little to weaken the Liberal government's hold on the House of Commons.

Library and Archives Canada, C-007774

basis as goods and profit," Mackenzie King told a cheering House. "The present government believes that the conscription of men for overseas would not be necessary." It was another of the carefully worded promises he would make more than once. Manion echoed the prime minister's sentiment, adding that protection of a "vulnerable" Canada came first.

Earlier in March, white smoke issuing from a chimney in the Vatican signified that the Roman Catholic Church had a new Pope. Eugenio Maria Giuseppe Giovanni Pacelli, who was born in Rome in 1878, would become Pope Pius XII. In the latter years of his career, Pacelli served as secretary of the Vatican's Department of Extraordinary Ecclesiastical Affairs, papal nuncio, and cardinal secretary of state, in which capacity he concluded a number of treaties with both European and South American nations. After his coronation, Pope Pius XI prayed publicly that the world would not stray from the path of reason: "We hope for peace, for that peace for which my predecessor prayed and for which he offered his life to God."

With Easter on the horizon, the homemaker with a few bucks to spare started thinking about a new dress. She leafed through the February issue of *McCall's* magazine, which presented a spread on spring fashions featuring "soft dresses in sheer fabrics." Although there were several colourful designs, "plain" was a key adjective. Hemlines were approaching the knee and the figure-eight waistline was introduced.

"Plain, pale colours" were deemed most interesting, especially those without collars. "This season you will see ever so many collarless dresses, and ever so many buttoned all the way down," the magazine said. Stripes and more stripes were promised, with seersucker, "the thin kind," as the fabric of the striped dinner dress. "The sensation of the season," according to *McCall's*, was the bias frock, "in one piece from shoulder to hem. It has lots of flared fulness [*sic*] which is casually gathered in by the belt."

Skirts were often longer at the back than at the front. The wide-shouldered, masculine suit, designed by Elsa Schiaparelli and made famous by Marlene Dietrich, was widely copied. While new, improved fabrics such as rayon provided various finishes, the emergence of nylon changed women's lives forever. Nylon hosiery became commercially available in 1938 and instantly eliminated the bagging and sagging of stockings. Not to mention that its sheer allure enhanced women's legs.

Newspaper ads offered pre-Easter wearables "from the smallest accessory to the tailored suit or dress." Dresses could be had in "pretty colored printed crepes in the cleverest styling." Party frocks were "outstanding creations in soft chiffons (and) crisp nets ... in lovely tulip shades so popular this spring." Coats were dressy and tailored, and along with suits were available in tweeds, worsteds, Poiret twills, and plain fabrics. Easter hats went for $1.95 to $6.95, middies for $1.25, blouses were $1.95 to $3.95, knitted pullover sweaters were $1.39, $1.95, and $2.95. Slacks "of nice quality wool faille" went for $2.95.

The Wonderbra was invented in Montreal in 1939 by Moe Nadler, founder of the Canadian Lady Corset Company. He established a vital connection with the New York City garment trade, licensed the Wonder-Bra trademark (the hyphen was soon discarded), and patented the diagonal slash design.

Men had their own fashion advisers, too. Although the editors were surely out of touch with bread lines and relief projects, the upscale men's magazine *Esquire* emphasized single- and double-breasted suits that were "more vogue than bizarre." Colourful, checked sports coats, high-ankle boots, and fedoras adorned male models. "One year ago, you would have been desperately out of style if you had put in an appearance wearing a square-front jacket," one blurb read, "but slip one on today and you'll go to the head of the class." Although probably not as classy as *Esquire*'s examples, men's topcoats could be had in Canada in March for $25 (tweeds), $20 (fleeces), $35 (Manx tweeds), and $35 (gabardines). In Toronto, suits and topcoats were going for $22.50, while a bankruptcy sale touted bargains at $16.50 for "all models and sizes." Eaton's was advertising the "cockade," the new spring style in "brant" hats. The hats were "broader in the brim with pronounced taper backward to crown." Price: $2.95.

The waistcoat, or vest, was still part of the male look and *de rigueur* for any sort of formal situation. Plus-fours, made popular by the Duke of Windsor, were just the thing for the golf course. Men wore suspenders to hold up their trousers and garters to hold up their socks. Paris men's garters — "Boosting your sox appeal" — ran print advertisements during the 1920s and 1930s that showed a male model sitting down with his legs crossed and his socks drooping. They carried such captions as, "And he wonders why success never comes" or, "And he wonders why she said NO." The company's slogan was, "No metal can touch you." The garters, manufactured by Albert Stein & Company, sold for twenty-five cents to $2.

Meanwhile, across Canada and the world, there was triumph and tragedy, disaster and drama, and a couple of hiccups from Mother Nature throughout the month.

Howard Carter, the archaeologist who discovered King Tutankhamen's tomb in 1922, died in England that March. He lived to the relatively ripe old age of seventy-four, despite the supposed curse of King Tut's Tomb. One legend has it that a stone tablet that was found when Carter's team opened the tomb, then mysteriously disappeared, was inscribed with the words, "Death will slay with his wings whoever disturbs the tomb of the Pharaoh." A year later, Lord Carnarvon, who had bankrolled Carter's expedition, died suddenly of pneumonia brought on by an infected mosquito bite. His abrupt demise had the popular press in a frenzy over the curse. One story had Carter's pet canary being bitten by a cobra, while another said Carnarvon's dog howled all night, then dropped dead at the same time as his master. Carter, however, led an undisturbed life after his discovery, dying of a blood disease in a London suburb.

At the Macdonald Brier bonspiel in Toronto, Bert Hall's rink from Kitchener, Ontario, won the men's Canadian curling championship by defeating the Ross Kennedy foursome from Winnipeg, 12–10. The seasoned Kitchener rink, wearing traditional white sweaters, led 8–3 after six ends. Manitoba rallied but Hall controlled the twelfth and final end for the victory.

In Halifax, a fire fanned by a strong ocean wind destroyed the Queen Hotel. The final death toll was twenty-eight, including several children. The headquarters of the Nova Scotia Liquor Commission and the Greek Orthodox church also burned to the ground. Damage was estimated at $800,000.

Out in Esquimalt, British Columbia, HMCS *Skidegate* led forty stout fishing boats out of the Royal Canadian Navy base for exercises at sea. They were starting a four-week training period in gunnery, minesweeping, signalling, naval navigation, and naval routine. It was a precautionary measure just in case the West Coast found itself at war in the Pacific once again. "We've been looking forward to this," said one fisherman, "and it means a few extras dollars for us in the slack season."

Mahatma Gandhi began a hunger fast in early March to punctuate his demands for reforms in the state of Rajkot. After almost a hundred hours, the state acceded to his demand; Gandhi was so weak at the end that he could not sit up.

Back in Canada, a fierce gale off Newfoundland wreaked havoc with shipping, sinking a small wooden freighter that was being towed to safety. And in northern British Columbia, flooding near Dawson Creek led to the reported loss of eight lives when ice in the East Pine River broke up.

The Way Things Were

WE'VE GOT MUSIC

Rock 'n' roll hadn't been born yet; neither had the Beatles. Elvis Presley was four years old. The music of 1939 was quite removed from what is available in this century. People hummed along to lyrics that actually rhymed, or snapped their fingers to a big-band sound that didn't assault the eardrums. One of the more popular programs was *Your Hit Parade*, broadcast Saturday nights by the CBS network. The show featured the top tunes of the week, based on phonograph record and sheet music sales, and was sponsored by Lucky Strike cigarettes. Some of the songs the Canadian radio listener might hear were, "If I Didn't Care," "Over the Rainbow" (memorably sung by Judy Garland in *The Wizard of Oz* movie), "Deep Purple," "South of the Border (Down Mexico Way)," and "Two Sleepy People." Bandleader Glenn Miller's "Moonlight Serenade" and "In the Mood" were also hugely popular. Vocalists Bing Crosby, Frank Sinatra, Helen Forrest, Jo Stafford, Billie Holiday, and Kay Thompson were favourites. Besides Miller, the top bandleaders included Benny Goodman, Artie Shaw, Harry James, Tommy Dorsey, and Paul Whiteman. Canada had Mart Kenney and His Western Gentlemen, and Bert Niosi's band.

Show Time. *Gunga Din* starred the irrepressible trio of Cary Grant, Victor McLaglen, and Douglas Fairbanks Jr., with Sam Jaffe as Gunga Din. "A cavalcade of action," said the theatre ads. "Kipling's ballad of heroism staged on a scale that beggars words!" Meanwhile, anyone seeking a change of pace could take in *The Little Princess*, starring Shirley Temple. One Toronto theatre offered "bargain morning prices": twenty-five-cent admission from 10:00 a.m. to 1:00 p.m.

Martin Brian Mulroney. He was born March 20 in Baie-Comeau, Quebec, to Benedict Mulroney, an electrician, and Mary Irene O'Shea Mulroney. Brian Mulroney served as the eighteenth prime minister of Canada from 1984 to 1993, when he was forced to resign. He is regarded as one of Canada's most unpopular leaders.

"Ya Dirty Rat!" It was like a plot out of a James Cagney prison movie. Three determined convicts at the British Columbia Penitentiary in New Westminster made a desperate bid for freedom after fashioning a hacksaw in the institution's machine shop. One of them (the skinny one) sawed through one of his cell bars, spread the two adjoining bars apart, and wriggled out. He then got the barrier gate open and unlocked all the cells on his tier. Joined by the other two, the trio attacked a guard and locked him in one of the cells before heading for the main yard. Another guard gave the alarm, however, and the three desperadoes were recaptured without getting a glimpse of the outside.

For Sale. The *Winnipeg Free Press* had a tidy selection of rooming and boarding houses for sale in its classified section. On Broadway, a fifteen-room building was offered for $1,800, or $1,000 cash. Rents were $75 per month. An eleven-room house on Langside was on the market for $450. Then there was this: "Special Appeal. In order to retain my job, I will sacrifice contents of my Rmg-H on Spence St. for $250."

April

Albania is a sliver of a country in southern Europe. It's quite mountainous and has a coastline of a little more than 200 miles along the lower edge of the Adriatic Sea. In 1925, Ahmet Muhtar Bey Zogolli, who had been born into an aristocratic family of landowners, was elected president of Albania. He took the name, Zogu. Then, in 1928, Zogu decided to become King Zog, claiming to be a direct descendant of the legendary Skanderberg, the Dragon of Albania, who led Albania in the fifteenth century. Once described as an "appalling gangster," King Zog became adept at political intrigue. He was no match, however, for Benito Mussolini.

Italy had begun its penetration of Albania in 1925, when President Zogu granted Italy mining concessions. Before long, the Italians were everywhere. Under Mussolini, they controlled the Roman Catholic school system, the *gendarmerie*, and, to some extent, the military. A banking crisis forced Albania's national bank to move its headquarters to Rome, effectively putting it under Italian control.

King Zog tried to fight back, but Mussolini's influence was too strong. Mussolini was also quite aware of Hitler's aggressive expansion of the Third Reich and didn't want to become the weakling in the fraternity of dictators. It would be embarrassing for a leader who imagined himself as a Caesar to have bullies like Adolf Hitler, Josef Stalin, and Francisco Franco kick sand in his face. So, Mussolini issued an ultimatum to the Albanian government that it accept Italian occupation of the country, but it refused. Il Duce decided to invade. Albania also had strategic importance because of its border with

Greece. Mussolini coveted Greece, which he viewed as an important link in his plans to dominate the Mediterranean.

On April 7, 100,000 Italian troops, supported by 137 naval units and 600 warplanes, landed in Albania. They struck all major ports simultaneously and had the situation under control within hours. There was no effective opposition from the Albanian army because it was dominated by Italian advisers and officers. King Zog fled, first to Greece and then to England.

In Britain, Parliament was recalled and military leaves cancelled. The fleet was put to sea. Prime Minister Chamberlain warned Italy and Germany to keep their hands off the Mediterranean. Lord Halifax, Britain's foreign secretary, noted that Italy's invasion had come on Good Friday, and said, "Not one act in this business could have more effectively silenced religious sentiment than the fact that it should have been on the day which for most Christians was the most sacred of the year." King George returned to London from Windsor Castle to get a one-on-one report on the situation from Chamberlain. A source

Library and Archives Canada, PA-130023

German Chancellor Adolf Hitler in full voice as he delivers an impassioned speech.

involved in planning King George and Queen Elizabeth's visit to Canada told a Canadian reporter that only a "whacking crisis," such as actual war, could halt the tour. Alarums such as the Albanian crisis didn't count.

In Ottawa, the special cabinet committee charged with planning the Royal Visit disposed of one more item in April. The locomotives that would pull the Royal Train were chosen, along with the engineers who would drive them. These were a couple of the final details in a planning process that had begun on October 8, 1938, when it was announced at Balmoral Castle in Scotland that Their Majesties would visit Canada in 1939. The prime minister had suggested a tour to King George personally while in London for the Coronation in 1937, believing that such a visit would do much to solidify Canada's emotional ties with the monarchy.

Prime Minister King was delighted when his office received the cable about the sovereign's decision. "It is a fine answer to the jingoes," he wrote in his diary. Prime Minister King also noted that this would be the "first time, in history, that Britain's Sovereign has been in North America; first time a British Dominion, other than India, has been visited by a reigning Sovereign. It adds much to the history of the Liberal party and I am glad it has come as a part of my career." At first, a straightforward visit to Ottawa, the Dominion's capital, was envisioned, but then King George changed his mind and decided he wanted to see more of the country. The Royal Couple would arrive on May 15 and depart on June 15.

The prime minister, as chairman of the Cabinet committee, was deeply involved throughout the entire planning process. During the latter months of 1938 and the early months of 1939, the committee tried not to be distracted by events in Europe as they wrestled with the myriad details of the trip. Officers in high places, from London to each province, were involved; the king had suggested he'd like to see all the provincial capitals. This was the framework upon which the prime minister and his committee fashioned the tour, with emphasis on giving as many Canadians as possible a glimpse of Their Majesties. An equally important goal was to show the king and queen as much typical Canadian life and society as possible.

Public functions, ceremonial affairs of all kinds, and presentations were ruthlessly winnowed from the thousands of proposals that flooded the committee. There had to be a fair number of formal affairs because, after all, this was the King of Canada, and his subjects needed to display their obeisance in the proper manner. However, long military parades and cavalcades full of local dignitaries weren't on the agenda. With one exception, there was no pecking order on who was to meet Their Majesties — it would depend on venue and circumstances. Children, young persons, and war veterans would be accommodated as much as possible.

Special postage stamps, a silver dollar, and two medallions would be issued to commemorate the visit. Radio would play a vital role, as the CBC was making elaborate plans to broadcast almost every waking moment. One key event was to be a message from King George to the Empire, broadcast from Winnipeg on May 24.

The king and queen would step ashore at Quebec City. The next day, they would take a train to see the rest of Canada. The CPR and CNR would share the honour of providing transportation: Canadian Pacific would handle the westward journey, and Canadian National, the eastward. A Hudson-type locomotive (later to be honoured with the designation, *Royal Hudson*) would pull twelve cars, finished in royal blue with gold and silver banding, on CPR tracks, with a Northern-type locomotive on the CNR tracks. On board, along with Their Majesties, would be lords and ladies in waiting, domestic servants, various functionaries and private staff, a doctor, RCMP bodyguards, and Prime Minister King, who was the official minister in attendance.

Mackenzie King had won the coveted post after insisting that no ministers in the British government accompany the Royal Couple. Lord Tweedsmuir was consultant-in-chief, but would keep to the background as much as possible. His one major suggestion, that he greet Their Majesties as they stepped ashore in Canada, was firmly rejected by Prime Minister King, who strongly felt that this function was the prime minister's job. It would be arranged for the governor general to pay his respects to his sovereign on board their vessel, leaving Prime Minister King at the bottom of the gangplank when the Royal Couple disembarked.

The 1939 budget, when presented to the House by Finance Minister Dunning, was a call to all Canadians to try a little harder. To help things along, Dunning proposed a tax credit equal to 10 percent of capital outlays to stimulate industry and promote employment. "The government proposes to offer what I believe will be a powerful incentive to all industries to go forward immediately" with plant expansion and modernization of machinery, Dunning said.

However, there would be no decrease in personal income taxes. "Much as I regret it, I am forced to ask our taxpayers to continue for the time being to bear approximately their present burdens because I am convinced that for us to give up tax revenues at this time would only cause greater burdens and probably other serious difficulties at a later date."

Dunning projected a deficit of $60 million for the fiscal year ending on March 31, 1940 — double the figure for the 1938 budget. A big chunk of this — more than $64 million — could be attributed to defence spending.

Dunning juggled Canada's complex tariff structure and came up with a number of winners and losers. The special 3 percent excise tax on imports to the United States and other most-favoured nations would be abolished. As a result, radio tubes would cost less, as would door mats; bananas and tomatoes would cost more. Duties on starch and woollen yarn would also be reduced. Dunning foresaw sales tax revenues down by $14 million over the coming year. All through his speech, the finance minister stayed with his main premise: the economy could only return to normal when private industry produced more jobs. "In these days, if the people as a whole, and business in particular, will not spend, the governments must," he said. "It is not a matter of choice, but of sheer social necessity."

Prime Minister King accepted Canada's steep plunge into the realm of deficits with equanimity. He was more interested, apparently, in his finance minister's clothes. "Lapointe and I were highly amused at his little vanities, dressed up with spats on, wearing morning suit with a flower in his buttonhole, but what was most amusing was the presence on his desk of two separate glasses — one with water, the other, a dark coloured glass, which, when he began to speak, we all came to see was whisky and soda," Mackenzie King wrote in his diary. "A little bottle of pills or pellets also laid out, all these taken at intervals during the time of speaking."

Mackenzie King was perhaps being a little harsh on Dunning, who had suffered a mild heart attack during his budget presentation a year earlier, collapsing in the House. He recovered sufficiently to return to cabinet, but pursued his duties with less vigour than before. He was, in fact, getting ready to step down after twenty-three years in public life. Elected to the Saskatchewan legislature in 1916, he became premier of that province before being lured into federal politics.

Dunning joined Mackenzie King's cabinet somewhat reluctantly: his initial assessment of his prime minister was not a favourable one. He once observed that this "charming, polite, hospitable, and inert mass" could only get in the way of any constructive action.* Despite this, Dunning served Prime Minister King faithfully during their long relationship.

The *Toronto Daily Star* called the budget a challenge to both industry and consumers and commented that "employed Canadians can do their share by refusing to yield to panic, and by resuming as far as possible, their normal buying habits." The Opposition leader, however, did not think much of Dunning's efforts. During the budget debate in early May, R.J. Manion called it barren of ideas and "entirely lacking in originality." He said he was convinced the Liberals "are on the skids and unable to turn back."

The rhetoric of confrontation continued unabated throughout April. On April Fools' Day, Adolf Hitler ratcheted up the tension by accusing Great Britain of destroying any chances for peace. In a speech before a crowd of 50,000 in the public square in Wilhelmshaven, Der Führer warned that Britain's pledge to support Poland would destroy the Munich agreement of 1938. "He who is willing to pull the chestnuts out of the fire for others must expect to get burned," Hitler said. The naval accord between the two countries was also in jeopardy. "I once concluded a naval treaty with Britain. I was motivated by the fervent desire that we would never again have a war with England. If, however, that wish does not exist on the other side, then the practical pre-conditions for concluding

---

* H.Blair Neatby, *William Lyon Mackenzie King*, Volume 3 (Toronto: University of Toronto Press), 15.

such a treaty have vanished." Hitler heaped derision on Britain, France, and other democracies generally, but made no definitive statement about war plans.

Prime Minister Chamberlain responded two days later by assuring the House of Commons that Britain meant business in its support of the European "peace bloc," pledging military aid to fight any kind of aggression. A "new epoch" had dawned in British foreign policy, he said, expressing surprise that his promise of support for Poland should have been misunderstood in any quarter. "A declaration of that importance is not concerned with some minor little border incident," he said. "It is concerned with bigger things which might be behind a frontier incident.... German assurances have now been flung to the wind. That is the fact which has completely destroyed confidence and forced us to make the great departure announced Friday."

Chamberlain also disputed charges that Great Britain had turned a cold shoulder toward Soviet Russia. "We welcome co-operation with any country, whatever may be its internal system of government." There were still ideological differences between Britain and Russia, he admitted, "but they do not count in a question of this kind. What we are concerned with is the maintenance of our independence and that of all states which might be threatened by aggression."

In Washington, President Roosevelt said the United States was ready to match "force to force" in defending the entire western hemisphere against aggression of any kind. Addressing the Pan-American Union, Roosevelt recalled his promise to defend Canada against attacks from overseas and — using firm language — extended that protection to all countries in South and North America. "The American peace which we celebrate today has no quality of weakness in it," he said. "We are prepared to maintain and to defend it to the fullest extent of our strength, matching force to force if any attempt is made to subvert our institutions or to impair the independence of any one of our group." He reminded his audience that all men "have within themselves the power to become free at any time," and said that peace and independence can only come when "our sister nations beyond the seas will break the bonds of the ideas which constrain them toward protracted warfare."

Then, in identical 1,217-word telegrams to Adolf Hitler and Benito Mussolini on April 14, Roosevelt urged them to guarantee peace for ten, or even twenty-five, years and offered to act as an intermediary toward that end. "You realize I am sure that throughout the world hundreds of millions of human beings are living today in constant fear of a new war or even a series of wars," he wrote. After noting that three nations in Europe and one in Africa have seen their independence terminated, Roosevelt wrote, "Nothing can persuade the peoples of the earth that any governing power has any right or need to inflict the consequence of war on its own or any other people save in the cause of self-evident home defence."

The messages asked specifically whether Hitler and Mussolini would assure the world that they would not attack thirty-one now-independent nations. "Such an assurance clearly must apply not only to the present day, but also to a future sufficiently long to give every opportunity to work by peaceful methods for a more permanent peace." He then suggested that the word "future" be construed as applying "to a minimum period of assured non-aggression — ten years at the least, a quarter of a century if we dare look that far ahead." Roosevelt assured them that the United States would be willing to act as a "friendly intermediary" in passing on any offers for peace from the two belligerent countries, or any others.

By April 20, Hitler's fiftieth birthday, there had been no response from Berlin. In Rome, however, Mussolini rejected Roosevelt's overtures, saying Italy would not be repressed by "messiah-like" messages from outsiders.

Less than a week later, Britain announced that it would conscript young adult males aged twenty and twenty-one to bear arms. The object "is not to wage war but to prevent it," Chamberlain told the House. The men would serve for six months in regular army units; 200,000 were expected to be drafted within the first year. Conscription in the United Kingdom shattered a British precedent that had existed for centuries.

Toward the end of April, the German chancellor called a time out — sort of. In a speech to the Reichstag, which was half defiant and half conciliatory, Hitler officially trashed the naval treaty with Britain and rejected Roosevelt's offer. However, he declared, "I am not aware of any purpose for which I should wage war."

Speaking for two hours and seventeen minutes, he made several points: the Germany-Poland non-aggression pact had been rendered invalid by Poland's rejection of Berlin's offer of a peaceful resolution to the Corridor problem; the Anglo-German naval treaty ceased to exist because of "war-mongering" Britain's insistence on regarding the Third Reich as a potential enemy; and Danzig must be allowed to return to Germany. (Danzig was a port city on the Baltic Sea, awarded to Poland by the Treaty of Versailles. The Danzig Corridor gave Poland access to the Baltic, but it separated Germany from East Prussia. Danzig was made a free city by the League of Nations in 1920. Although the Corridor was mainly settled by Poles, the city itself was predominantly German.)

Hitler's only answer to Roosevelt's insistence on a peaceful solution was to note that it seemed as though there was now a "Monroe Doctrine" for Central European nations as for the Americas. Although declaring that Germany would never again enter a conference room unwanted, he said he would be "very happy if these problems could really find their solution at the council table."

Prime Minister King took the high road about Hitler's speech. "I feel it is on the whole, a remarkably good speech, and justified from his point of view," Mackenzie King wrote:

> I think the British should take immediate advantage of his readiness to begin anew. I know nothing that seems to me worse than the alliance recently made with Poland, Romania and Greece, and attempted alliance with Russia. It is all in the wrong direction. From the point of view of other parts of the Empire, it is most unfair.

Almost to the end of August, Prime Minister King believed Hitler to be a rational man, that he would come to his senses and realize the consequences of his actions. The German army's march into Czechoslovakia shook that belief, as did the threats against Romania and Poland. The Reichstag speech had given Mackenzie King hope; he appeared to be more annoyed with Chamberlain than Hitler. What the prime minister longed for was tranquility, and he grasped at any positive straw.

Despite the reference in January's throne speech about "anxious and continuous consideration" of events in Europe, this was supposed to be a year for mending domestic fences. The party had triumphed in the 1935 general election and Prime Minister King had pencilled in a new vote for the fall of 1939. His job was to steer the Liberal ship to another successful result at the polls, and there was much to be done on the national scene. Hepburn's Ontario and Duplessis's Quebec would need careful handling, and there was the never-ending task of keeping the farm bloc fat and quiescent out west. The king and queen's visit would certainly give a boost to the government's fortunes, as well.

Adversaries interpret restraint as military weakness or lack of will, and appeasement is the ugliest face of restraint. The ring of jackboots in March and the heavy breathing in April were the strongest indications yet that the willingness of Western powers to bend at Munich in September 1938 was leading to something very bad. The only question was, when? The twin terrors of Continental Europe — Hitler and Mussolini — were running amok like schoolyard bullies terrorizing the second graders.

Safe in his lair on the other side of a very wide ditch, Roosevelt talked tough but he wasn't at Munich. Neither was Mackenzie King, who carried the euphoria of Chamberlain's "peace for our time" mindset into 1939. Prime Minister King's foreign policy as his own secretary of state for external affairs was, perversely, based on internal affairs with an emphasis on national unity. Despite the trauma of the previous nine years, deep divisions festered between the neutralists, the isolationists, and the pacifists on one side, and the imperialists, who would unquestioningly follow their sovereign into battle, and ordinary Canadians who — when they thought about it at all — realized that if Britain went to war, so would its Dominions, on the other.

Prime Minister King was the great compromiser, the arch-enemy of precipitate actions or precipitate decisions. Muddle through as long as possible until you are reasonably certain your actions won't damage yourself, your party, or Canada, as the case may be, seemed to be his *modus operandi*. He became a master at invoking that unctuous little phrase, "Parliament will decide." It was a handy evasion and it served him well when dealing with the League of Nations or members of the Empire, as well as with the voters, of course. As 1939 progressed, however, it became apparent to the prime minister that compromise would perhaps not be an option anymore. But not yet. Not in April.

The international news that mom and dad picked up on the radio was not easy listening, but for any children in the house it didn't matter. For many of them, the biggest event on the airwaves was the *Little Orphan Annie* show. Six days a week, in the late afternoon, this wildly popular children's series would air for fifteen minutes. It starred Little Orphan Annie herself, Daddy Warbucks, Sandy, her faithful dog ("Arf! Arf!"), and various villains. For proof of purchase (box top, label), Ovaltine, the show's long-time sponsor, would send young listeners a secret decoder ring or pin. The kids could then unscramble secret messages read over the radio.

In the evenings, the radio was Canada's primary source of entertainment. There was a wide variety of programs offered, often in fifteen-minute segments. Among those the Rayner family listened to in 1939 were *The Green Hornet*, *Adventures of Charlie Chan*, and *Amos 'n' Andy*. (When the Rayners were on relief in the mid-1930s, my father acquired — for five precious dollars — a second-hand mantel radio. The very first program we listened to was *Amos 'n' Andy*.)

Other shows that helped pass the time in the evenings were *Doc Savage*, *The Shadow* ("Who knows what evil lurks in the minds of men? The Shadow knows," followed by that weird laugh), *Easy Aces*, *Edgar Bergen and Charlie McCarthy*, *Terry and The Pirates* (with the announcer stretching out the words: "Terrrryyyy and the Piiiirates!"), *Burns and Allen*, *Fibber McGee and Molly*, *Challenge of The Yukon* (later called *Preston of The Yukon*), *Jack Benny*, and *Big Town* (starring Edward G. Robinson and Claire Trevor). There were also full-length dramas, variety and musical shows, operas, recitals, and philharmonic hours.

Daytime radio was another matter. Then, the soap opera ruled. The popularity of this form of escapism has drawn much learned thought. Listening to the agonizing and drawn-out episodes gave the homebound woman a connection with her own economic and social condition. The conflict coming through the speakers could well be the dramatization of their own loves, marriages, and destinies.

Ma Perkins, *The Guiding Light*, and *Pepper Young's Family* were among the most popular programs, which ran daily in fifteen-minute segments from 10:00 a.m. to 6:00 p.m. Other popular serials were *The Romance of Helen Trent*, *Stella Dallas*, *Young Widder Brown*, and *John's Other Wife*. Some of the plots even made the transition to television and ran for decades.

All of these could be found on the four American networks. The CBC also had its full share of shows listed in the programming schedules of each daily paper. The Canadian Broadcasting Corporation started a radio network on CNR passenger trains. And, in 1933, the Canadian Radio Broadcasting Corporation took over the network. In 1936, the CBC was officially formed.

There was a decent assortment of radio sets available. Viking brand mantel sets were offered at Eaton's for $39.50 and up, while console floor models sold for $59.50 to $98.50. Throughout the month, Simpson's department store in Toronto advertised discontinued, five-tube Philco full-size console models for $49.50. "Receives all Standard United States and Canadian Broadcasting and Chain Stations," a newspaper ad claimed. Many outlets offered sets that ran on cumbersome batteries, not unlike those in an automobile. It was also wise to stock up on spare vacuum tubes.

On the legal front, there was a lot of excitement. Early in 1939, two radio personalities got themselves in hot water over a scheme that could easily have been the plot of a prime-time drama. In April, a shame-faced Jack Benny pleaded guilty to jewel smuggling in a New York federal court. He was fined $10,000 and given a suspended sentence of one year and one day. Back in January, George Burns, star of the *Burns and Allen Show*, had been fined $8,000 and given a similar suspended sentence. He also pleaded guilty. Both Burns and Benny had become enmeshed in a plan to avoid paying duty on jewellery brought into the United States from Europe. The mastermind was Albert N. Chaperau, soldier of fortune and self-confessed smuggler, who lured show business and café society celebrities into his illegal operations.

On April 5, the Supreme Court of Canada ruled that Eskimos should be considered Indians under the terms of the British North America Act (they became known as Inuit later). The issue arose when the federal government, trying to avoid responsibility for the Inuit in Quebec, claimed they were under provincial jurisdiction. The court ruled that when the Act was originally adopted, there were few, if any, Inuit in Canada and that they inhabited Rupert's Land. When Canada absorbed Rupert's Land, the federal government agreed to take responsibility for the Natives there. Rupert's Land subsequently became part of the province of Quebec.

At Buckingham Palace, King George kept one eye on the dispatches from his ministers, while getting wrapped up in planning for the trip to Canada. So much so that he and Queen Elizabeth were forced to give up one of their favourite outings: going to the races at Newmarket. King George had come quite a way from the little boy who once trembled at the sight of his father.

The future king was born on December 14, 1895, at York Cottage, Sandringham. He was christened Albert Frederick Arthur George, Bertie to his family. Bertie's childhood was not unhappy, but his father, the Duke of York (later to become King George V), was intolerant of his children's failings. Young Prince Albert was so tense around his father that he became excruciatingly shy. His older brother, Prince Edward, was outgoing and mercurial, and Albert slipped into the background, nervous and easily frightened. He developed a stammer that became a serious speech defect.

During his schooldays, the prince became withdrawn and depressed. His stammer was exaggerated as he was forced to write with his right hand, although he was naturally left-handed. Despite finishing at the bottom of his class, he moved on to Dartmouth, the naval institution that was a traditional stop for young royal males. Bertie was sidelined by a severe attack of appendicitis for a number of months, but he seemed to emerge from his shell as his naval career progressed. As a sub-lieutenant aboard the dreadnought HMS *Collingwood*, Bertie saw action at the battle of Jutland and wrote home to the family that it was "certainly a great experience to have been through."

The prince's naval career ended in 1917 when he underwent an operation to remove a duodenal ulcer. He was twenty-one and had matured into a hard-working, conscientious, and humane officer. The interwar years were somewhat aimless for Bertie. As second in line to the throne, he had no future to prepare for. He learned to fly, went to Cambridge to complete his formal education, and got married. His bride was Elizabeth Bowes-Lyon. Eventually, they had two daughters, Elizabeth and Margaret Rose.

In 1936, George V died. A few months later, Bertie's older brother, King Edward VIII, abdicated to marry Wallis Simpson. Bertie was thrust into the limelight quite unprepared. Some earlier disastrous attempts at public speaking had forced him to consult a voice coach, who concentrated on the prince's breathing. This helped considerably; the new King George VI, not all that robust and still diffident, was able to speak with only a slight hesitation. In 1939, the king had become a popular monarch along with his beautiful, assured queen.

The Way Things Were

STANLEY CUP FINAL

The Boston Bruins defeated the Toronto Maple Leafs, four games to one, to win the 1939 Stanley Cup. It was the first time the National Hockey League had gone to a best-of-seven final series, but the playoffs leading to the Boston-Toronto showdown were cumbersome. The Montreal Maroons had folded the year before, leaving a seven-team league, so the NHL decided that six of the seven teams would make the playoffs. (The other teams in the NHL that season were the Montreal Canadiens, Detroit Red Wings, Chicago Black Hawks, New York Rangers, and New York Americans.) There was an awkward mixture of three-game and seven-game matches, with the Bruins and the Maple Leafs ultimately qualifying for the final. The Leafs won only one game, 3–2 in overtime, while the Bruins took the others, 2–1, 3–1, 2–0, and 3–1.

The 1938–39 All Star Team consisted of Frank Brimsek of Boston in goal; Eddie Shore and Dit Clapper of Boston on defence; Syl Apps of Toronto at centre; and Gordie Drillon of Toronto and Toe Blake of Montreal as wingers. Art Ross of the Bruins was the coach.

William Ian Corneil Binnie. This future jurist was born April 14 in Montreal to James Corneil Binnie and Phyllis Mackenzie Binnie. He served as associate deputy minister of justice from 1982 to 1986. Mr. Justice Binnie was a senior partner at a Toronto law firm when appointed to the Supreme Court of Canada in 1998. Mr. Justice Binnie has an extensive background in commercial, corporate, and international law. At the time of his appointment, he was considered an expert on constitutional matters.

Hopping It. Winners of a month-long hopscotch competition in Toronto were June Mark, age nine; Bertha Russell, ten; Freda Dollery, eleven, and Gwen Spelligue, twelve. The competition was sponsored by Simpson's department store.

Stocking Up. Simpson's announced it had 24,000 pairs of "ringless chiffon stockings" in popular shades. The fully fashioned stockings, "of a flattering yet serviceable silk," were on sale for fifty-seven cents a pair (two for one dollar).

Chinese Freeze-Out. Vancouver City Council pondered a petition put forth by white waitresses claiming that they weren't allowed to work in Chinese eateries. The ban against non-Asian waitresses was apparently "in the interest of good morals."

May

On the sixth day of May, the king and queen left the English shores on a historic voyage to the New World. The departure of the *Empress of Australia*, pride of the Canadian Pacific Steamships fleet, was made in the best tradition of British pomp and circumstance. Flags and bunting flew, bands played "God Save The King" and "O Canada," a twenty-one-gun salute thundered out, wave upon wave of cheers erupted from the packed throngs in Portsmouth harbour, not to be drowned out by the roar of warplanes overhead.

As the Royal Couple walked up the gangplank to the gleaming white liner, they left behind their two daughters and the Queen Mother. There were no tears and no sorrow. Little Princess Margaret Rose, nine, held tightly to her grandmother's hand. Princess Elizabeth, thirteen, waved and waved. The queen blew kisses and the king saluted. Then, as the *Australia* was tugged away, he threw a bouquet of flowers to his mother on the dock. "They fell at her feet. She picked them up and pressed them to her heart," a reporter wrote later.

Soon the ship and its precious cargo were lost to sight on their way down the English Channel. The bands, the crowds, and the honour guards departed. It's not hard to imagine the nervous pacing and prolonged scrutiny of naval charts at the Admiralty back in London, nor the need to moisten dry mouths at Westminster. The German pocket battleship *Deutschland* was known to be lurking off the coast of Spain. What if Adolf Hitler, in a fit of suicidal bravado, decided to send her against the *Empress of Australia* in a ghastly opening gambit of total war? The fast battle cruiser HMS *Repulse*, after being rejected for the duty of taking the Royal Couple to Canada at the last minute, would accompany them for only three days before returning to home waters. That would leave two light cruisers, HMS *Southampton* and HMS *Glasgow*, as escorts

The trip itself had been in question for some time. The king himself had been torn between duty to England and to the Empire. With every ominous dispatch from the Continent, he agonized over whether he would be deserting his subjects at home in time of crisis. There were other voices raised against the trip, too. Some cabinet members thought it was a waste of time, sending the sovereign, already in frail health, on an arduous journey through an empty land, visiting one jerkwater town after another. Chamberlain, on the other hand, was well aware of the schism between duty to the Empire and isolationism in Canada. The Royal Couple had to go to demonstrate the mother country's connection to one of its most strategic Dominions. He persuaded the king and the cabinet.

The switch from the *Repulse* to *Empress of Australia* was made on April 27, just days before the scheduled departure. The warship had left Gibraltar for England earlier in the month, fully prepared to make room for two Very Important Passengers. However, with the situation in Europe reaching a scary level, the king didn't think it was a good idea to deprive the Royal Navy of one of its premium fighting ships. The *Repulse's* two sister ships, HMS *Hood* and HMS *Renown*, were in dry dock for refitting, so the decision was made to keep the *Repulse* at home and ready to fight ("Fast enough to catch the enemy, powerful enough to destroy it").

For Queen Elizabeth, the trip to Canada must have been an exciting adventure. She was a sophisticated woman, but not a world traveller. She was born Elizabeth Angela Marguerite Bowes-Lyon into the Scottish nobility, which, because of the peculiar English snobbishness surrounding royal lineage, meant she was officially a commoner. It didn't matter to the Duke of York, as Bertie was known in the 1920s. She was vivacious and popular, and he despaired of winning her hand. But he did, shyness or no shyness, and neither one of them regretted the marriage.

Fog. Ice. The cold, implacable North Atlantic. By choosing the fast northern route to Canada, rather than the more leisurely southern swing, a tactical error had been made at the planning table. Four days into the voyage, a violent storm descended on the *Australia* and her escorts. Tables were tossed about as huge waves rolled repeatedly over the 21,000-ton liner. According to a report from on board, the king and queen apparently enjoyed the fury of the storm. "Both are good sailors and they spent some time on deck ... watching the boisterous sea." Within twenty-four hours, the sea had flattened out, covered by a blanket of fog. The *Australia*'s speed dropped dramatically and the foghorns began blaring incessantly. Aboard the two cruisers, lookouts were told to keep a sharp eye out for impending collisions.

"For three and a half days we only moved a few miles," the queen wrote to her mother-in-law, Queen Mary. "The fog was so thick that it was like a white cloud round the ship, and the foghorn blew incessantly. Its melancholy blasts were echoed back by the icebergs like the twang of a piece of wire. Incredibly eerie and really very alarming, knowing that we were surrounded by ice and unable to see a foot either way. We very nearly hit a berg the day before yesterday, and the poor Captain was nearly demented because some kind, cheerful people kept on reminding him that it was just about here that the *Titanic* was struck and *just* about the same date."

The *Australia* only covered 172 miles in little more than three days, inching through the fog and carefully bumping aside the ice floes. Once, when the fog lifted briefly, an iceberg "the size of Windsor Castle" was spotted nearby. Back on shore, hands were wrung as tight schedules suddenly acquired a measure of anxious fluidity. In London, the press demanded that heads should roll for choosing the storm-prone northern route, but at the Admiralty and Canadian Pacific offices, officials shrugged. No one can predict the weather. At least, the admirals told themselves, the nasty weather would keep any Nazi raiders at bay.

By May 14, a Sunday, the fog lifted for good and the battered flotilla steamed at nineteen knots toward the Gulf of St. Lawrence. They were two days behind schedule. On Monday, the day the king and queen should have been arriving in Quebec City, the *Australia* skirted Newfoundland's Cape Race and the islands of St. Pierre and Miquelon, their snow-capped hills gleaming in the sunlight. In Canadian waters now, the *Australia* was met by two RCN destroyers, HMCS *Skeena* and HMCS *Saguenay*. The next day, bonfires blazed on both sides of the Quebec shore as the flotilla travelled up the St. Lawrence. Crowds thronged in riverside towns to catch a glimpse of the liner. Near midnight, scarred from the ice and looking a little weather-beaten, the *Australia* anchored off the Ile d'Orleans, just downriver from Quebec City. The Royal Couple seemed none the worse for wear, despite the protracted crossing, looking relaxed and happy. "I have been able to have a good rest," the king wrote to his mother.

While the *Australia* was still duelling with the ice, the painful moment that everyone in Ottawa expected had arrived. Because the Royal Couple would now not dock until at least May 17, the tour schedule had to be revised. The Quebec timetable was left untouched, for political reasons more than anything else, so a hurried scalpel was taken to the Ontario portion. The four days scheduled for Ottawa were trimmed to two and a half (with an approving nod, no doubt, from the rest of the country). Brief stops in Cornwall and Brockville were

Stepping ashore in Canada at Wolfe's Cove, the Royal Couple are greeted by Prime Minister William Lyon Mackenzie King (nearest to the gangway) and Justice Minister Ernest Lapointe.

replaced by a slow-speed run-through of these communities. Kingston, where Their Majesties had been scheduled to spend several hours, was pencilled in for a thirty-five-minute limousine tour. That did it. So, despite the snarling cries from short-changed civic officials in the background, the tour would be back on the rails, so to speak, by the time the Royal Train reached Toronto.

King George VI and Queen Elizabeth finally stepped onto Canadian soil at Wolfe's Cove on May 17. It was 10:32 a.m. The cheers of 250,000 people echoed across the Plains of Abraham, said one report, describing the scene as one of splendour and serenity. At the foot of the gangway were Prime Minister William Lyon McKenzie King and Justice Minister Ernest Lapointe. They were in court dress, with their cocked hats tucked under their arms, ready to greet the Royal Couple. Then the pomp began. "God Save The King" was played. Quebec's lieutenant-governor, Ésioff-Léon Patenaude, was introduced, along with members of the federal cabinet and other dignitaries. The king inspected an honour guard from the French-speaking Royal 22nd Regiment.

Riding in an open limousine, a blanket tucked around their legs, the Royal Couple passed through the narrow, cobblestoned streets of the Lower Town to the Quebec Legislative Assembly up on the heights. As they passed, the balconies were crowded with onlookers and Union Jacks were in evidence everywhere, as were portraits of Their Majesties. The response of Quebecers to the Royal Couple was formidable. The oft-voiced disdain of French-Canadians toward the British Crown was nowhere in evidence. They had been urged to show love and respect, and they did exactly that. The Roman Catholic Church had made a point of supporting the visit, and the French-Canadian press had, for the most part, followed suit. So Prime Minister King's first major concern had proved groundless. There would be no cold shoulder from the province of Quebec.

Another nagging concern was Maurice Duplessis. The premier was a noted and volatile drinker. What shape would he be in when it was time to meet the King of England? Well, Duplessis was sober. When he greeted the king and queen at the Legislative Assembly, he was elegant, distinguished, and subdued. A deep bow was followed by a welcoming handshake and a correct, positive, and brief speech. In French, he expressed "the sentiments of joy, respect, loyalty, and affection of the entire Province of Quebec." At the head of the reception line was Rodrigue Cardinal Villeneuve, who, as a prince of the Church, had no misgivings about monopolizing the sovereign's attention for several minutes. (Cardinal Villeneuve also knew his influence had much to do with the positive reaction of his flock.)

Then it was off to a glittering luncheon at the Chateau Frontenac, where the banquet room was decorated with red roses and delphiniums. (During the planning stage, Prime Minister King was shocked to discover the flowers were to be blue. Sensing a Tory plot, for blue was the adopted colour of the Conservative Party, he ordered them changed to red.) "Today, as never before, the throne has become the centre of our national life," the prime minister reminded the 300 guests (but not Duplessis, who had mysteriously vanished). Then the king stood up for his first public address in Canada. There was tension among those who knew of his background, but His Majesty carried off his speech with only a little stammer in English and hardly any in French.

"Mr. Prime Minister," he said.

> I am deeply moved by your words of welcome to the queen and myself on behalf of the Canadian people. I recognize that this moment is historic. It is the first time that a British king has crossed the Atlantic. I stand today on the soil of North America. Here, in the past two centuries, through loss and through gain, the British Commonwealth of Nations has been largely moulded into its present form. This is also the first visit of the sovereign to one of his overseas Dominions. It is fitting that it should be to the senior Dominion of the Crown. I am particularly pleased that, on the day of my arrival in Canada I should have the pleasure of meeting not only my ministers but all the members of my Privy Council for Canada. You, in Canada, have already fulfilled part of the Biblical

promise and obtained dominion from sea to sea. You are now engaged in fulfilling the latter part of that promise in consolidating government from the river to the ends of the earth, from the St. Lawrence to the Arctic snows. The Queen and I are looking forward, with anticipation too great for expression, to seeing all we possibly can of this vast country. Particularly do we welcome the opportunity of greeting the men and women who are the strength and stay, and of seeing something of the younger generation, so soon to become the generations of the future.

When the time came to head for the lieutenant-governor's mansion, where the Royal Couple would spend the night, Duplessis had resurfaced, mumbling something about family problems. The prime minister invited him to share a ride to the mansion, but wasn't impressed by his first close encounter with Duplessis. "He absolutely had nothing intelligent to say all day," Mackenzie King later wrote.

The next day, the Royal Couple caught a train. It was quite a train, with its twelve polished and gleaming coaches precisely arranged. The king and queen travelled at the rear, their two coaches somewhat insulated from the noise and soot of the engine. The very last car, with its observation platform, contained bedrooms for Their Majesties, all facilities, and separate bedrooms for the senior staff. There was a fitting room and a private office for the king. A clever communication link with the engineer allowed him to buzz the Royal Couple when he spotted crowds along the track. He would then slow down while Their Majesties rushed out to the observation platform and waved.

The second coach had a large lounge, a dining room, a kitchen, an office, and two more bedrooms for the staff. Each coach carried the royal coat-of-arms. Prime Minister King, as minister in attendance, had special quarters in one coach, along with his staff. There was also room for the RCMP, members of the Intergovernmental Committee, stenographers, valets, maids, and railway workers, plus lots of space for baggage. All the cars were air-conditioned and contained radios and telephones. Pulling it all was a Hudson-class locomotive. Number 2850 would haul the Royal Train all the way to Vancouver, a feat that earned this class the designation, "Royal Hudson," by command of the king.

What the general public didn't know was that a quite undistinguished pilot train ran along the tracks half an hour ahead of the Royal Train. It carried more RCMP officers, members of a Scotland Yard detachment, communication personnel, a darkroom, extra baggage cars for the surplus from the Royal Train, and the press. The pilot train's primary function was to ensure safety and security for the Royal Couple, should any untoward development occur, be it a farm wagon stuck on the tracks or an IRA bomb. The reporters knew this, of course. As a *Time* magazine correspondent wrote:

> If a bridge fails, if a freight train gets shunted to the main line, or somebody leaves a bomb on the track it will be 30 minutes before the train bearing King George VI and Queen Elizabeth across Canada this week comes upon the wreckage of its pilot train and the mangled bodies of 56 correspondents and twelve photographers who are covering Their Majesties' trip.

Montreal awaited the king and queen on May 18. After a warm welcome from 40,000 people during a fifteen-minute stop in Trois Rivières, they arrived in Canada's largest city. Normally cosmopolitan and haughty, it was seething with pride and excitement. In what would be reported as the largest turnout of the tour, more than a million people crowded the sidewalks along the twenty-three-mile route through the city from Park Avenue Station. The sight of the king and queen in their open limousine, flanked by the 17th Duke of York's Royal Canadian Hussars, "wrenched," as *Le Devoir* wrote, "from normally unemotional breasts clamours that in the eyes of the passing foreigner, could win Montreal a name for abandoning itself unrestrainedly to public demonstrations, especially when they are grandiose." The *Toronto Daily Star* called the cheering the most remarkable sound in Canadian history, "one endless cheer 24 miles long and over four hours' ceaseless duration."

Every public and private building was lavishly decorated. It was Ascension Day in the Roman Catholic Church and bells were ringing. Montrealers lucky enough to live along the route sold seats in their upstairs windows. "If you had a really wide window, you might take in enough money that afternoon to pay an entire month's rent," William Weintraub wrote in his book *City Unique*. More than 50,000 French-speaking schoolchildren packed Montreal Stadium, while McGill Stadium was equally packed with English-speaking youngsters.

The smirking mug of Camillien Houde, the mayor of Montreal, was much in evidence. An erratic politician with a well-developed anti-British fixation, he had publicly declared that Quebec would side with Italy against Britain should there be a war only two months earlier. After using blackmail (a threat to cancel a civic reception) to get a seat in the vehicle immediately following that of the Royal Couple, he appeared at the train station, hand outstretched, grinning like a buffoon. "The king and queen had gotten off their car and were shaking hands with Camillien Houde and his wife before any of us could reach the platform," groused Prime Minister King in his diary. Later, while standing on the balcony at City Hall with the Royal Couple before the cheering crowd, Houde archly remarked to the sovereign, "Some of those cheers are for you also."

The prime minister did not have a good evening. Somehow he was persuaded to go to the formal banquet at the Windsor Hotel on his own, not with the king's party. When he arrived, he discovered that there was no seat for him at the dinner table; when that was straightened out, he found himself stuck in a wasteland of minor guests far from the Royal Couple. "I feel very hurt that I should have been let down in this way," he wrote in his diary, "and all against my own repeated statements that I felt we were making a mistake in having me go as I did with members of my staff instead of with the king as Prime Minister as well as Minister in Attendance ... I am beginning to find it has been a desire on the part of our own people not to push Canada too far to the fore; they succeeded tonight in pushing Canada out of the picture altogether."

* * *

While the press and the politicians were rather narrowly focused on the Royal Tour, other things were going on, both in Canada and the world, throughout May. May Day was marked in Danzig by Nazi-led violence. Demonstrators stoned the Polish cathedral and defaced its doors and those of other Polish establishments with graffiti. In Silesia, a Polish theatre troupe was beaten up. The Warsaw government, unfazed, again rejected German demands for the return of the Danzig Corridor. Over in Moscow, May Day was celebrated by the biggest military display ever in Red Square. Six hundred warplanes roared over the Kremlin as the Red Army paraded its might. The bayonets of thousands of soldiers glinted in bright sunlight, while tanks and artillery pieces added a noisy counterpoint. "Whoever tries to step on the threshold of our home will be destroyed," a commissar announced.

In Ottawa, the House extended its session into the early hours of May 3 to debate the budget. Harry Leader, a Liberal backbencher from Portage La Prairie, announced he would vote against the budget because it did little to help the Prairie farmer. Conservative Leader R.J. Manion voted against the budget the next day, too. Speaking during the final day of the debate, he asked the Liberals, "How are you going to convince the voters this time?" He called for an immediate election. "I challenge them," Manion said, repeating his familiar claim that the government party was on the skids. Despite these dissenters, the Liberal majority passed the budget easily.

A decision to decrease the acreage bonus for western farmers brought a protracted defence from James Gardiner, the agriculture minister. "In order to have the western area financed," he said, "it is necessary to maintain confidence in the minds of the people that the area can be made to maintain farmers' homes." Rejecting calls to leave the bonus alone, he added, "I would not ask the people of Canada to pay $4 million a year for rehabilitation, and an additional twenty-five to thirty million to tide them over until we can get a more permanent policy."

Manion criticized Gardiner for abruptly lowering bonus without any consultation. "The minister maintained the Wheat Board would be abolished and there would be no modified acreage bonus system," he said, pointing out that Gardiner also changed his mind on the price per bushel for wheat, in addition to changing the bonus. Agnes MacPhail, an Independent MP, warned against driving the West into mixed farming. "I think it is time Easterners realized that if the surplus acreage in Western Canada were turned into mixed farming, the distressed area in agriculture ... would then be spread over the whole Dominion," she said to the House. Later, Prime Minister King, who dearly (and vainly) hoped to prorogue the House before the Royal Visit began, introduced a motion for Saturday sittings and drew a sharp retort from J.S. Woodsworth. The CCF leader called Mackenzie King's plan "railroading" Parliament.

It was raining in Ottawa on May 19, a persistent drizzle that dampened not a single spirit. Certainly not that of the queen, who stepped out on the observation deck when the Royal Train paused for some shunting manoeuvres in the rail yard. "But the view is beautiful," she said. According to a newspaper reporter, who happened to be close by, the queen "looked radiant. She wore a blue top coat with a fur neckpiece off her shoulders. Despite the somewhat chilly weather, she made no attempt to protect her neck." Moments later, a "loyal and joyous" Ottawa surrendered itself to the Royal Couple.

At Dominion Square, the immense crowd waited patiently. Then the clip-clop of horses' hooves provided counterpoint as the scarlet and gold of the Royal Canadian Dragoons came into view. Finally, the crowd stirred and murmured. There, *right there*, were the king and queen. In an open carriage, they rode past khaki-clad ranks of soldiers presenting arms. Everywhere Their Majesties went, to every function, the streets were densely packed. The king, with the queen almost continuously at his side, also got a lot accomplished during the shortened visit. The king gave Royal Assent to a number of bills before a joint session of the Senate and the House of Commons. There was a dinner for the inhabitants of both chambers and the Royal Couple, along with luncheons, a garden party, a formal dinner, a quiet stroll with the governor general, and lots of hands to shake.

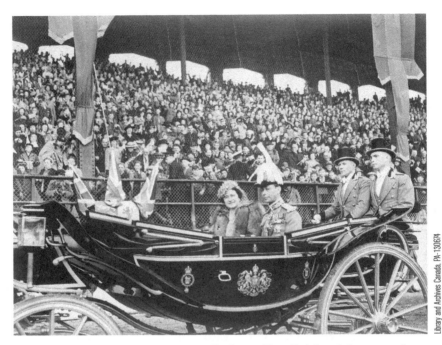

Lansdowne Park in Ottawa is crammed with loyal subjects as King George and Queen Elizabeth pass by in an ornate carriage.

Library and Archives Canada. PA-130674

The highlight of the second day was the Trooping of the Colour on the king's official birthday. The queen laid the cornerstone for the new Supreme Court building. Making her first public utterance, she gave a short speech about the rule of law. On their last half day in Ottawa, the king unveiled the new War Memorial. Afterwards, he and the queen spontaneously approached the immense crowd — many of them veterans — and were virtually lost among their subjects for half an hour. The "common touch" they displayed was an inspiring moment that dispelled any notion that this was going to be a remote, impersonal visit by a foreign monarch. That incident along with many other taxing moments had the prime minister fretting constantly: the Ottawa segment was the federal government's responsibility and, as the top man, the buck stopped at him. Prime Minister King didn't really relax and enjoy himself until the tour was almost half over. His Majesty also began to relax a little while in Ottawa and stopped worrying about minor glitches. The enthusiastic response wherever the Royal Couple went was a tonic. The queen, as usual, was serene, inquisitive, and resourceful.

That afternoon, May 22, the Royal Train passed through Cornwall and Brockville, as well as a few other towns along the way, slowing down in spots when the crowds pressed close to the tracks. It didn't stop until Kingston. There, because of the revised schedule, the Royal Couple were spirited through town so quickly that the crowd of 70,000 men, women, and many, many children didn't get much chance to cheer for, let alone see, Their Majesties. While there, however, the queen presented new colours to the Royal Military College.

The train parked on a siding outside Cobourg for the night, then pulled into the North Toronto CPR station at 10:30 the next morning. This station, built during the Great War, had been abandoned in 1930 when Union Station opened downtown and the first bites of the Great Depression ate into the passenger traffic. It was swept out, beautified, and polished up just so the Royal Train could stop there. Mitchell Hepburn was on the immaculate platform to greet the Royal Couple. Another overflowing crowd was also on hand (despite heavy rains overnight), their cheers mingling with the roar of a twenty-one-gun salute. After fifteen minutes, the Royal Procession moved out.

"Thunderous, fervent cheers rose from Yonge Street, packed from curb to roof on each side as Their Majesties turned south to begin their Toronto visit," the *Toronto Daily Star* reported. "The roar had a note, it seemed, that no other Canadian crowd had yet given." The Royal Couple, the newspaper said, "drove through the line of humanity that stretched away and was lost in the grey mists of the downtown." Yonge Street was described as a "canyon of cheers." Estimates of the welcoming crowd ranged up to two million.

Their Majesties were officially welcomed at the Ontario Legislature, where the king noted that "the people of Ontario, the central province off the Dominion, have in their great qualities made a very significant contribution to the national progress of Canada."

The Royal Couple's stay in Toronto was just as busy as any other day, but it included one of the most heart-warming pauses of the tour. In the music room at the lieutenant-governor's residence, Their Majesties had a private audience with Canada's famous Dionne quintuplets. Each one of them — Yvonne, Annette, Cecile, Emilie, and Marie — it was reported, put baby arms around the queen's neck and kissed her. Queen Elizabeth kissed each one of them back.

The rest of the day included a luncheon, tea at Queen's Park, and a visit to Riverside Park, where 25,000 children, including some that were ill and in stretchers, cheered as Their Majesties stood up in their open limousine and waved.

At Woodbine Park, where they watched the running of the King's Plate, the crowd's eyes were on Prime Minister King and Premier Hepburn. The pair's public feud over the stewardship of the Liberal party had turned into active dislike, but they were all smiles that day, as they accompanied the Royal Couple. In fact, the Toronto visit must have had a calming effect on them, because Hepburn arranged for Mackenzie King to meet the quints and the prime minister arranged for the Hepburn children to meet Their Majesties. After Woodbine, the Royal Couple visited a hospital, where they met 250 disabled veterans. Then a quick

Peering from the windows of their train, the Dionne quintuplets arrive in Toronto to meet the Royal Couple.

peek at Exhibition Park, where more thousands of children had been waiting for three hours to see them. When the Royal Train pulled out of Union Station at 7:45 p.m., it was almost two hours behind schedule. The big Hudson engine sped Their Majesties through many small communities without even slowing down, bringing disappointment and tears to many loyal Canadians hoping to catch a glimpse of them.

"One feels almost heartless to rush by some localities without a word," the prime minister told his diary. "But it would be physically impossible to do more than the king and queen have been doing. As a matter of fact they have had really hard physical work, which they have performed with wonderful charm and readiness, patience and cheerfulness."

At White River, the king and queen gave the Natives and outdoorsmen an unexpected treat when they stepped down from their coach as the locomotive was being serviced. Navigating the muddy, unpaved main street of the raw settlement, they paused to chat with some of the townsfolk.

As the train sped toward the north shore of Lake Superior, people gathered to wave in clearings, next to rude shacks, and in nondescript hamlets. Schreiber was another brief, scheduled stop, and it was that afternoon, May 25, that the king received word that his mother had been involved in a traffic accident. It quickly became apparent that the Queen Mother had received only a few bruises when her Daimler was broadsided by a lorry. Relieved, Their Majesties continued on their journey toward Manitoba.

After the dense population centres of the East were dealt with, the tour developed an orderly, familiar aspect at almost every stop. Apart from the provincial capitals — Winnipeg, Regina, Edmonton, Victoria — where the presence of legislatures meant more elaborate ceremony, the pattern was almost predictable. A greeting on the station platform, an affair of some sort at city hall, perhaps a trip around town. Now and then, however, there was a little added spice to the program.

At the Lakehead, the twin cities of Port Arthur and Fort William had been battered by a vicious storm the night before, so they were decidedly tattered when the Royal Train arrived. Their Majesties ignored all that, though, and did their usual gracious thing, even meeting a seventy-seven-year-old Ojibway chief. At Brandon, there was another wave of children among the 50,000-strong welcoming throng, prompting the prime minister to write, "Nothing more stirring or more moving ... the gathering of the children there was the finest scene on the entire trip." When the Royal Couple moved into the crowd, "here it was nearly midnight," he wrote, "and His Majesty there in the middle of the great throng, talking to everyone.... At one stage, the queen was by herself, the length of a car, without any other person, police or attendant, the king remaining behind, talking to some others. Wonderful cheering ... an unforgettable scene. The finest of the trip this far."

A late-night drive through Moose Jaw's business district took on the unworldly aura of a movie scene. According to a reporter, the "massed mile of Main Street ... was glittering with lights. It was an amazing sight. The whole street strung with lights, thousands of people massed eight and ten feet deep along the sides." It was 6:00 a.m. at Swift Current, and the Royal Train didn't even raise a shutter, let alone slow down. Nevertheless, there was a band playing on the platform with

Curtseying nervously, Joyce Evans, daughter of the city clerk at Port Arthur, presents a bouquet to Queen Elizabeth.

Library and Archives Canada. PA-211025

people singing. At Medicine Hat, where the train did stop, the king spoke to a former member of the North-West Mounted Police and a veteran of the Zulu and Sudan wars.

It was raining in Winnipeg when the Royal Couple arrived (although the Rayner children scarcely noticed). A long, slow, dripping-wet procession forged its way along Main Street from the CPR station at Higgins Avenue, then turned west on Portage Avenue.

At the Royal Couple's insistence, the top was lowered on the limousine. "I shall hold up my umbrella," said the queen. His Majesty, stoic and bare-headed in his greatcoat, made do without one. Again the crowd was enormous, congregating especially at the famous, windswept corner of Portage and Main. Along Portage, the decorations brightening the grim façade of the massive Eaton's department store stood up well in the downpour, as did those on the Hudson's Bay Company store a few blocks away.

A welcome at city hall and a visit to the Manitoba Legislature were on the itinerary, as was a luncheon at the Fort Garry Hotel. May 24 was Empire Day, or Victoria Day to some ("The twenty-fourth of

Library and Archives Canada, PA-122957

King George addresses the British Empire in a radio broadcast from a temporary studio at the Manitoba Legislature.

May is the queen's birthday. If we don't get a holiday, we'll all run away!"), so King George VI sat in the lieutenant-governor's suite at the Legislature to make a radio address to the British Commonwealth and the United States. His theme, spoken with scarcely a stammer, was unity among diverse cultures. "For a long period in history it was the mind of Europe which led the march and fixed the aims of progress in the world," he said in part.

> But that tide of inspiration is no longer running as it did in time gone by. The Christian civilization in Europe is now profoundly troubled and challenged from within. We are striving to restore its standards, though the task is long and hard. Asia, too, is changing fast, and its mind is deeply disturbed. Is this not a moment when the Old World in its turn might look for hope and guidance to the achievements of the new?

The soggy procession that day included a drive along the south side of the Assiniboine River, where the toffs lived, a short stretch of Salter Street, which was not the classiest part of town, and French-speaking St. Boniface across the Red River.

At Regina, there was a welcome at the station, the few words spoken at city hall, tea at the RCMP barracks, ceremonies at the Saskatchewan Legislature, and a state dinner at Government House. It was the children, however, who once again took charge, as they seemed to do at many western stops. There were 50,000 of them, from all over the southern part of Saskatchewan. They massed along Victoria Boulevard to watch their king and queen go by and took up every available space at the exhibition grounds as the Royal Couple's limousine circled the track twice, for their benefit.

While the East had its pomp and formal dress, the West had a carnival spirit. There were co-ed bands and cheerleaders in Winnipeg. Clowns appeared in Saskatchewan, and wheat sheaves decorated Regina City Hall. Cowboy yells and war whoops sounded in Calgary, not to mention the carefully constructed Indian encampment, with its inhabitants wearing war bonnets and Native finery for Their Majesties. Calgary had the reputation of being a cow town, so its welcome was a bit more ebullient than many others. The aforementioned yells mingled with regular cheering as more than a million people came in from around Southern Alberta for the show. There were seventeen bands at various locations along the parade route. And there were 40,000 schoolchildren.

As May turned into June, the king and queen were immersed in the silence of the mountains at the Banff Springs Hotel. After ten days of unremitting attention, they deserved a break from the crowds and the adulation. As a Toronto reporter put it, "They were not half an hour in the great empty echoing hotel that they drank their first full draft of the exquisite stillness and the divine beauty of the Bow Valley; and the hills as they began to melt into the burial of the night." Alone and unattended, they went for a walk in the dusk. Nobody followed. The next day, Their Majesties were driven to Tunnel Mountain, where they enjoyed a spectacular view of the surrounding peaks. Then they crossed the valley to Mount Norquay. Surrounded by wildlife, the king had his movie camera whirring constantly. Their Majesties also went for a ride in a sixty-year-old buggy, delighting the queen. "I simply must ride in one," she had said.

After a day and a half alone to relax and recharge their batteries, the Royal Couple returned to their duty. After church (it was a Sunday), the entire party motored deep into the Rocky Mountains to Field, British Columbia, along a gravel road thorough Kicking Horse Pass, which was as scary as it was awe-inspiring. There, they all got on the train again and plunged deeper into the mountains. The train stopped at Craigellachie, where the last spike of the transcontinental railway was driven in 1885. The children were there, too, bearing wildflowers. After brief walkabouts at Revelstoke and Kamloops, the Thompson and Fraser canyons were safely navigated before the Royal Train emerged abruptly into the flat delta of the Fraser Valley.

Vancouver was the end of the track, and the visit to the great port city had a different atmosphere. It had stopped raining and the Pacific Ocean on the city's doorstep added an invigorating extra dimension to their trip.

When the Royal Train pulled into the CPR station on the shore of Burrard Inlet, the 15th Coast Brigade of the Royal Canadian Artillery shot off a roaring salute. A guard of honour was inspected, then Their Majesties headed out by limousine along streets lined with military personnel (and thousands of ordinary citizens) to city hall. After the formalities were over, the motorcade wended its way for almost forty miles through city neighbourhoods, with a stop at Shaughnessy Veteran's Hospital and a swing around the University of British Columbia campus. The streets and the playgrounds were teeming with children but the polygot nature of cosmopolitan Vancouver was also much in evidence. Gents in formal attire jostled for a view with diminutive ladies in Oriental dress. There were loggers, Natives, Japanese fishermen, and representatives of a wide array of ethnic groups.

"The streets were lined and at times crowded all the way," the prime minister wrote later. "A pleasant feature was to see the Chinese in their costumes, particularly one street of little children.... We passed through a long street where many present were Scotch, many in kilts." One report had 25,000 Scots massed on a hillside, bagpipes wailing.

Arriving back at the brand-new Hotel Vancouver on the corner of Burrard and Georgia streets, which had opened only days earlier, Their Majesties attended a luncheon hosted by the City. Then there was more travel, over streets and bridges. First, the king and queen visited Hastings Park, where a "concentration" of children waited, then crossed over to the North Shore by one bridge and returned by another before heading for the CPR dock. There, the *Princess Marguerite* was waiting to ferry them to Victoria. Through Lions Gate, she went, escorted by the RCN, an RCMP vessel, Native war canoes, and scores of pleasure craft. There were a lot of ships whooping.

Staid, proper, reserved, and British to the core, Victoria went overboard. When the *Princess Marguerite* rounded Ogden Point well after dark, ghosting into the Inner Harbour, she was greeted with a festival of lights. The Parliament Buildings and the Empress Hotel, both of which fronted the harbour, were outlined with electric lights. Other public buildings were also ablaze. And, waiting patiently as salute had boomed out and the honour guard was inspected, Their Majesties were taken for a drive around downtown streets washed in the flickering light of torches held up by Boy Scouts and Sea Cadets. "All the crowd saw was the flash of Their Majesties' faces as they passed," one newspaper reported, "strange in the vivid, weird, conflicting slabs of magnesium light. But that was enough. The cheers never ceased until their car turned in through the gates and up the avenue of oaks and maples that led to Carey Castle which is Government House."

The next day was consumed by ceremonies at the British Columbia Legislature, a presentation of new colours to the RCN, a luncheon at the Empress, and dinner at Government House. At the luncheon, the king gave another radio address, and this time it was a heartfelt message to Canadians:

> To travel through so grand a country is a privilege to any man, but to travel through it to the accompaniment of such an overwhelming testimony of good will, from young and old alike, is an experience that has, I believe, been granted to few people in this world … In the course of this journey I have seen the old settled parts of the Dominion which have a long history behind them, and I have seen the newer parts, of which the first settlement is still within the memory of living men. When I remember that here I am as far from Ottawa, as Ottawa is from London, I realize something of the vastness of Canada. When I saw the broad plains, changed by pioneers to the uses of men, and the mighty mountain ranges through which they cut their roads, I began to understand the qualities of the Canadian people.

When it was time to leave Vancouver Island, Prime Minister King summed it all up this way: "Without question Victoria has left the most pleasing of all impressions. It was a crowning gem — a note of splendour at the end of a long journey and the beginning of the return trip." With 10,000 people massed around the Inner Harbour and singing, "Will Ye No' Come Back Again," the Royal Couple boarded the Canadian

National Steamships vessel the *Prince Robert* for the trip back to the mainland.

There was scarcely a vacant spot along the way as Their Majesties' motorcade rolled from Burrard Inlet through Burnaby to New Westminster. In the Royal City, whose name was selected by the king's great-grandmother, Queen Victoria, the streets "were packed to suffocation" as the vehicles headed for Queen's Park. Although there were 11,000 children there, with 2,700 of them performing May Day dances, the Royal Couple's limousine only circled slowly around the track without stopping. A five-mile circuit of the small city, under twenty-eight elaborate welcoming arches, ended at the rail station on the bank of the Fraser River below the British Columbia Penitentiary. New locomotive power, in the form of a huge, throbbing Northern class engine, awaited them at the head of the Royal Train, because the return journey would now be along CNR tracks.

Chilliwack, at the head of the valley, was the last official stop in British Columbia, with a crowd of 10,000 pushing against the barriers and cheering. Then came the interior of the province and the long, empty plateaus before the train reached Jasper, Alberta.

There were several Canadians celebrating something other than the Royal Visit that May. These were the lucky few in line for a share of approximately $140,000 in the Irish Hospital Sweepstakes after Blue Peter won the English Derby at Epsom Downs. There were three winning tickets in Canada on the winner: one shared by twenty-five factory workers, the other two split among four ticket holders. The Irish Sweeps was launched in 1930 as a means to defray hospital costs. However, early in the Great Depression, so many tickets were sold in Britain, at 10 shillings a pop, that the government — alarmed over the loss of sterling to the Irish Free State – made the lottery illegal. Canada and the United States followed suit, precipitating an elaborate smuggling operation in both directions across the Atlantic. Because the tickets were illegal, buyers had to use pseudonyms, working through shadowy agents. There were police and post office crackdowns on the illegal operation from time to time, but this forerunner to the entirely legal Lotto 6/49 remained popular despite official disapproval.

Meanwhile, Nazi Germany and Fascist Italy began thumping the drums of war. Boasting of an "invincible bloc of 300 million people," they signed the Pact of Steel. It committed each country to supporting the other in time of war. Among the ominous phrases tossed about were "impending decisions" and "a reckoning" to come. In Moscow, the Soviet Union rejected an alliance with Britain and France, saying the Anglo-French effort to build an anti-aggression front was "insufficient and ineffective."

The Way Things Were

IN THE POLLING BOOTH

From the mid-1930s to the end of the 1950s, Prince Edward Island general elections were a sure thing for betting types. The Liberal party just won and won and won — usually by a land-slide. On May 18, Premier Thomas A. Campbell's Liberals won twenty-six of thirty seats. This was not quite as overwhelming as 1935, when they took all thirty under the late Walter Lea. For almost twenty-five years, until the Conservatives finally took power in 1959, Prince Edward Island was a Liberal stronghold. Even without the prodding of an effective opposition, Premier Campbell's government managed some positive legislation. It set up a provincial police force, brought in regulations governing the public service, and established a national park.

Trash Talk. The view from atop Winnipeg's infamous dump was the subject of a tongue-in-cheek feature in the *Free Press*. "Montreal has its Mount Royal, and San Francisco its Nob Hill, and no one will deny that these eminences offer a brave view indeed of the cities they command," reporter Ben Malkin wrote. "But Winnipeg, with its huge garbage dump on Saskatchewan avenue, need take a back seat to no city in the matter of views." The other two hills might be natural phenomena, he wrote, but the panorama available from the crest of the city's man-made, and odorous, elevation was just as spectacular. The dump covered several acres and was estimated at twenty-five feet in height. It had been spreading out and up for more than sixty years. "A homely enterprise, the city dump, but in its ways, a magnificent one, and its results are there for everyone to see," he wrote. (The dump was eventually landscaped and is now a popular tobogganing hill during the winter months.)

Padlock Law. In Montreal, a superior court judge dismissed a challenge to Quebec's so-called Padlock Law. The law, which was aimed at fighting Communist influence in the province, was meant to protect, not punish, the judge said, and was therefore quite proper.

Dance Steps. The Winnipeg Ballet Club was formed early in 1939. Its first performances were part of a pageant called "Happy and Glorious," honouring King George VI and Queen Elizabeth's visit. The company's two short dances were called "Kilowatt Magic," about hydro-electric power, and "Grain," about Manitoba's leading export. The Royal Couple never actually saw the pageant. In 1953, Queen Elizabeth II gave the company permission to call itself the Royal Winnipeg Ballet.

June

It came to be known as The Voyage of the Damned. In the spring of 1939, a boatload of Jewish refugees fleeing Nazi Germany took to the high seas in a desperate quest for a safe haven. Canada was among the countries that turned them down.

The transatlantic liner, the MS *St. Louis*, left Hamburg on May 15 with 907 penniless Jews who had been hounded from their homes and businesses, then stripped of all their possessions, by means of an increasingly onerous emigration tax. All that each of them had left was a precious landing permit for Cuba. The passengers had hoped to stay in the island nation while they waited for their chance to get on the United States quota list, but when the *St. Louis* anchored in Havana harbour on May 27, the permits were declared invalid. While the refugees sweltered aboard the liner under the hot Caribbean sun, desperate entreaties were made on their behalf to other Central and South American countries. One by one, each government rejected the Jews.

Forced to leave Havana on June 2, the *St. Louis* steamed toward the uncertain waters of the United States and Canada. Quickly, the Jews discovered they were just as unwelcome up north. The United States responded to their appeal for sanctuary by sending a gunboat to shadow the *St. Louis* as it approached the coast of Florida.

From Ottawa, the response from the Dominion government was equally as harsh: no Jews need apply.

That the refugees even attempted to breach Canada's rock-solid bulwark of governmental anti-Semitism was an illustration of their desperation; the exclusion of Jews had long been a cornerstone of Canadian immigration policy. Early in the century, thousands of Eastern European Jews had immigrated to Canada, causing alarm in some quarters because they tended to stick together in the ghettoes of Montreal, Toronto, and Winnipeg, rather than help colonize farmland across the country. The urban and industrious Jews were especially abhorred in Roman Catholic Quebec, where the Church characterized them as alien, dishonest scoundrels who had killed Christ and who would rather conduct business than live off the land.

In 1923, Mackenzie King's cabinet endorsed (without bothering to consult Parliament) revisions of existing immigration regulations. The new guidelines created a separate class for Jews, who now had to seek a special permit from the cabinet before they could enter the country. During the early years of the Great Depression, cabinet orders-in-council loaded the dice even more against European Jewry. One stipulation required immigrants to bring enough capital with them to establish and maintain a farm; another that all non-farming immigrants be British or American.

When King's Liberal government regained power in 1935 (after the five-year mandate of the equally obdurate Conservative prime minister, R.B. Bennett), the official enforcer of anti-Semitism in Canada was Frederick Charles Blair. Tall and spare, with the rimless glasses of a prim, no-nonsense schoolmaster, Blair was director of the immigration branch. According to one observer, quoted by authors Irving Abella and Harold Troper, Blair believed "that people should be kept out of Canada instead of being let in."* He was self-righteous, inflexible and prejudicial. How prejudicial? Here is part of a letter on file in immigration branch records:

> I suggested recently to three Jewish gentlemen with whom I am well acquainted, that it might be a very good thing if they would call a conference and have a day of humiliation and prayer, which might profitably

* Irving Abella and Howard Troper, *None is Too Many* (Toronto: Lester Publishing Ltd., 1983), 7.

be extended for a week or more, where they would honestly try to answer the question of why they are so unpopular almost everywhere ... I often think that instead of persecution it would be far better if we more often told them frankly why many of them are unpopular. If they would divest themselves of certain of their habits I am sure they could be just as popular in Canada as our Scandinavians.*

On November 23, 1938, a Jewish delegation pleaded with King and Immigration Minister Thomas Crerar to admit 10,000 refugees. King pointed out politely that the jobless situation was still acute, and that his first duty was "the avoidance of strife ... maintaining the unity of the country" and fighting "the forces of separatism." In any event, the cabinet would have none of it. At a meeting the next day, King asked his ministers to view the problem "from the way in which this nation will be judged in years to come, if we do not play our part ... in helping to meet one of humanity's direst needs." The cabinet would go no further than helping resettle Jews in some "land other than our own."

The *St. Louis* carried 907 Jews, not the 10,000 mentioned in November, but the political leaders of Canada found even that total too much to swallow. In a letter to O.D. Skelton, under-secretary of state for external affairs, Blair contended that no country — let alone Canada — would be able to "open its doors wide enough to take in the hundreds of thousands of Jewish people who want to leave Europe; the line must be drawn somewhere."

His comment followed the stance taken by Justice Minister Ernest Lapointe. On June 7, Lapointe, who was acting as the government's official voice in Ottawa while the prime minister was travelling across the country with Their Majesties, said he "emphatically opposed" allowing the *St. Louis* to dock at a Canadian port. As King's Quebec lieutenant, Lapointe was well aware of French Canada's blatant anti-Semitism, so he was not about to rock the refugee boat, so to speak, in his boss's absence.

---

*Immigration Branch Records, File 594182/5, Letter to F.N. Schlanders, September 13, 1938

While the *St. Louis* and its "cargo of despair" loitered off the coast of Bermuda, waiting for some country to welcome them, intense efforts were made by pro-Jewish factions to sway Washington and Ottawa. On June 8, while heading for the American capital on the Royal Train, King received a telegram from a group of concerned citizens, including: Sir Robert Falconer, past-president of the University of Toronto,; Elleston Flavelle, a wealthy businessman; Anglican bishop R.J. Renison; *Saturday Night* editor B.K. Sandwell; and University of Toronto Professor George Wrong. They wrote:

> As a mark of gratitude toward God for the happiness which has been vouchsafed the Canadian people in the visit of their king and queen, and as evidence of the Christian charity of the people of this most fortunate country, we, the undersigned Christian citizens of Canada, respectfully suggest that, under the power vested in you as Prime Minister of our country, you forthwith offer to the 907 homeless exiles on board the Hamburg-American ship *St. Louis* sanctuary in Canada.

In his diary, King's one-line acknowledgment of the petition read, "Received, this morning, a message about immigrants."

Describing a luncheon at the White House with the Royal Couple and President Franklin Roosevelt, King later wrote, "The question of the immigrants on the ship 'St. Louis' came up. The President explained the situation to the king. Added that he thought I too had my immigration laws which placed certain restrictions. I said nothing about the wire which I had received or about the situation itself. It is much less our problem than that of the U.S. and Cuba."

As the *St. Louis* headed back to a cruel Europe, Bishop Renison delivered a parting shot about the government's lack of charity. "Here in Canada, we ought to be helpful and happy," Renison said in Toronto, "but I can't help but think of that ghost ship that sails the Atlantic tonight carrying nearly 1,000 refugee Jews who came from the Old World toward this land of hope and glory and plenty. I think of them with death and suicide in their hearts, returning to the country whence they came."

In any event, the 907 damned voyagers did not return to Germany — at least not right away. A League of Nations refugee committee had persuaded Britain, France, Belgium, and Holland to find room for them. The 288 accepted by Britain were the luckier ones; the others remaining on the Continent eventually disappeared into the jaws of the Holocaust.

Meanwhile, King, his cabinet, Quebec, and the rest of Canada turned their attention to other things that month. One was the departure of King George and Queen Elizabeth for England after their brilliant tour of the Dominion. They sailed on June 15 from Halifax — the same port that had been declared off-limits to the Jewish refugees only days earlier.

Back on June 1, while the boatload of Jews were being told they had to leave Havana, the Royal Couple were at Jasper Park for another much-appreciated break from the crowds and the fanfare. Their base was a luxurious private cabin on Lake Beauvert, some distance from the main lodge. From there, they explored the wilderness.

During a morning walk, the Royal Couple became enchanted by the antics of a bear cub they encountered in the woods. While the mother bear kept a wary eye on Their Majesties (who remained a safe distance away), the cub played a game of hide-and-seek while scampering up and down a tree trunk. The king spent several minutes filming "the little black ball of fur" with his movie camera. The queen gathered coloured rocks and picked wildflowers. In the afternoon, the king and queen motored eighteen miles to Glacier of the Angels on Mount Edith Cavell. At the edge of the ice, they were delighted to find themselves enveloped by a sudden, brief snow squall. "Something we wanted, but hadn't expected," the king said later.

The fate of the *St. Louis*'s refugees was well below the horizon of those accompanying Their Majesties on the Royal Visit, but other world events were of continuing interest, and concern. Although the king had earlier suggested he might be able to help with diplomatic efforts, "this trip keeps the international situation out of sight as well as out of mind," Prime Minister King wrote. "This will all [be] to the good for the king and queen but it proves how far from reality we are in such an atmosphere."

King George's advisers were cool to the prime minister's suggestion that His Majesty have direct, informal chats with some of the press correspondents accompanying the tour. "I pressed my view that it was to the interest of Hitler and Mussolini to know the king's desire for co-operation as against conflict in all things that pertained to the relations of the nation," Prime Minister King wrote in his diary. However, nothing came of it.

While at Jasper, the prime minister was also given a thorough briefing on the European situation by A.C. Cummings, a Fleet Street correspondent. Cummings told King that the German General Staff had given Hitler a full report on what the army would require to fight a war. He also said that recent successes had turned the Nazi dictator into a megalomaniac. Mackenzie King was still willing to give Hitler the benefit of the doubt, however, although he could "have changed very much in the last year or two."

From Jasper, the Royal Tour continued on to Edmonton and "one of the great surprises of the trip," as the prime minister would write later about the crowds awaiting the Royal Train. A sizeable percentage of Alberta's population had gathered in the provincial capital to greet Their Majesties. The motorcade from the CNR station traversed a wide, two-mile stretch of Portage Avenue, where bleachers had been constructed on either side — it was vacant land originally cleared for a housing project that had been killed by the Great Depression — and packed with 68,000 loyal subjects.

"School children from different districts, schools, etc.; also Indians, bands and the like were really a thrilling sight," King wrote. While the solid mass of people cheered and cheered, the king and queen were driven up one side of the avenue, then down the other. Finally, the thin line of Boy Scouts guarding the right-of-way succumbed to the crowd and thousands surged forth to surround Their Majesties. The Royal Party was extricated, with some difficulty, and made its way to the Legislative Buildings.

The animosity between Premier William Aberhart and Lieutenant-Governor John Campbell Bowen almost ruined the visit, though. Aberhart, whose relations with the stiff and proper Bowen had been deteriorating since his radical Social Credit party had formed the government a few years before, found himself shut out of a tea reception for the Royal Couple in the lieutenant-governor's suite. This was apparently in retaliation for Aberhart monopolizing arrangements for the formal dinner later that evening at the Macdonald Hotel, which was properly Bowen's prerogative.

However, the spectacle of a premier being banned from a function in his own building was too much for the prime minister, who remarked later of Bowen that "he is not a big enough man for a position of the kind." King latched onto Aberhart and his wife and ushered them into meet the monarchs, even arranging for Aberhart's two daughters to join them. The icy atmosphere of the gathering did not escape King George, who remarked to the prime minister that he thought the lieutenant-governor "might have forgotten differences for one day."

Finally, the crowds and the feuding functionaries headed for their beds, and so did the Royal Couple as their train headed into the dark night. As it steamed eastward across the Prairie for the next two days, the towns rolled by with the regularity of a system timetable: Wainwright, Unity, Biggar, Saskatoon, Watrous, Melville, Portage La Prairie. And like the passenger trains that stitched the West together, the Royal Train paused regularly, if only for a moment.

At Unity, where "there were literally a couple of miles of people, mostly children," the huge Northern locomotive came to a brief stop, then slowly pulled its royal passengers past row upon row of youngsters. In Saskatoon, there was the usual civic ceremonial and a quick drive around while huge crowds cheered and sang. At the station, the throng broke through the barriers and once again the Royal Couple was hemmed in by excited subjects. Another estimated 30,000–40,000 waited in the gathering summer darkness at Melville to see the king and his radiant queen. At Portage La Prairie, they attended a United Church service, "which was conducted throughout with great dignity."

In contrast to the glittering reception during the trip westward,
Winnipeg was an unofficial stop on the way back. While the train was
being serviced at the CNR station at Main and Broadway, the Royal
Couple met wounded Great War veterans, who had been brought into
the city from the Deer Lodge military hospital on the western outskirts.
Then it was time to say goodbye to the West — and time for one last
stirring sight. At Whittier Park, just across the Red River in the suburb
of St. Boniface, 18,000 Manitobans gathered to wave farewell as the
gleaming, blue-and-silver Royal Train passed by the racetrack along a
high embankment.

Taking a stroll along the tracks while the Royal Train pauses for servicing, the Royal Couple are trailed by RCMP officers.

Along the sparsely-populated Canadian Shield north of the Great Lakes, the crowds were smaller but no less enthusiastic. At Redditt, the normal complement of 300 souls ballooned to more than 12,000 schoolchildren and adults — including hunters, trappers, lumberjacks, and prospectors from the northern wilderness. Everyone cheered and clapped and waved from behind temporary fences as the king and queen strolled along the tracks during a service stop. Two nuggets of Northern Ontario gold were presented to Their Majesties at Sioux Lookout and the king chatted with a ninety-eight-year-old veteran of the Zulu war. At Fire River, Gogama, and Capreol, there were more schoolchildren and veterans.

In the mining town of Sudbury, the normal welcoming festivities were spiced up by a visit underground. Wearing safety helmets and protective outer garments, the Royal Couple plunged down a shaft at a speed of 1,500 feet per minute to watch machines extracting nickel ore half a mile below the surface at the Frood mine.

After this, came southwestern Ontario and the two most frantic days of the Royal Visit.

As the train approached Toronto, the crowds got bigger and bigger, until another huge throng had to be held at bay during a brief, unofficial stop at Union Station. But if the Royal Couple thought they had seen big crowds before, the numbers would pale against the multitudes awaiting Their Majesties in the industrial and agricultural heartland of Ontario. There were easily two million people (with another estimate of four million) gawking, cheering, singing, waving, curtsying, tossing flowers, shaking the royal hands, and making presentations. "Enormous" was the prime minister's favourite adjective for discussing the massed throngs.

From Kitchener (where William Lyon Mackenzie King was born when the city was still called Berlin), through Stratford, Chatham, Windsor, London, Ingersoll, Woodstock, Brantford, Hamilton, and St. Catharines, "there seemed to be a continuous stream of people."

In Hamilton, where "I got personally a great reception part of the way," King found the sight particularly stirring. "At the Fair Grounds, we had the finest scene thus far of young children arranged in stands and around the entire circle ... The king and queen enjoyed it immensely."

Windsor was another highlight. "It was easily the finest display of the whole tour, with the river on one side and people between the train and the river," he wrote. "Detroit vessels lighted up ... skyline of Detroit visible on one side, and on the other, people and children massed on [the] banks."

All was not tea and scones, though. The Royal Train fell seriously behind schedule, necessitating some higher speeds that left thousands of schoolchildren in tears because all they saw was a blur as Their Majesties rattled by. And for the first time during the tour, the king seemed a little edgy, wanting to keep things moving. Perhaps he sensed the end of this extraordinary adventure was in sight and he'd be home soon. Fatigue was creeping in, too. Both the king and queen begged off a side trip under Niagara Falls because of tiredness. Besides, "he wanted to have a haircut," and the queen remarked that she hadn't had her hair dressed since Jasper.

Late in the evening of June 7, the king and queen passed over the iron railway bridge spanning the Niagara Gorge and into the United States. Immediately, there was a distinct change in the atmosphere. An American engine now pulled the Royal Train. The familiar escort of four red-coated RCMP officers had been replaced (despite the despairing protests of the Royal Couple) by comically serious Secret Service agents and other American law enforcement officers. Guns, never in plain view in Canada, seemed to sprout from every hip.

The British Foreign Office, personified by the supercilious British Ambassador to the United States Sir Ronald Lindsay and his wife, had intended that the prime minister be left behind with the Mounties, but Prime Minister King had a powerful friend in Washington: the president. FDR had made it plain that his Canadian friend was not to be treated as a colonial nobody, so King remained in his official role as the minister in attendance.

The fears in some quarters that the Royal Couple would lay an egg south of the border were immediately swept away by their reception in New York State. A massed crowd cheered as Cordell Hull, the U.S. Secretary of State, greeted the Royal Visitors. Another estimated one million curious Americans showed up to have a gander at the Royal Train as it headed south. The next morning, in Washington's Union Station, President Franklin Delano Roosevelt shook hands with King George VI of Great Britain. It was a historic occasion, one that wasn't overlooked by pundits and historians: the leader of a democracy that had wrestled its freedom from the British yoke was welcoming a direct descendant of the eighteenth-century English king who had precipitated the American Revolution.

"How are you? I'm glad to see you," Roosevelt said as the king's tanned face broke into a broad smile.

"It is indeed a pleasure for Her Majesty and myself to be here," King George answered.

Then, as a Canadian reporter put it, "the Royal procession moved off, with a glittering military display, through Washington's broad avenues and spacious squares. A hot sun beat down, causing the queen to open her parasol." Along the way, "the king and queen heard American voices raised in roars of welcome almost rivalling the cheers that greeted Their Majesties during their … progress across a continent and back."

Through lunch at the White House, a garden party at the British Embassy, and a state dinner that evening back at the White House (while a torrential thunderstorm pelted the city), FDR and his wife, Eleanor, chatted and bonded with "two very nice young people" from London. Prime Minister King was relegated to the background during much of the first day, although the president made sure his friend "Mackenzie" was not entirely forgotten.

The Brits tried hard to lose him, though. They acted as though the Royal Couple's twenty-two days in Canada were an annoying prelude to the actual purpose of the trip. For instance, as King recalled later, a memo saying "Prime Minister may be requested to be present as Minister in Attendance" had been altered, with the "may be" replaced with "will not be." He was shunted off to stand in lonely anterooms and entrance halls, and to be firmly upstaged by the Lindsays at public appearances.

"There has evidently been a good deal of discussion and unpleasant-ness with respect to the arrangements as to matters of precedence with regard to my coming as Minister in Attendance, etc.," King later wrote. "I could not help thinking ... that if one had been inclined to be censorious, one could have made a good deal of the failure of the British Ambassador and his suite to pay any attention to the P.M. of one of the Dominions, and leave him talking with chauffeurs and others while he was entertaining the king and queen. So far as the British Embassy was concerned, it was quite clear that they were for keeping me out of the picture."

The next day, ten official engagements were wedged into eleven hours, including having the Royal Couple shake hands with more than 300 Congressmen in the cool rotunda of the United States Capitol. There was also a sail down the Potomac River to Mount Vernon, a visit to the National Cemetery at Arlington, and tea on the White House lawn with 500 Boy Scouts and 300 Girl Scouts. After a dinner at the British Embassy, the Royal Entourage returned to their train. The next morning, they were in New Jersey, with New York City on the agenda.

Gotham went gaga, as a *Winnipeg Free Press* headline put it, from the minute the king and queen stepped ashore from an American warship onto the island of Manhattan. Hard-boiled, blasé New Yorkers assembled in their millions, from the Battery — where Mayor Fiorello LaGuardia ("The Little Flower") greeted them, until they escaped five hours later along the Henry Hudson Parkway. Highlights of the fifty-mile tour of the city included one million children massed in Central Park, a quick tour of the World's Fair in Flushing Meadow, and a visit to Columbia University. While 13,482 New York cops — the largest detail in the city's history — kept a lookout for anarchists and party-poopers, the motorcade sped along streets lined with an estimated three million onlookers.

In one raucous blur of a day, which seemed an inevitable climax to the delirious scenes witnessed earlier in Washington, King George and Queen Elizabeth had become celebrities. As the prime minister noted later, "The king and queen have had to, more or less, play the role of movie stars and encounter not a few of their obligations and treats." The queen, especially, captured America's hearts. Pert, gracious, pretty — and young — she was the star of the show, and many a cynical Yank, suspicious of Britain's motives, found himself drowning in the depths of those magnetic, violet-blue eyes.

Sixty miles north of New York City was Hyde Park, the Hudson Valley estate owned by the Roosevelt family. There, the Royal Couple, Prime Minister King, and their hosts caught their breaths after the hectic pace of the previous three days. On the fourth day, a Sunday, the Royals attended church, went swimming with Franklin, Eleanor and their son, Elliott, and joined in an old-fashioned American picnic. (Also present were ambassadors, bishops, neighbours, and politicians, as well as some Morgenthaus and Astors.) Much to the delight of the American press, the Royal Couple sampled America's official comfort food, the hot dog. ("Push it in your mouth and keep pushing it until it's all gone," was FDR's advice to the queen.)* Roosevelt also drove his visitors about the estate "in my old Ford," and the king, the president, and the prime minister found time in the evenings to discuss the worsening situation in Europe.

Farewells were said at the train station just before midnight on Sunday, June 11. As Prime Minister King later put it, "Everyone, I think, felt that the visit had been the greatest possible success."

There remained four more days in Canada of crowds, cheers, children, and presentations before Their Majesties embarked for home. At Sherbrooke, the principal centre of Quebec's Eastern Townships, "an immense concourse of people were assembled" to greet the Royal Couple. The next stop was Lévis, across the St. Lawrence River from Quebec City, where a plaque was unveiled. Then Their Majesties were borne eastward for a whirlwind glimpse of the Maritime provinces.

Included was a 100-mile drive from the train station at Newcastle, New Brunswick, to Fredericton. At the halfway mark, the Royal Entourage stopped for tea at a guest house and, according to one report, a minor crisis occurred over the lack of a bathroom. King George apparently resorted to relieving himself against a barn on the banks of the Miramichi River while his Mountie escort discreetly looked the other way.

Onward to St. John and Moncton, where there were more children. At Moncton, according to the prime minister, they were "banked in a mass as far back as the eye could see." In driving rain

---

* Will Swift, *The Roosevelts and The Royals* (New York: John Wiley & Sons, 2004), 3.

that soaked the large crowd at Cape Tormentine, the Royal Party boarded the destroyer, HMCS *Skeena*, for the two-and-a-half-hour journey to Prince Edward Island. After a long and elaborate luncheon at Government House in Charlottetown (and more crowds lining the streets), the king and queen returned to the mainland. Following a slight delay at New Glasgow, Nova Scotia, when the locomotive had gone astray, Their Majesties spent their last night in Canada on a quiet siding near Truro.

The king wore his Admiral of The Fleet uniform and the queen her favourite shade of blue for the functions marking the final day. Following a luncheon at the Nova Scotian Hotel, Their Majesties said farewell to their Dominion of Canada. In a radio address beamed across the country by the CBC and around the world by the BBC, the king spoke in English and French of "a welcome of which the memory will always be dear to us."

> We leave your shores after some of the most inspiring and illuminating weeks in our lives. From the Atlantic to the Pacific, and from the tropics to the Arctic, lies a large part of the earth where there is no possibility of war between neighbours, whose people are wholly dedicated to the pursuits of peace, a pattern to all men of how civilized nations should live together ... By God's grace yours may yet be the example which all the world will follow.

The queen described how touched she had been by the women and children she had met and their warm welcome. "This wonderful tour of ours has given me memories that the passage of time will never dim," she said. *"Au revoir et que Dieu vous benisse."*

King George took away more than fond memories from Canada. He was quite a different ruler than the one who had disembarked at Quebec City a month earlier. Now, instead of adhering to the rigid view of the monarchy that consumed his forebears, he had realized that a sovereign must keep in touch with the people. During some key conversations with Prime Minister King, His Majesty intimated that he was now much closer to his subjects. He was also more comfortable with the job that had been thrust upon him.

And by the time the *Empress of Britain*, with the king and queen waving from the topmost deck, headed for a brief visit to the former Dominion of Newfoundland before crossing the Atlantic, the press — and most certainly the people of Canada — had revised their view of the Empire. One correspondent, while noting that King George was "a statesman in his own right," emphasized that the Royal Couple "are just good, decent people, modest and unassuming, and with a simple, natural air about them that makes you like them."

Even more fulsome — and certain that Canada was firmly wedded to the mother country — was *Globe and Mail* staff writer Douglas R. Oliver. Here is how he described the last moments of the Royal Visit on June 15, 1939:

> They've gone. Out to sea in the heart of flaming sunset. Their Majesties sailed tonight, the broad white wake of another "Empress" trailing final curtain across the bright drama of the past four weeks — ending a Royal crusade as colorful and commanding as when a Richard stirred to conquest for humanity's sake and marched in England's name, with justice at his sword-point and with freedom on his shield.
>
> Nine thousand triumphant, if travel-straining, Canadian miles are behind them. Eleven million Canadian people have now — if never before — fallen prisoner to their unaffectedness and charm. On Canadian life, on Canadian scene — from Cariboo to Chateaugay, by timber line and fishing stream and glacier glare and outcropped gold and empty granary, they have left their mark imperishable, their influence inviolate. In the smoke and din of tall cities they have been heard. In the hush and freedom of peaceful green pastures, they have had their say. And now their story

here is finished, and their song here has ended. And they have said farewell.

And as they turned to go and wave their hands, in their young eyes a sudden glory shone, and we were dazzled by a sunset glow — and they were gone.

As we scribble these phrases in the comparative gloom of the rangy dockshed, trying to put down as rapidly and as well as we know how the glory and the pathos of farewell which brings one's best British blood pounding up into one's throat, their home-headed ship is fast outbound, a great white smear merging rapidly with the horizon's sweep. The figures of our king and queen — standing on the bridge, waving, waving, waving back — are growing indistinguishable. And suddenly the world grows cold, and a vast emptiness sweeps upon us, and something very human, and, oh, so understanding, seems to have gone out of life, and one wonders when, if ever, they'll pass this humble way again.

In Ottawa, meanwhile, an orphan Parliament had limped to a close. When Sir Lyman Duff, Chief Justice of the Supreme Court of Canada, prorogued Parliament on June 3, the three main characters were absent. Prime Minister King was aboard the Royal Train (and quite content to be there instead of in the House of Commons), Opposition Leader R.J. Manion was on holidays, and the governor general, Lord Tweedsmuir, had gone fishing.

Partisan skirmishing between the Liberal-controlled Commons and the dominant Conservatives in the Senate enlivened the final hours of Parliament. The main issue was the Central Mortgage Bank Bill, designed as a vehicle giving the government control over mortgage funding, with a maximum interest rate of 5.5 percent on urban property and 5 percent on farms. The Tories, led by Senator Arthur

Meighen, attempted to amend the bill by making it apply to farm properties only, but the Liberal majority in the Commons — backed by the Conservative, Co-operative Commonwealth Federation, and Social Credit MPs — called Meighen's bluff by a vote of 86–1 against the amendment. The Tory Senator grumpily backed down.

In the public accounts committee, as Southam-Company correspondent Charles Bishop put it, "verbal pistols were popping in the trenches till the last minute over the machine gun contract. They were shouting and gesticulating till the bell rang over to report or make no report. With the session over, the enquiry flops, not in the middle, but not much beyond."

Gerry McGeer, the flamboyant Member for Vancouver-Burrard, was in the midst of summing up the evidence when another Liberal entered the committee room and said, "You might as well quit talking, Gerry, Parliament is dead."

Among the fifty-seven bills given Royal Assent by Justice Duff was the Prairie Farm Assistance Act, which offered a degree of insurance in the event of crop failure or low prices. Also passed was a bill establishing a defence purchasing board, as well as amendments to the Fisheries Act, the Canadian Grain Act, and the Canadian Wheat Board Act. Of the fifty-seven measures, thirty-four were divorce bills involving couples from Quebec, which did not have its own divorce legislation. The bill establishing the purchasing board was given detailed scrutiny. It called for a three-man board to supervise all defence purchases of $5,000 or more, and also placed a limit on the profits that might be made on contracts given without tenders.

Amid the political news, the war news, the royal news, and the images of refugees wandering aimlessly around the Atlantic, was a cheery update from Canada's five famous daughters, the Dionne quintuplets. A report to an Ontario Dental Association meeting in Toronto revealed that X-rays had been taken and the quints' teeth — all 100 of them — were in perfect condition.

The Way Things Were

THE FUNNY PAPERS

By the end of the 1930s, most metropolitan daily newspapers offered a wide selection of comics. Black-and-white strips appeared somewhere in the back of the paper from Monday through Friday, while separate colour sections ran on Saturdays. *Little Orphan Annie* probably topped the list as most-read, but there were other favourites, too. *Terry and The Pirates*, *The Lone Ranger*, *Popeye*, *Flash Gordon*, and *Charlie Chan* had their followers. Today, it might be hard to find such once-popular strips as *Moon Mullins*, *The Gumps*, *Tillie The Toiler*, *Willie Winky*, *Bringing Up Farther*, *Gasoline Alley*, or *King of The Royal Mounted*. The golden age of comic books was just dawning in 1939. Action heroes such as Superman, Batman, and The Lone Ranger entranced the kids as they battled evil in issue after issue. Although there were genre comic books such as *Amazing Comics* and *Detective Comics*, most titles focussed on individuals: Tarzan, Buck Rogers, Charlie Chan, Billy The Kid, Little Orphan Annie, and such niche personalities as Betty Boop.

Pulp Fiction. Attracting a large readership among adults were the pulps. The term, which derived from the cheap newsprint the magazines were printed on, similar to that supplied to newspapers by pulp mills, described low-cost magazines in various formats. These ranged from adventure and crime to romance, science fiction, and western. The standard newsstand price was ten cents a copy. Usually, the covers (printed in full colour on glossy paper) featured a half-naked woman, whether the contents justified it or not. The magazines' titles also often offered more than they delivered: *Amazing Adventures*, *Phantom Detective*, *Astounding Stories*. Notable, long-running heroes who found a homes there included Doc Savage, Conan the Barbarian, Buck Rogers, The Continental Op, The Shadow, Tarzan, Zorro, and Flash Gordon. Some famous authors got their start writing for the pulps. These included Isaac Asimov, Ray Bradbury, Erle Gardner, Zane Grey, Dashiell Hammett, and Jack London.

Show Time. Every Canadian lad who saw this movie dreamed of living Huck's carefree, barefoot life. *Huckleberry Finn*, starring Mickey Rooney, was more than "great adventure," as the ads promised: it was a great escape.

July

Heat and wheat. International developments aside, these were the stories making headlines for several weeks. Early in the month, the death toll from the excessive temperatures was reported at twenty-one. The fatalities were attributed mostly to the heat and drowning. On July 12, the *Winnipeg Free Press* reported that "Winnipeggers ran for shelter before the summer's worst heat wave." Downtown temperatures reached ninety-seven degrees. No casualties were reported, but some office buildings closed early because of the "impossible" working conditions. Among the closures were the CNR's general offices. A couple of weeks later, the West was scorched again, with Lethbridge, Alberta, reporting 101 degrees.

All this warmth had crop forecasters veering between optimism and pessimism. First, a high-ranking executive of the Canadian Bank of Commerce "sat back in his chair and discussed the country's general situation," according to a newspaper report. "The western wheat situation looks like a 100 percent crop this year," he said. "Moisture conditions are the best they have been in ten years. Fields in Saskatchewan as bare as my blotter two years ago are flourishing today. The western farmer will get his money this year." Then came a prediction of 400 million bushels of wheat — the second largest crop since 1928. All that was needed was rain.

Well, the rainfall came over a wide portion of the Prairies, prompting the *Winnipeg Free Press* to exclaim, MANNA FOR MANY. However, the heat didn't go away. Considerable crop damage was reported during the latter part of the month. "I don't think I've ever seen a good crop take so much damage from heat in the third week in July as this one," J.G.

Harvested wheat being delivered by wagon to a Manitoba elevator. The Prairies had a banner crop in 1939.

Gardiner, the agriculture minister, said in Winnipeg. Damage ranged from five to ten bushels per acre in an extensive area of Saskatchewan and part of western Manitoba. The damage could get even worse for stubble crops of all kinds, Gardiner said, if the heat didn't moderate. Apparently, the eventual harvest was adequate enough, because it was announced in August that Great Britain had bought five million bushels of Canadian wheat. The purchase of another five million bushels was expected.

British Prime Minister Chamberlain did a lot of talking during the month. Tough talk, some of it. First, on July 3, he revealed to the British House of Commons that German "tourists" were reported to be flooding into Danzig. "Reliable reports indicate that intensive measures of a military character are being carried out in the free city," he said. "Large and increasing numbers of German nationals recently have arrived … ostensibly as tourists, and a local defence corps is being formed under the name of Heimwehr [home defence]." He assured the House two days later that Britain would take "any step which may seem necessary" to solve the Danzig problem.

This brought a response from a Nazi spokesman in Berlin, who repeated Germany's claim to the Danzig Corridor. "Morally, the right to Danzig is ours," he said. "Just as we have a moral right to everything else we have taken with the exception of Bohemia-Moravia, but we had to do that to create a strategic frontier for ourselves. Czechoslovakia was like a fist thrust deep into the middle of our back, and it was a matter of necessity for us to take it."

Chamberlain's statement came two days after 20,000 British troops marched past King George and Queen Elizabeth during the welcoming festivities marking their safe return from Canada. According to press reports, "a great congregation" joined Their Majesties at a thanksgiving service in Westminster Abbey the day before Chamberlain made his statement. Canon F.P. Barry led the prayers for peace. Backing up his tough talk with hard cash, Chamberlain's government prepared to extend credits of up to $250 million to finance the export of war materiel to friendly countries. This sum, which was in addition to $50 million already committed, would go to such threatened European nations as Poland and Romania. This brought furious charges of "bribery" from the German press.

On July 10, Chamberlain again stressed that Britain was "firmly resolved" to stand by Danzig. He said recent occurrences in the free city had raised fears that Germany might use surreptitious methods to gain control. Any one-sided attempt to alter the status of Danzig would not be considered "a purely local matter," he said. "We have guaranteed to give our assistance to Poland in case of a clear threat to her independence which she considers it vital to resist with her national forces, and we are firmly resolved to carry out this undertaking."

The prime minister then moved on to the subject of Russia. On July 19, he told the House that he was hoping that a British-French-Russian mutual assistance pact would be in play by early August. Later that day, he said a joint British-French military mission would go to Moscow to seek an agreement. The British representative was Rear Admiral Sir Reginald Aylmer Ranfurly Plunkett-Ernle-Erle-Drax.

* * *

Arthur Neville Chamberlain was a member of an active political family. His father, Joseph Chamberlain, was Britain's colonial secretary at the turn of the century. He devised Imperial Preference as a way to keep the Dominions from straying too far from the Empire. Born in 1868, Neville Chamberlain spent several years managing his father's plantation in the Bahamas before returning to England and entering politics. He was first elected as a Conservative MP in 1918 and succeeded Stanley Baldwin in 1937 as prime minister. As Conservative leader, Chamberlain led the party's policy of non-intervention in European affairs into the quicksand of appeasement. He was sympathetic to Germany, believing it had been badly treated at Versailles following the Great War, and was receptive to some of the demands being made by Adolf Hitler. Chamberlain's attempts at accommodation to avoid another war was okay with Hitler, who began snatching up various parts of Europe. Chamberlain's appeasement reached its zenith (or nadir) at the Munich Conference in September of 1938. He agreed to let the Nazis have the Sudetenland, a slice of Czechoslovakia that was largely populated by Germans. Chamberlain thought this would be the end of Hitler's ambitions. He was wrong.

Adolf Hitler's beginnings were many times more modest than those of Chamberlain. Born in 1879 in an inn on the Austrian-Bavarian border, Hitler's father was a retired customs official who, as an illegitimate child, used his mother's name, Schicklgruber, for many years. Schicklbruber senior tried to stick his son with the name Adolf Schicklgruber, but he was overruled and the young boy became Adolf Hitler (a variation of Hiedler). Young Adolf's early years were as undistinguished as his beginnings, but the first stirrings of a future obsession came when he was in his twenties. Decorated twice, wounded twice, and also temporarily blinded by gas during the Great War, Corporal Hitler was tortured by Germany's defeat at the hands of "a gang of wretched criminals."

By 1920, Hitler had begun formulating a credo that would become the building block of the National Socialist party, otherwise known as the Nazis. One of its major points was a union of all Germans into a Greater Germany. When he was jailed for treason in 1924, Hitler wrote

Mein Kampf (*My Struggle*). By the 1930s, Hitler and his Nazis had steadily taken control. Through violence, double-crossing, arson, lies, outright murder, and an appeal to German patriotism, the National Socialists hardened into a single-minded police state with the goal of not only achieving a stronger Germany, but also of world domination.

Hitler spent some of July 1939 in his mountain lair in Berchtesgaden planning an attack on Poland. He relaxed by dabbling in culture, attending the Day of German Art festival in Munich. That weekend was warm and sunny, prompting one observer to write, "let's forget the filthy British hate propaganda for a day."

The Nazi leader also received a letter from Mahatma Gandhi. Addressed to "My Friend," Gandhi wrote, "It is quite clear today that you are the one person in the world who can prevent a war which may reduce humanity to the savage state. Must you pay that price for an objective, however worthy it may appear to you to be? Will you listen to the appeal of one who has deliberately shunned the method of war not without considerable success?" The letter ended, "Anyway, I anticipate your forgiveness if I have erred in writing to you. I remain, your sincere friend, Sd. M. MK. Gandhi."

There is no record of any reply. Perhaps the Führer was concentrating on agricultural problems: his obsession with Poland had left Germany short of farm workers. Some 200,000 Polish farm labourers, who for decades had migrated across the border for the harvest, weren't available because of the crisis in their homeland. In addition, the Nazis were short about 800,000 domestic workers. The labour pool was empty because of the concentration on industrial production. There were about 21.6 million Germans employed, with almost two million jobs unfilled. Other foreign workers — Slovaks, Hungarians, Bulgarians, Italians, Japanese, Dutch — were imported to fill the gap, boys in the Hitler Youth were ordered into the fields, and there was talk of calling out the army.

Meanwhile, trade negotiations were under way in Moscow. A cautious Hitler saw the negotiations as the beginning of a stronger alliance with the once-hated Russians. These talks were not connected with the secret trade negotiations between British officials and a high-ranking German bureaucrat. Britain was offered non-aggression and non-interference guarantees, as well as an arms reduction treaty. In return, Britain would return former German colonies, promise economic co-operation, and recognize the German sphere of influence over Eastern and Southeastern Europe. And, under a restructuring of global trade, Soviet Russia and China would become German markets. These talks never reached any official diplomatic level, but, along with Chamberlain's frosty attitude, they may have led to the reported softening of Germany's attitude. The usual threats against Poland and reports of military preparations in the Nazi press were replaced by a flood of optimistic reports that the Danzig question could be solved by peaceful negotiations. Still pessimistic about avoiding war, Prime Minister Chamberlain said, in a speech at the end of the month, that he still had hopes "we may yet find a way to escape from the present nightmare into the sunlight of peace."

On July 1, Dominion Day, Vincent Massey, the British High Commissioner to Canada, echoed Chamberlain's pessimism in his radio message from London. Solemnly focusing on England's war preparations, he said, "I'm afraid we cannot yet see very much blue sky on the international horizon. To a casual observer, London might seem to be following its normal summer routine," but the reality was quite different. "Air raid shelters, large and small, are evidence of this widespread preparedness."

In Canada itself, Dominion Day was observed quietly. Prime Minister King was at his Kingsmere retreat, rearranging furniture and writing in his diary about Chamberlain's attitude. "I don't believe the world will go to war over Danzig," he wrote. "England has protested too much as to what she and France will do, putting herself into a position devoid of possibility of retreat."

King also mused about the timing of a federal election. Going to the people was not strictly necessary in 1939, for the mandate granted the governing party five years in office. Normally, however, a government would seek a new vote of confidence every four years, especially if it had a good issue or a decent record. King had been carefully setting the stage for a 1939 election as early as January. The throne speech, the budget, and certain pieces of legislation were intended to be voter-friendly. His careful pronouncements over conscription and isolationism were designed to calm a populace that was prone to sudden vapours. The compromise over the Wheat Board was a prime example of putting the party ahead of any messy principle involving the right thing to do. The European situation was a major complication, and King had probably accepted the fact Canada would be at war before the year was out. Since the wisest path is always to prepare for an eventuality you can control, he began tinkering with dates.

Meanwhile, Conservative leader R.J. Manion was in Queenston Heights, Ontario, where he made a speech touching on history, tariffs, and unity. Speaking in the shadow of the Sir Isaac Brock Monument, he sketched the lengthy history of Canada and said that unity of purpose and effort today was the price to pay for future greatness. On the subject of tariffs, he floated the idea of implementing regional levies to benefit one section of the country: "It might apply in the East and not in the West."

Manion kept himself quite busy in July. Like everyone else, he expected an October election and was laying the groundwork for a successful bid to take over the government. Manion had been Opposition leader for four years, having replaced R.B. Bennett after the Tories lost the 1935 election. He was a medical doctor, who was decorated for heroism at the Battle of Vimy Ridge. Manion was elected as a Unionist to the House of Commons in the 1917 election and continued as a Conservative MP. He was appointed railways minister in the Bennett government of 1930, then lost his seat along with several other Conservatives in the 1935 election. After being chosen as party leader, he was returned to the House in a by-election.

Mid-July found Manion in Quebec, where he ventured 130 miles into the province by motorcade. Travelling by easy stages, he sought to determine what level of support Quebec would give his Tories in the next election. He was also "pleasantly surprised but still skeptical" to learn that Premiers Hepburn and Duplessis would support him in that campaign. In the Gaspé, he said welfare was demoralizing Canada's young people. "The greatest resource the Dominion has is its youth," he said, "yet we are ruining them with relief instead of giving them opportunities to work, to develop themselves and their country." Manioin also returned to one of his favourite topics: the merger of the CPR and CNR systems. He hinted that a future Conservative government would make it compulsory for the two rail giants to co-operate and eliminate duplicate services.

Manion was in tough competition against a veteran, wily politician. Prime Minister King was completing his twentieth year as leader of the Liberal Party, and his stewardship — although rocky in parts — was not being seriously challenged. King had a successful early career as a labour expert, serving as a deputy minister of labour and as a consultant for the Rockefeller Foundation. Chosen party leader in 1919, he skated on the very edge of contempt for the Crown during the constitutional crisis of 1926. In order to hang on as prime minister, King manipulated Governor General Lord Byng — hero of the great Canadian victory at Vimy Ridge and one of the finest persons in the history of Canadian public affairs — to win the inevitable election. The Beauharnois Scandal of the late 1920s, however, temporarily cost King his post. Although not even remotely involved with the bribery and corruption surrounding the construction of the Beauharnois Canal, he was tainted and the Liberals lost the 1930 election.

Despite being on vacation, King did attend to a few items of business in July 1939. Among a list of appointments to various organizations was Robert C. Vaughan as chairman of the Defence Purchasing Board. It would be a temporary, unpaid job for Vaughan, who was a vice-president with the CNR. His long experience in procurement with the railway, King said, "made him particularly suited to set up and put into operation the machinery of the purchasing board." The DPB was King's political brainstorm early in the year as an attempt to defuse the Bren Gun Scandal. The concept never took off, though. Given the "authority to purchase munitions, materiel and stores; and negotiate contracts for construction and repair of defence buildings, bases and projects," this authority was not sufficient to meet wartime needs. Before being replaced by the War Supply Board in September, the Defence Purchasing Board only managed to authorized $43.7 million worth of goods, with three-quarters of the orders placed after the war started. One of the problems, as C.D. Howe pointed out, was a limit of 5 percent on any profits to be made.

On July 26, 1939, the United States abruptly cancelled its trade agreement with Japan. Secretary of State Cordell Hull, with the approval of President Roosevelt, summoned the Japanese ambassador in Washington and told him the pact would end in six months. There had been growing tension between the two nations and it was believed the United States was concerned about Tokyo's commodity manoeuvring. The decision, which caught both capitals by surprise, came two days after Great Britain's agreement with Japan to recognize its "special requirements" in China. These "requirements" apparently included an intensification of the anti-British boycott. Missionaries were told that they faced expulsion from China and British goods were swept off the store shelves in Peking by Japanese police. Those products that remained were wrapped in paper bearing the inscription, "Death to Britain."

The sudden focus on the Pacific didn't raise any eyebrows in Ottawa, but it did fuel growing fears about Japanese influence on the West coast. Alderman Halford Wilson, the poster boy for anti-Asian intolerance in Vancouver, regularly warned about the Japanese menace to Canada. He would later declare that Japanese business owners had "different standards of living" and tried to circumvent normal labour practices.

With the drone of politics on Parliament Hill stilled for the moment, Canadians devoted more of their attention to local matters. In Vancouver, a dispute arose over employment of chop suey waitresses. Montrealers took the No. 17 streetcar on weekends to Belmont Park, where they could ride the scenic railway or watch a flying trapeze act. In Calgary, a mother and daughter were arrested and charged with assault causing bodily harm after they attempted to tar and feather a nurse.

One special event that July was the mass marriage of 105 couples in Montreal Stadium. As 20,000 invited guests — uniformed members of the Young Catholic Workers organization — watched, the brides in white and the grooms in blue suits were joined in holy matrimony by Archbishop Georges Gauthier and 104 supporting priests. Music from an organ at home plate was piped through the stands, accompanying choirs singing marriage songs. Four hundred guests collapsed because of the heat during the ten-hour ceremony.

In its thirtieth year, the Girl Guides of Canada held their Second National Camp July 14–21 at Rothesay, New Brunswick. Each province was represented, and activities included powwows, discussion groups, and sightseeing jaunts. Meanwhile, at a swimming camp in the Strathroy district of Ontario near London, Boy Scout Cubs were scared right out of their trunks by a tornado that ripped through the area. No injuries were reported, though property damage was estimated at $250,000.

Somewhere in Canada, the Conklin Shows had probably come to town. Conklin, which billed itself as the "World's Finest Show," was uniquely Canadian. In 1937, the mix of rides, games, sideshows, and midway concession stands was awarded a contract by the Canadian National Exhibition in Toronto, the world's largest fair. This was a big boost to the circus's bottom line, allowing it to continue offering a version of its wares to small town fairs each summer. In 1939, Conklin Shows was advertising "gigantic, scintillating skylights ... a million laughs on the glittering gayway, 50 startling midway attractions, spectacular free acts and a rainbow of colour." Sideshows included the Ro-Lo Funhouse, World's Fair Freaks, Baby Thelma Fat Show, and a "Sally" girl show. For rides, there were the Auto Speedway, Tilt-A-Whir, the Octopus, twin Ferris wheels and, of course, a merry-go-round. Apart from the CNE, Conklin offered mostly small-town shows. For the bigger cities, Ringling Brothers-Barnum & Bailey would bring in its circus train. Gargantua, billed as the largest gorilla in captivity and "the world's most terrifying creature," was a star attraction.

On July 12, the Great Lakes area was transfixed by a huge meteor streaking across the night sky. "It was a fearsome sight," said a St.

Thomas, Ontario, policeman. "I have never seen anything like it. It looked like a huge flying teardrop flying through the air." Heading slightly to the northwest, the meteor lit the sky for several seconds. The next day, a farmer near Dresden, Ontario, sold an eighty-eight-pound chunk of the meteor for four dollars to representatives of the London Life Insurance Company. They turned it over to the University of Western Ontario in London. Just over a week later, another meteor streaked across the British Columbia sky in broad daylight. Hundreds of residents of the Lower Mainland watched the fireball until it disappeared over the North Shore mountains near Vancouver. "It shot over the sky in an arc and was intensely bright in spite of the daylight," said William Gifford of Crescent Beach, who was sitting on his verandah. "There seemed to be a tail of sparks behind it."

In other space news, astronomers kept their instruments trained on Mars as the Red Planet approached within thirty-six million miles of the earth. This was the closest conjunction of the two planets in fifteen years, and scientists hoped to learn something about our mysterious neighbour. Toward the end of the month, Mars hung in the night sky like a bright jewel. In Mexico, witch doctors predicted earthquakes and the end of the world.

On July 8, the Royal Mail Ship *Nascopie* slipped out of her berth on the Montreal waterfront and headed down the St. Lawrence. The *Nascopie*, a 2,500-ton steamship-icebreaker, was making her annual voyage to the Arctic. On board were supplies for remote trading posts and other goods ranging from babies bottles and canned peaches to drums of gasoline. A special shipment was part of the cargo for this trip: medallions commemorating the Royal Visit were to be passed out to 1,500 Inuit schoolchildren in Arctic communities. They would be the last schoolchildren in Canada to receive them. The *Nascopie* also carried passengers, including Mounted Policemen, doctors, and missionaries. Some of them wouldn't return for five years.

The *Nascopie* was one of the Arctic's most historic vessels. Beginning in 1912, she sailed for thirty-four years to the northern outposts, reaching as far as Ellesmere Island, 800 miles from the North Pole. During the Second World War, she was fitted with naval guns as protection. In 1947, the *Nascopie* struck an uncharted reef, broke in two, and slid into deep water during a storm.

As July continued to unfold, the British government had to wrench its attention from the threat in Europe to one in its own backyard. The Irish Republican Army had embarked on a campaign of violence in England that culminated in July with a plot to blow up the parliament buildings. The IRA, a terrorist organization devoted to the union of Northern Ireland and the Irish Free State, came into being after the Irish Revolt of 1916. For years, the group's home turf was the subject of violent activities, but in 1939 the "S Plan" specifically targeted England. The campaign (*S* for Sabotage) was aimed at civil, military, and economic targets in an attempt to force Britain to loosen its hold on Ireland. The strategy was devised by Sean Russell, the IRA's chief of staff; the actual plan was conceived by Seamus O'Donovan in 1938.

In January 1939, the IRA declared war on Britain. A communiqué directed to Foreign Secretary Lord Halifax said, "The government of the Irish Republic, having as its first duty towards its people the establishment and maintenance of peace and order here, demand the withdrawal of all British armed forces stationed in Ireland." This was followed by attacks in London, Birmingham, Liverpool, and elsewhere. (One London subway attack was thwarted when a toilet attendant spotted a suspicious parcel.) After the frequency of attacks increased, the House of Commons was told on July 24 that blowing up Parliament was likely part of the "S Plan." Sir Samuel Hoare, the home secretary, also told the House that the IRA was being "actively stimulated by a foreign organization." He produced a copy of the plan, which had been obtained by British police.

"It is a very remarkable document," Sir Simon said. "It is not the kind of irresponsible, melodramatic document that one sometimes discovers in searches of this sort. It is a very carefully worked out staff plan — the kind that might be worked out by a general staff setting out in detail the way in which a campaign of sabotage could be successfully carried out against this country." He disclosed that police had seized 1,000 sticks of gelignite, 1,000 detonators, and hundreds of pounds of other explosives — "enough to cause millions of pounds worth of damage and the loss of at least 1,000 lives." Although "S Plan" listed several general targets, such as transport, industry, armament factories, newspapers, and "civil utilities," Hoare did not spell out the specific threat against Parliament.

Within days, legislation was passed giving Scotland Yard and other police organizations broad powers to curb the attacks. Special guards were put around scores of famous public buildings, including the royal palaces, Westminster Abbey, and the parliament buildings. Both the House of Commons and the House of Lords were closed to the public. Suspects were rounded up for deportation. The campaign involved 15,000 officers in the London area alone. Reports from London also indicated a "great exodus" of IRA men and women immediately prior to the crackdown. Despite the heightened security, however, a suitcase bomb exploded at King's Cross tube station, killing one person and injuring fifteen.

The Way Things Were

CIGARETTE BREAK

Cigarette brands available in 1939 included a few choices still on the shelves today: Macdonald's Export, Player's, Sweet Caporal. Those that went up in smoke during the intervening years, however, were such offerings as Winchester, Buckingham, Guinea Gold, British Consols, Turret (available in packs of ten), and Spud, the original menthol cigarette. An advertisement in the May 29, 1939, issue of *Life* magazine promised — under a picture of a smiling female model holding a cigarette — that "you pay the usual cigarette price for a Spud, but you get menthol value!" For decades, Player's packs featured the familiar cameo of a bearded Royal Navy sailor. Also for decades, the Macdonald Tobacco

Company sponsored the Macdonald Brier, Canada's national curling championship. The provincial playdowns were sponsored by British Consols. In 1939, there were no restrictions on sports sponsorship or on advertising, and no health warnings.

Cigars and pipe tobacco were also freely available. Mischievous little boys would grab an unguarded phone, call the drugstore, and ask whether they had Prince Albert in the can. When the druggist gave a cautious affirmative, they'd shout, *"Better let him out!"* before hanging up, and dashing away amid peals of laughter.

Real Estate. "Properties for Sale" was one of the busiest listings in newspaper classified sections. There were some good bargains. A home in Toronto, "one of Forest Hill's best," was on the market for $37,500. At the other end of the scale, a solid brick bungalow, only three years old, was being offered for $5,300. Electric refrigerator and stove were included.

Naked Truth. In the East Kootenay region of British Columbia, some Doukhobor families lost their communal home when foreclosure proceedings forced them onto the street. They attempted to stage a nude protest against the harsh actions of the mortgage-holders, but it was short-lived. An estimated 5,000 other Doukhobors in the region also faced eviction.

Market Basket. During the last summer of peace, hamburger was nineteen cents a pound and steak, twenty-nine cents. Depending on your location, apples were ten cents a basket and peaches, nineteen cents. A fourteen-ounce bottle of brand-name ketchup was on sale for nineteen cents. Tea was seventy-five cents for a one-pound bag and lettuce was five cents a head.

Show Time. *Tarzan Finds a Son!* was another in the series of jungle epics starring Johnny Weismuller and Maureen O'Sullivan. According to the publicity, "Tarzan's jungle love-call thrills again!"

August

On the Continent, damp handshakes and the nervous clearing of throats in diplomatic circles became more prevalent as August stumbled toward its inevitable climax. In Canada, the languor over the Royal Visit was giving way to expressions of concern about the worsening European situation — except among the ruling Liberals, who were definitely feeling their oats.

Early in the month, the party threw an elaborate wingding in Toronto to celebrate Prime Minister King's twenty years at the helm. Five provincial premiers were among the 3,500 guests, but John Bracken of Manitoba was not among the province's twenty-five-man delegation. He had begged off because he was too busy organizing a trade mission to Europe. (That Bracken still thought that there would be a calm and collected Europe to trade with marked him either as an incurable optimist or a provincial hayseed woefully ignorant of international affairs.) Also absent was Ontario's Mitchell Hepburn. No reason was given, but Hepburn, an onion farmer as well as a politician, would probably claim he was tending his 40,000-onion crop. Nevertheless, "the most remarkable manifestation of loyalty and confidence yet given a Canadian public man was tendered Mr. King at the Royal York Hotel," gushed a *Toronto Daily Star* reporter. A modest King insisted the tribute was for his colleagues, and the "great principles of Liberalism," as much as it was for him. During his speech, he also said that he would not commit the country blindly on any issue.

Instead of paying real attention to the governing party's self-absorption, ordinary Canadians were busy deploring the stiff-necked bureaucrats at the post office. It came to light that those caught sending ticket stubs to the Irish Hospital Sweepstakes were being denied mail service. A Toronto doctor blew the whistle on this apparently routine punishment, when he complained that the postal folks' zeal put one of his patients at risk. Dr. James Cotton informed the deputy postmaster in Toronto that "my report on a serious heart condition of a patient was not delivered. As a result, the man nearly died." The post office's tactics, he said, were "worse than regulations in dictator countries." The ban applied to everyone in the house, a spokesman said, whether the individual had broken the law or not. "The ban lasts indefinitely and applies to all those using the mails illegally for purposes to defraud, including those dealing with Irish Sweepstakes or other lottery tickets." The ban could be lifted through an appeal to the postmaster-general, though, along with a promise not to do it again.

The month's first shivers of real apprehension came from China, which is about as far away from Danzig as one can get and stay on dry land. British Prime Minister Chamberlain told the House of

Library and Archives Canada, PA-061678

Mail boxes line a rural road. Mail delivery was much more frequent in 1939 than it is today.

Commons that Japanese indignities against British citizens in China had his "blood boiling." The harassment, including such incidents as denying access for hours at a time to British compounds and smashing an Englishman's watch because it was set for local, not Tokyo, time, was exasperating enough, that even though distracted by the central European situation, Chamberlain said he might dispatch a fleet to the Far East. "I don't say this as a threat, but really as a warning," he said, while admitting that the last thing Britain wanted at the moment was a two-hemisphere war. "Even in the presence of those insults and injuries which have been afflicted upon British people in China by the Japanese, we must remember there are limits to what we can do at this time to help our people there."

Chamberlain's attention was soon wrenched back to the Continent. On August 18, German troops poured into Slovakia prior to massing on the Polish border. Slovak radio listeners were stunned to hear an English-speaking voice announce in reassuring tones, "Owing to the existing situation, Germany has taken military possession of Slovakia." A "defence agreement" between the two countries was described in reliable quarters as placing the small republic's armed forces under Nazi control. Germany had also begun insisting that Poland was not really a nation at all, that a large proportion of the population consisted of alien peoples who were being oppressed by the Poles, and that this oppressed majority must be rescued. A map published in a German newspaper purported to show that the Poles occupied only the central portion of the country, while Germans, Czechs, Letts, Ukrainians, White Russians, and Lithuanians lived in the outer regions.

This disturbing development was closely followed by another shock: Germany and Soviet Russia were negotiating a non-aggression treaty. At 10:53 p.m. on August 14, Joachim von Ribbentrop, the German foreign minister, sent a *MOST URGENT* coded telegram to Count von der Schulenburg, the German ambassador in Moscow. The telegram ordered the envoy to contact Soviet Foreign Minister Vyacheslav Molotov personally and read to him (but not give him a copy) its contents, which included Ribbentrop's request to meet with Joseph Stalin. The telegram spent some time discussing "the ideological contradictions between National Socialist Germany and the Soviet Union," adding that "there is no doubt that German-Soviet policy today has come to an historic turning point." In asking for an opportunity to present the Führer's views, the telegram said:

> The crisis which has been produced in German-Polish relations by English policy, as well as English agitation for war and the attempts at an alliance which are bound up with that policy, make a speedy clarification of German-Russian relations desirable. Otherwise, these matters, without any German initiative, might take a turn which would deprive both Governments of the possibility of restoring German-Soviet friendship and the possibility of clearing up jointly the territorial questions of Eastern Europe. The leadership in both countries should, therefore, not allow the situation to drift, but should take action at the proper time. It would be fatal if, through mutual lack of knowledge of views and intentions our peoples should be finally driven asunder.

Stalin, Molotov, and Ribbentrop did meet in Moscow late on the night of August 23. A *MOST SECRET! STATE SECRET* memorandum later set down other problems. Japan was one of them, with Stalin remarking that he wished to improve relations, but that there were limits to Russia's patience with regard to Japanese provocations. "If Japan desired war, it could have it," Stalin said. As for Italy, he wondered why small, mountainous, and thinly-populated Albania was so important. (Strategic value, Ribbentrop replied.) Coming finally to England, Stalin and Molotov commented that the recent British military mission to Moscow never did spell out exactly what it wanted. After Ribbentrop gave his opinion that England was weak and "wanted to let others fight for its presumptuous claim to world domination," Stalin eagerly contended that the British army was ineffectual, the British Navy no longer deserved its previous reputation, and its air arm lacked pilots. "If England dominates the world in spite of this," he said, "this was due to the stupidity of the other countries that always let themselves be bluffed. It was ridiculous, for example, that a few hundred British should dominate India." As they parted early in the morning of August 24, Stalin assured Ribbentrop that "on his word of honour, the Soviet Union would not betray its partner."

A terse communiqué on the front pages of Moscow's morning newspapers said Ribbentrop was on the way to conclude a "no-war" pact. In Berlin, jubilant Nazis said they had struck a death blow to British and French hopes of dragging Russia into a peace alliance, and that a triumphant victory was certain in Germany's dispute with Poland. Warsaw said it would fight aggression despite any German-Soviet treaty. Reports from Britain said officials in London were "shocked and startled" by the news, but not plunged into gloom. There was still some hope that this treaty wouldn't affect the Anglo-French peace initiative. As Parliament (which had just voted itself a two-month holiday) met for an emergency session, the government said it would remain "steadfast and unaltered" in its support for Poland.

It appears as though Britain and France never had a chance to lure Soviet Russia into the fold. In pledging their support for Poland, they also accepted Poland's stand against any diplomatic incursions by Moscow. This fed Stalin's extreme paranoia about the Western nations' motives. He had become convinced that they were conspiring to throw the whole strength of the German army against the U.S.S.R. So, despite the bitter ideological gulf between himself and Hitler, he had sought an accommodation with Berlin. Upon reading a telegram from Stalin, Hitler pounded his fist on the dinner table and exclaimed, "I have them! I have them!"* He was talking about the Soviets, not the Western allies. He had his gaze focused on the Ukraine, a rich wheat-growing region on the Black Sea. First, he'd have victory in the West, then war with an unsuspecting Russia.

Molotov, in a speech to the Supreme Soviet toward the end of the month, declared that, "On the one hand, Britain and France demanded military help from the U.S.S.R. in the case of aggression

---

* Chronology of World War II, 1939 *http://www.islandnet.com/~kpolsson/ww2hist/ww21939.htm.*

against Poland.... On the other hand, precisely Great Britain and France brought Poland on the scene, who resolutely declined military assistance on the part of the U.S.S.R. Now, try reaching an agreement regarding mutual assistance when assistance on the part of the U.S.S.R. is declared beforehand to be unnecessary and obtrusive."

In Ottawa, Prime Minister King noted the "terrible shock and surprise" felt in England, and wrote in his diary, "It is an appalling position ... for England and France, but not so bad as to have begun a war and found themselves deceived by an ally before it was under way." He then called the fateful cabinet meeting that would decide how to respond to a declaration of war. There was some debate, but "general agreement and unanimity" was reached: The cabinet's position was that Canada should go to war if Great Britain did so. However, Parliament would be consulted before any fatal steps were taken. King then summed up the position succinctly:

> The cabinet is of one mind. It is united in its view of the present European situation and the procedure to be followed in giving expression to what we believe to be the will of the Canadian people with respect to whatever situation may develop. We regard it of supreme importance at this critical hour that the country should remain united and this end can best be met by proceeding with caution with respect to every step to be taken as the situation may develop. At the same time, that we were taking all possible precautionary measures to meet any and every eventuality.

"Proceeding with caution..." Ah yes, the Prime Minister King way.

In Quebec, the Soviet-German deal appeared to have a positive effect for Canada. French-Canadians had long regarded Germany as a bulwark against Russia, and (like Lindbergh) did not want a weakened Reich to lose any war. Now, according to a newspaper report, they had realized that the "two Godless countries" were capable of being pals. This attitude was not unanimous, however. Despite some quiet support for the federal government, dissenting voices were being heard across Quebec. It was reported that Frederick Dorion, a Conservative organizer in the province, branded the historic Liberal support for Great Britain as false and unacceptable. "How can we see that we are drawn into a war which may result from the treaty signed by Great Britain and Poland?" Dorion asked. "Have we taken part in that agreement? Has Canada made some pledge which she must now respect? Is there on our part any reason at all why we should participate in a war the issue of which must be unfavourable to us, like the issue of 1918?" Canada has nothing to gain and everything to lose, he added. His stand was echoed by Maxime Raymond, a Liberal MP from Quebec.

Paul Gouin, leader of L'Action libérale nationale, claimed that "the province of Quebec is opposed to Canada being engaged in a conflict which is none of our business." French-Canadian cabinet ministers played down the dissent, claiming that Quebec was in Canada's corner in any war effort short of conscription.

Across the Dominion, a sense of unease began to creep in. Wives and mothers looked on with a sinking feeling as their menfolk stared out the window for long minutes, waiting for the word that their militia unit was being activated. Around the fires at hobo jungles, vagrants spooned up their beans and talked nervously of the Great War. Most of them were too young to have experienced trench warfare, but like the military brass, they assumed the next war would be fought along the same lines as the last one.

That call came for many. Howard Graham, a reserve army officer who would eventually become chief of the general staff, contributed his thoughts to the book *The Good Fight: Canadians and World War II*. "What a fool I had been to spend time and money these past seventeen years on military affairs," he wrote. "Yet, I thought, I must be honest. I was only one of hundreds of militia officers with families across Canada who would be feeling the same unhappy situation."

Militia units were first called out to protect coastal defences and industrial points. Among these were the 15th Coast Brigade, the 1st Searchlight Regiment, and the 5th (B.C.) Coast Brigade, Royal Canadian Artillery. Soon afterward, the voluntary mobilization became widespread. The Rocky Mountain Rangers were assigned defence duties in Kamloops, British Columbia. The Regina Rifle Regiment was sent to guard the Regina airport. Special attention was given to the Welland Canal after a bomb plot was uncovered. Some of the other units called up were Cape Breton Highlanders, Halifax Rifles, New Brunswick Rangers, Princess Louise Fusiliers, St. John Fusiliers, 2nd battalion of the Canadian Scottish, and the Irish Fusiliers of Canada. The Irish Regiment of Canada was put on active duty. The Eastern and Western Air Commands of the RCAF began making regular patrols over the Atlantic and Pacific Oceans.

Despite the rattle of obsolete weaponry in the armouries and the smell of mothballs from Great War uniforms wafting through the air, Canadians still had their major August diversions to look forward to. These were the Canadian National Exhibition in Toronto and the Canada Pacific Exhibition (now known as the Pacific National Exhibition) in Vancouver. Both fairs offered the usual mix of midway rides, cotton candy and hotdogs, sideshows, and entertainment, including swine and other livestock competitions and other farming fare in the agricultural barns.

At the CPE, which was the largest fair in the Pacific Northwest at the time, the British Columbia Telephone Company held daily draws for free long-distance calls to anywhere in the province. It also featured a "Voice Mirror," which played your spoken words back to you. The British Columbia Electric Company was showing "Cinderella" kitchens. "Special privilege" tickets for the fair were three for one dollar.

The CNE was opened by Viscount Maugham, the Lord Chancellor of Great Britain, on August 18. Among a group of events sponsored by the *Toronto Daily Star* was a special presentation of the Royal Tour. The centrepiece was the world premiere of a colour motion picture depicting Their Majesties' visit to Canada. It was culled from "thousands and thousands" of professional and amateur films. At the same time, another diversion attracted Torontonians at Union Station. The Maharajah Bahadur of Benares arrived from Chicago with his staff, members of his family, and plenty of luggage. The party took over the entire 16th floor of the Royal York Hotel. Reported to have an annual income of £1 million, the maharajah was breezing through town on a quick tour of Toronto, Ottawa, and Montreal before heading to New York and home.

At about the same time that Ribbentrop was sealing the deal with Molotov, Hitler sent a strongly-worded memorandum to Chamberlain. After stating that "Germany has never sought conflict with England and has never interfered in English interests," he wrote:

> The unconditional assurance given by England to Poland that she would render assistance to that country in all circumstances regardless of the causes from which a conflict might spring, could only be interpreted in that country as an encouragement thenceforward to unloosen, under cover of such a charter, a wave of appalling terrorism against the one and a half million German inhabitants living in Poland. The atrocities which since then have been taking place in that country are terrible for the victims, but intolerable for a Great Power such as the German Reich which is expected to remain a passive onlooker during these happenings.

In conclusion, Hitler said it wasn't up to him to initiate a *détente*. "The question of the treatment of European problems on a peaceful basis is not a decision which rests on Germany but primarily on those who since the crime committed by the Versailles dictate have stubbornly and consistently opposed any peaceful revision," he wrote. "Only after a change of spirit on the part of the responsible Powers can there be any real change in the relationship between England and Germany."

In reply, "His Majesty's Government" sent a message to Hitler advising him that Britain was still determined to aid Poland and meet force with force. The note was delivered personally to the German chancellor at Berchtesgaden. Meanwhile, King George had returned to London from Scotland to meet his senior advisers. In France, trains full of troops rumbled toward the German border. Shipments of gold bars and securities worth $71 billion were being transported to Canada for safekeeping aboard liners and warships. (Under heavy guard and in sealed baggage cars, the treasure was whisked to Montreal in the dead of night after arriving on Canadian shores. The gold went into the Bank of Canada vaults in Ottawa and the securities were deposited at Sun Life Assurance Company in Montreal.) Sea transportation was also being arranged to ferry a British Expeditionary Force across the English Channel.

British nationals were being advised to leave Germany and Americans in England were given a similar message. The German Embassy in London advised all Germans to leave Britain immediately, and hundreds did. These included press attachés, the editor of the official Nazi news agency in London, and mechanics for the German airline Lufthansa. Royal Navy destroyers escorted vessels across the North Sea from Scandinavia. Reservists were alerted to expect mobilization. Blackout restrictions were posted in London. The German battleship, *Schleswig-Holstein*, dropped anchor in Danzig harbour (it would fire a few rounds at Polish positions on September 1). In Cairo, Egypt, forty cases packed with the sarcophagus of King Tutankhamen, along with treasures found in his tomb, were moved to a secret underground location for safekeeping.

American President Roosevelt made another appeal to Britain, Germany, and Poland to back away from the brink. In his message to Hitler, Roosevelt noted that he had not received a reply to his April 14 communiqué, and wrote, "But because of my confident belief that the cause of world peace — which is the cause of humanity itself — rises above all other considerations, I am again addressing myself to you with the hope that the war which impends and the consequent disaster to all peoples everywhere may yet be averted." The president then repeated his main points: no acts of hostility between Germany and Poland for a stipulated period, a common accord to solve any controversies, and submitting of these controversies to impartial arbitration. In closing, he appealed "in the name of the people of the United States and I believe in the name of peace-loving men and women everywhere" for Germany to agree to his proposal. While London said that it appreciated the president's initiatives, they were rejected by Berlin.

Prime Minister King sent a similar plea. The people of Canada, he wrote to Hitler, "are prepared to join what authority and power they possess to that of the other nations of the British Commonwealth in seeking a just and equitable settlement of the great problems with which the nations are faced." Making a direct appeal to the German chancellor, he wrote:

> On behalf of the Canadian people, but equally in the interests of humanity itself, I join with those of other countries and powers who have appealed to you in the firm hope that your great power and authority will be used to prevent impending catastrophe by having recourse to every possible peaceful means to effect a solution of the momentous issues of this period of transition and change in world affairs.

Roosevelt also sent a long message to King Victor Emmanuel of Italy on August 23 urging him to lend a hand. Referring to his previous offer in April to have America act as an intermediary in the European crisis, Roosevelt wrote:

> Were it possible for Your Majesty's Government to formulate proposals for a pacific solution of the present crisis along these lines you are assured of the earnest sympathy of the United States. The Government of Italy and the United States can today advance those ideals of Christianity which of late seem so often to have been obscured. The unheard voices of countless millions of human beings ask that they shall not be vainly sacrificed again.

Two days later (although it had to be a coincidence) Benito Mussolini told Hitler that Italy was not ready to go to war over Poland.

> If Germany attacks, and Poland's allies open a counterattack against Germany, I want to let you know in advance that it would be better if I did not take the initiative in military activities in view of the present situation of Italian war preparations, which we have repeatedly previously explained to you, Fuehrer, and to Herr von Ribbentrop.
>
> … I consider it my implicit duty as a true friend to tell you the whole truth and inform you about the actual situation in advance. Not to do so might have unpleasant consequences for us all. This is my point of view and since within a short time I must summon the highest governmental bodies of the realm, I ask you to let me know yours as well.*

Hitler did delay his attack against Poland, for a week. On August 26, a newspaper dispatch quoting a source on the Polish frontier said, "The turning point, the informant contended, came at 2 a.m. today. At that time, he said, an order to begin operations along the Polish border and at Danzig at 4:30 a.m. was rescinded, and telephone and telegraph communications with foreign countries were returned after an interruption of seven hours."

At Westminster, a sense of nervous anticipation filled the air. Chamberlain's words that August were much more despairing than those in July. "God knows I have done all that is possible in efforts for peace," the grave-faced prime minister told the House. "If war comes, we shall be fighting to prevent destruction of those principles which hold all possibility of peace and security for the peoples of the world. We have a united country behind us. As we think, so shall we act unitedly."

---

* Benito Mussolini to Adolf Hitler, August 25, 1939, *http://avalon.law.yale.edu/20th_century/ns058.asp*

Chamberlain outlined in general terms the last-minute diplomatic dialogue between England and Germany. Although Hitler "wished for an Anglo-German understanding of a complete and lasting character," his insistence on regaining Danzig had not wavered. Chamberlain then went on to outline some moves the government had taken: Air defences had been placed in a state of instant readiness. Anti-aircraft defences had been deployed and manned. RAF fighter and reconnaissance squadrons had been brought to war strength. Coastal defences had been manned, and units of the Territorial Army were ready to protect important points. The Civil Defence organization was on a war footing. As for the Royal Navy, Chamberlain said it was already in an advanced state of preparedness.

"The Admiralty has also assumed control of merchant shipping, acting under the powers conferred by the Emergency Powers Act, and written instructions have already been issued to merchant shipping on various routes," the prime minister said. "The British people are said sometimes to be slow to make up their minds, but having made them up, they do not readily let go. The issue of peace or war is still undecided, and we still will hope, and still will work for peace; but we will not abate no jot of our resolution to hold fast to the line which we have laid down for ourselves."

Sifting through the events of those last days of August, it is not hard to conclude — from the safe perspective of hindsight — that the Third Reich wasn't actually serious about attaining a peaceful solution. Bearing in mind that Hitler had already scheduled an invasion of Poland earlier in the month (before being dissuaded by whatever agency), the last-minute flurry of communiqués with Great Britain had to be window-dressing. When a note from the British was delivered to Hitler at 10:30 p.m. on August 28, he promised to reply the following day. It came in the form of a distorted summary of the events leading up to the crisis, and a demand that a Polish envoy report to Berlin immediately. Britain's rejoinder, just before midnight on August 30, was answered as Ribbentrop read out a lengthy document in rapid German. When Ribbentrop was asked for a written copy, his reply was that it was too late anyway because the Polish diplomat hadn't arrived by the midnight deadline. The Polish ambassador to Germany was finally granted a face-to-face meeting with Ribbentrop on the evening of August 31. The ambassador then tried to contact Warsaw, but couldn't get through because all communication between Poland and Germany had been severed by the Nazi government.

That same day, Poland ordered full mobilization. According to press reports, it "caused the Eastern Europe situation to take a dangerous step toward a showdown. The move aroused indignation in Berlin." A special council was established to deal with defence of the Reich "for the duration of the present foreign political tension." German secret police seized the Danzig railway station and raised Nazi swastikas above its roof.

In London, the ministry of health ordered the "precautionary" removal of 1.5 million schoolchildren from London and other key urban centres. Besides the children, 40,000 of whom were from the London area alone, the evacuation order included 1.5 million "cripples, the blind and expectant mothers." They would be taken to "places of safety." The ministry's announcement said:

> Evacuation, which will take several days to complete, is being undertaken as a precautionary measure in view of the prolongation of the period of tension. The government is fully assured that the attitude of quiet confidence which the public have been displaying will continue, that no unnecessary movements which would interfere with the smooth operation of the transport arrangements will take place.

The evacuation brought some hand-wringing from the press. "The government's portentous decision increased the strain of Europe's war of nerves to an almost unbearable pitch," one dispatch from London said. "The schedule of evacuation is one of the most poignant in the history of the world."

That last weekend of August, Members of Parliament began drifting back to Ottawa from fence-mending chores in their ridings. No announcement had yet been made, but everyone expected Parliament to be recalled any day. The cabinet was told not to stray too far from Ottawa. J.S. Woodsworth, pale and haggard, had one additional duty to perform before attending the session. He had to persuade the national council of the CCF that the party's sitting MPs must vote "Nay" to any declaration of war by Canada. That he failed would become evident in September, when the question of war was called in the House. Manion, who was concentrating on Ontario after his foray into Quebec, was only a few hours from Parliament Hill.

King had one personal demon of his own to deal with: O.D. Skelton, the fervent isolationist, who was still the prime minister's closest adviser in external affairs. All year, despite King's blunt rejection of isolationism, Skelton patiently pleaded the case for neutrality. In those nervous days of August, it was a distraction that King did not need. Finally, he told his old friend that the path he advocated would rend the Dominion asunder. There could be no compromise this time. The distraught Skelton tendered his resignation. The prime minister let it sit on his desk for two days. Then, realizing that there could only be one proper course of action, Skelton withdrew his resignation and continued in his post.

Because of such pressures, King wasn't exactly feeling chipper. He was having bouts of sleeplessness, and when he did nod off, his dreams were disturbing. Around 4:00 a.m. one morning, he "got down beside little Pat [his dog] and talked to him in the basket. He seemed to be understanding everything that was being said to him." The days were warm, however, and King managed to rejuvenate himself by sunbathing on the Kingsmere lawn. Surrounded by the ominous dispatches from Europe, he began sketching the face the government would present when calling the House back into session.

Mackenzie King had already primed Canadians earlier in the month by reminding them that the War Measures Act was still on the books. Passed at the outbreak of the Great War, it had never been repealed. "It finds its place today in Chapter 206 of the Revised Statutes of Canada and is entitled, An Act to Confer Certain Powers upon the Government-in-Council in the Event of War, Invasion or Insurrection," he said in a public statement. "The provisions of this act are exceedingly comprehensive. They apply to war 'real or apprehended.' Were the War Measures Act not already upon our statutes I would in the existing circumstances have considered it advisable and necessary to summon Parliament immediately for the purpose of the enactment of a similar statute."

In a meeting on August 28, Cabinet agreed that the defence of the Dominion would be stressed. "We are agreed it is important not to let impressions get abroad that there is to be any expeditionary force which indeed it is not the intention of the government to have, if possible, to resist," he later wrote. On the very last day of the month (after a brief panic when telegraphic communications with England had been cut for seven hours and fear that Great Britain was imposing censorship), Mackenzie King still held to his belief that Danzig was not worth fighting for. Although there were still a few "hopeful" messages from Europe, the prime minister went to bed at midnight on August 31 "feeling very concerned."

The premier retail destination in Western Canada, the Eaton's store dominated Portage Avenue in Winnipeg for many years.

The Way Things Were

MAIL-ORDER DAYS

Today, Canadians use the Internet to do a lot of their shopping. Back in the day, they used mail-order catalogues. The T. Eaton Company dominated the market. Other companies distributing catalogues were Simpson's, Dupuis Frères in Montreal, and — for short periods of time earlier in the century — Army & Navy, Morgan's, Woodward's, and the Hudson's Bay Company.

There was another mail-order house called Nerlich & Co., which has been almost forgotten today. Founded in 1858 by Henry Nerlich, a watchmaker who was born in Prussia, Nerlich & Co. occupied a substantial building in 1939 at 146–48 West Front Street in Toronto, with show rooms in Winnipeg and Montreal. In its earlier years, Nerlich's touted "fancy goods, toys, dolls, games, novelties, fancy china, and glassware," but eventually expanded its inventory.

Timothy Eaton put out his first catalogue in 1884. It was thirty-four pages long. Simpson's followed suit ten years later. The catalogues played a major role in Canadian life during the first half of the century. Not only did they offer everything from baby bibs to farm implements, they also gave consumers outside urban centres access to reasonable prices and a wide selection of goods. The thick catalogues had other uses, too. For instance, they made serviceable goalie pads for pickup hockey games. Many of their pages found their way into the privy, too.

Some selections from Eaton's catalogues in the late 1930s included women's "good-fitting and durable" foundations, $1.95 to $2.95, with corselettes at twenty-eight cents and girdles at $1.49; men's overalls at $1.95; boys' all-wool bloomers at $1.95 and knee pants at fifty-nine cents a pair; poultry fencing at $4.29

for ten rods; hot water boilers, nine dollars; chemical toilets, $9.65. The familiar line of Viking outboard motors was on sale for $56.50 (1.6 HP), $98.50 (5 HP), and $169.50 (8.5 HP).

Eaton's closed down its mail-order operation in 1976 (and eventually disappeared entirely from the retail scene), Dupuis Frères gave up its catalogue in 1963, and Simpson's (by then part of Simpson's-Sears) in the 1980s.

Show Time. "The Greatest Adventure Known to Man" was the tagline for *Stanley and Livingstone*, starring Spencer Tracy and Cedric Hardwicke. The movie presented a somewhat fictionalized version of how *New York Herald* reporter Henry Stanley was dispatched in 1869 to find Dr. David Livingstone, a missionary who had vanished in Africa. There is some doubt that Stanley actually uttered the famous phrase, "Dr. Livingstone, I presume."

Sticky Situation. In the culmination of a long running case, a woman and her daughter were convicted in a Calgary court of assault after attempting to tar-and-feather a nurse. The mother told the court that the nurse and her husband had a "lewd and lascivious" relationship.

September

War came to Canada on Sunday, September 10, 1939. It was precisely one week after Great Britain herself had declared a state of hostilities with Germany. Some newspapers put out extra editions and the CBC briefly interrupted its programming of American radio shows to announce that Canada had indeed joined the fray. There was very little shouting, and definitely no bugles blowing. As one Vancouver newspaper reporter wrote, "Canada shouldered arms in silence."

Nevertheless, thousands of volunteers descended on recruiting centres and armouries, swelling the lines that had begun building a few days earlier. Men from the hobo jungles, relief camps, and street corners queued up, along with breadwinners who were giving up precious jobs to fight for their country. There were men dressed virtually in rags, husbands wearing their Sunday best, college kids, farm boys, mothers' only sons. Many of them could have used a good bath. Many more needed a good meal. Some lines early in the month were so long it took two or three days to process everybody.

In Ottawa, the march to war was a measured one. On September 7, the gallery was packed and the benches full as the House of Commons met in special session. Tradition, protocol, and all the formalities were observed at a glacial pace, as if it were just another day on Parliament Hill. The Speech from the Throne, read by the governor general, contained the government's request that it be given the power to defend Canada and to co-operate with Great Britain in an effort to "resist further aggression."

The next day, Prime Minister King, his tired face drawn from the final efforts of shepherding Canada toward war, his hands trembling a little bit, made probably the most important speech of his political career. It was not a riveting address, because King had decided to use the points raised by Opposition Leader R.J. Manion as a basis for his own. His remarks came out as if he was reading a brief before the Supreme Court of Canada. Mackenzie King started out quietly and, as he later wrote, "felicitously." The prime minister of Canada did not thrust himself out of his seat on the government's front bench, chest puffed out, hands grasping his lapels like Sir John A. Macdonald or Sir Wilfrid Laurier would perhaps have done. Instead, he made a speech that seemed to be disjointed.

He promised, once again, that there would be no conscription measures taken at this or any other stage by his government. All the steps up to the present, he said, "were taken in a state of apprehended war," which would change to a state of real war if Parliament approved the government's resolution. "As regards action in other theatres of war and the means and measures that might be taken, certain essential information touching the character of British and allied action and contemplated plans must be available before any intelligent and delicate decision could be made as to Canadian action even in the immediate future," King said. "On this all-important aspect of co-operation in defence, the Canadian government, like the governments of other of the Dominions, is in consultation with the British government. We will continue to consult with the purposes of determining the course of action which may be regarded as most effective."

He said that $82 million had been committed to the rapid expansion of manpower, as well as air training and naval facilities. As for continental defence, the highest priority would be given to the St. Lawrence River and the Gulf of St. Lawrence. "It may be said with assurance that a determined national effort to bring our industry and agriculture to the highest efficiency and to keep them at that high level will be of the utmost importance to the common cause," King added.

Ernest Lapointe, King's Quebec bulwark for many years, delivered a much more powerful speech. He began by saying, "I hate war with all my heart and conscience, but devotion to peace does not mean ignorance or blindness." He then listed some of the many reasons why Canada was so inexorably bound to Britain — consular affairs, the criminal code, trade, shipping, contracts, and agreements — before turning to the accepted definition of neutrality in international law: "Neutrality may be defined as the attitude of impartiality adopted by a third state towards belligerents, such attitude creating rights and duties between the impartial state and the belligerents." He then asked, "Could such an attitude of impartiality be possible in Canada during a war, having regard to the present international situation? Could Canadians in one section of the country compel other Canadians in other sections to remain neutral and to enforce such neutrality even against their own king?" Such a development, he said, would only encourage the enemies of England. He did emphasize strongly, however, that Quebec would never countenance conscription. "I will go further than that," he said. "When I say the whole province of Quebec, I mean that I personally agree with them."

Maxime Raymond, another Quebec Liberal, who had already publicly expressed his opposition to Canada's involvement, said that Canada was not in any way obligated to help Poland. "The agreement of 1867 made no provisions for defending the countries of Europe, and the Canadians of Quebec do not recognize any other military duty than that of defending their country, which is Canada," Raymond said. "Let us not incite them to put an end to that agreement by imposing upon them other obligations."

R.J. Manion pledged the active co-operation of his Conservative Party, and urged that mobilization and co-ordination of industry should be undertaken without delay. War profiteers, he said, should be dealt with harshly. "Our best offensive is the offensive in a far-off land," he said, adding that it would be in national interest to keep men with dependents who are sent overseas "as far as possible from danger."

By this time, J.S. Woodsworth was no longer the leader of the CCF. He had resigned two days earlier, on September 6, when the party's national CCF council turned down his plea that all members vote against any declaration of war. Nevertheless, he rose once more to try to persuade the House that fighting a European war — any war — was folly. In an impassioned speech, full of sorrow at the path he saw his country taking, Woodsworth pleaded for Canada to stand aloof and "not resort to brute force." He talked of watching children planting a rose garden at the Peace Arch on the Canada-American border south of Vancouver, during which they held a "fine ceremony," exchanging national flags and singing songs. "I take my place with the children," he said. "I am going to take my place besides the children ... because it is only as we adopt new policies that this world will be at all a liveable place for our children who follow us."

His voice was a lonely one. "True to the principle he has so consistently advocated, this kindly, courageous man nailed his colours to the mast and sailed off on the lonely route where conscience is the only compass," the *Vancouver Daily Province* later wrote.

In the end, there was no recorded vote on the government's resolution that Canada go to war. Woodsworth was the only Member who stood to signify his "Nay." M.J. Coldwell, who spelled out the CCF party's position in place of Woodsworth, Manion, and everybody else — including the grumblers from Quebec — voted in favour of war. King and his cabinet colleagues must have smiled inwardly when Manion made his lengthy address, because his main point was that Canada came first and must defend herself. This was precisely the scenario they had drawn up in August.

It was the prime minister's inspiration to have King George sign the proclamation sending Canada to war. Normally, the governor general, as representative of the Crown, approved such documents, but King thought that the sovereign's signature would do much to cement the bond that had formed during the Royal Visit. He approached the governor general with the suggestion, and Lord Tweedsmuir "agreed completely and in fact was quite enthusiastic." On Sunday, September 10, King anxiously waited for a signal from England. Then, the code room informed him at 10:55 a.m. that a dispatch had arrived and was being decoded. It read: "No. 307. Following for Prime Minister begins: Your telegrams 301 and 306 and unnumbered of the 9th of September. Have just returned from Royal Lodge, Windsor, where H.M. the King received me and gave his approval to your submission at 1:08 p.m." That meant that Canada had officially been at war since 8:08 a.m. Ottawa time.

King wrote that both he and Skelton — on opposite sides of the neutrality debate for so long — could express a great feeling of relief "that at last uncertainty had been removed." The prime minister also wrote in his diary how important he thought the monarch's signature was: "With the issuance of the Proclamation of the state of war in the name of the king on identical terms with the Proclamation issued on behalf of the U.K. and with all action taken voluntarily on Canada's part, it may now be said that from now on Canada stands as a nation not only among the nations of the British Commonwealth, but as a nation among the nations of the world — a young nation with a bright light in her eyes and the spirit of idealistic youth. A Sir Galahad among other nations."

Most Canadians heard about King George's approval of Parliament's momentous decision shortly after it was made public, although those travellers on the transcontinental trains had to wait. Many of them got on the train in time of peace and got off with the country at war. And, as King wrote in his diary, "There will, I fear, be plenty of war before the end comes."

But how did the Second World War begin, exactly?

Like this:

On August 31 at 5:30 p.m., Berlin time, Adolf Hitler released Directive No. 1 to senior commanders of the German Army "for the conduct of the war." Poland would be attacked on September 1, but the neutrality of Belgium, Holland, Luxembourg, and Switzerland would be respected. "Western forces are not to be attacked until fired upon." The next day, as his troops moved into Poland, Hitler issued a proclamation to the army. It read, "The Polish State has refused the peaceful settlement of relations which I desired, and has appealed to arms.

> Germans in Poland are persecuted with bloody terror and driven from their houses. A series of violations of the frontier, intolerable to a Great Power, prove that Poland is no longer willing to respect the frontier of the Reich. In order to put an end to this lunacy, I have

no other choice than to meet force with force from now on. The German Army will fight the battle for the honour and the vital rights of reborn Germany with hard determination. I expect that every soldier, mindful of the great traditions of eternal German soldiery, will ever remain conscious that he is a representative of the National-Socialist Greater Germany. Long live our people and our Reich.

Then, in a rambling speech to the Reichstag, a speech filled with self-justification and a decidedly one-sided analysis of the European crisis, he warned that those who tried to compare the Germany of the day with the Germany of the past were deceiving themselves. He declared that he was determined to solve both the Danzig and the Corridor questions, and to seek peaceful co-existence with Poland. Fire was exchanged at 5:45 a.m. on the frontier, he said, adding that bombs would be met with bombs and poison gas with poison gas.

"As a National Socialist and as a German soldier, I enter this battle with a stout heart," he said. "My whole life has been nothing but one long struggle for my people, for the restoration and for Germany.... One word I have never learned; that is surrender ... I would therefore like to assure all the world that a November 1918 will never be repeated in German history." His final words were, "I would like to close with the declaration that I once made when I began the struggle for power in the Reich. I then said that if our will is so strong that no hardship and suffering can subdue it, then our will and our German might shall prevail."

The same day, September 1, Prime Minister Chamberlain rose up to address the House of Commons in London. "The time has come when action rather than words is required," he said. "Now that all the relevant documents are being made public we shall stand at the bar of history knowing that the responsibility for this terrible catastrophe lies on the shoulders of one man — the German chancellor, who has not hesitated to plunge the world into misery in order to serve his own senseless ambitions." Chamberlain pointed out that despite the urgent necessity for a reply to Britain's suggestion that Poland and Germany open negotiations, Germany didn't even bother to reply. He also noted Ribbentrop's strange, high-speed recitation of a German communiqué and his refusal to provide a written copy in August.

The British prime minister then read out the ultimatum passed on by telegram to Berlin earlier that day:

> Early this morning the German Chancellor issued a proclamation to the German Army which indicated clearly that he was about to attack Poland. Information which has reached His Majesty's Government in the United Kingdom and the French Government indicates that German troops have crossed the Polish frontier and that attacks upon Polish towns are proceeding. In these circumstances it appears to the Governments of the United Kingdom and France that by their action the German Government have created conditions, namely, an aggressive act of force against Poland threatening the independence of Poland, which call for the implementation by the Governments of the United Kingdom and France of the undertaking to Poland to come to her assistance. I am accordingly to inform your Excellency that unless the German Government are prepared to give His Majesty's Government satisfactory assurances that that the German Government have suspended all aggressive action against Poland and are prepared promptly to withdraw their forces from Polish territory, His Majesty's Government in the United Kingdom will without hesitation fulfil their obligations to Poland.

Chamberlain then drew a comparison between the events of 1939 and 1914, and declared that Great Britain was in a more favourable position now than it was then. "We have no quarrel with the German people, except that they allow themselves to be governed by a Nazi Government," he added. "As long as that Government exists and pursues the methods it has so persistently followed during the last two years, there will be no peace in Europe.... If out of the struggle we again re-establish in the world the rules of good faith and the renunciation of force, why, then even the sacrifices that are entailed upon us will find their fullest justification."

On the morning of September 3, an interpreter nervously translated the contents of a British telegram for Adolf Hitler. After pointing out that Germany had not replied to the earlier note, and had in fact intensified its attacks on Poland rather than withdrawing, the telegram read:

> I have the honour to inform you that, unless not later than 11 a.m. British summer time today, September 3, satisfactory assurances to the above effect have been given by the German Government and have reached His Majesty's Government in London, a state of war will exist between the two countries as of that hour.

According to a witness, Hitler sat motionless for a long spell, gazing into space. Then, after the deadline had passed, Ribbentrop told the British ambassador that Germany refused "to receive or accept, let alone to fulfill" the ultimatum. Shortly afterwards, Lord Halifax handed the German charge d'affaires in London a formal note stating that, "I have the honour to inform you that a state of war exists between the two countries as from 11 a.m. today, September 3."

Chamberlain then made a direct radio broadcast to the German people. He told them that Britain and France were not at war with Germany because their government lied to them and their leader, Hitler, could not be trusted to keep his word: "In this war we are not fighting against you, the German people, for whom we have no bitter feeling, but against a tyrannous and forsworn regime which has betrayed not only its own people but the whole of Western civilization and all that you and we hold dear."

In Ottawa, Prime Minister King was awakened at 6:20 a.m. and told that the Nazis had invaded Poland. The cabinet met at 9:00 a.m. and immediately plunged into preparations for the war they knew was coming. The proclamation of the War Measures Act — which gave the federal government sweeping powers of arrest and detention, censorship, and control over shipping and transportation — was approved. Other orders-in-council were put into motion, including one ordering mobilization. The Wartime Prices and Trade Board was also established to scrutinize rent, sugar, milk, coal, steel, timber, and other goods. During the war, the board operated out of thirteen regional centres and 100 local ones. In 1941, it would impose wage and price controls. King also shuffled his cabinet that first week in September. James Ralston was plucked from the legal profession to become finance minister, replacing Charles Dunning, who was in ill health, and Norman Rogers took over the national defence portfolio from the inadequate Ian Mackenzie.

Parliament would be summoned for a special session on September 7 — six days hence. Why wait so long? King knew that Great Britain would honour its commitment to Poland and that war would be declared before the weekend was out. The Members of Parliament could easily be in Ottawa by Monday, September 4, or Tuesday at the latest. Most of them were already in the capital, anyway. So why wait almost a week to "let Parliament decide?" According to journalist and author Bruce Hutchison, who was as close to the prime minister as any newspaperman, it was a calculated delay in order to get war materiel shipped across the line from the United States. Hutchison says King received a call on his private telephone from President Roosevelt, who asked him whether Canada was at war. Not yet, King replied. Thereupon, Roosevelt turned to his advisers gathered in the White House and said, "You see, I was right!" Being legally neutral, Canada could then receive American war supplies without violating the U.S. Neutrality Act.

In a diary entry for September 5, King wrote that he spoke with Roosevelt and Cordell Hull about the fact Canada was not yet at war. He wrote that, "The messages evidently were intended as a friendly gesture to indicate sympathy and readiness to co-operate insofar as might be possible."

For almost a whole week, Roosevelt rushed across the border what munitions his country could spare, as well as aircraft for training purposes. Providentially, the Canadian cabinet had placed an order in the United States on August 25 for $7 million worth of airplanes.

So, with a united cabinet behind him that first Friday in September, Prime Minister King then read a statement to the journalists gathered outside his office door. "In the event of the United Kingdom becoming engaged in war in the effort to resist aggression, the Government of Canada has unanimously decided, as soon as Parliament meets, to seek its authority for effective co-operation by Canada at the side of Great Britain," it said. "Meanwhile, necessary measures will be taken for the defence of Canada."

A special edition of the *Canada Gazette*, the government's official publication, was issued. It announced the existence of "A state of war with the German Reich."

With winter looming (as it usually does in Canada), military planners realized that the original plan of billeting 60,000 men outdoors in army camps was not a good idea. So commanders of the various units — infantry, artillery, cavalry, special services — were told to find accommodation indoors. Some strange billets were requisitioned. Since the summer fair season was over, exhibition buildings were a popular choice. Many armouries squeezed in as much accommodation as they could. Colleges, a disused hotel in Montreal, a macaroni factory, even private homes took their share of men. Toronto's 53rd Field Battery bedded down its other ranks in the Women's Building at the Canadian National Exhibition Grounds, while the officers established their mess in the ladies' washroom. The billeting solution wasn't perfect, and many soldiers still ended up outdoors, kept warm only by a greatcoat left over from the Great War, if they had one.

Those ancient uniforms were actually still being issued, until commercial tailors began producing more of the modern battledress design than there were recruits. Equipment was another worrisome point. As Major-General A.G.L. McNaughton, the army's chief of staff before the war, noted, "Except as regards rifles and rifle ammunition, partial stocks of which were inherited from the Great War, the country has no reserves of equipment and ammunition. About the only article of which stocks are held is harness. The composition of a modern land force would use very little horsed transport." There was not a single modern anti-aircraft gun in the entire country, only enough ammunition for ninety minutes' fire from obsolete field guns, sixteen tanks, and a few operational military aircraft but no bombs for them.

The flood of volunteers soon ebbed to a trickle after recruiting standards were stiffened. Only accepted were "men perfectly fit, mentally and physically, for all active service conditions of actual warfare in any climate, who are able to march, can see to shoot, and hear well." Those with bad teeth were turned away and told to get them fixed before trying again. The army was not about to pay anyone's dental bills. As the lineups lessened, recruitment posters went up. This one, from the Royal Canadian Artillery and the Royal Canadian Horse Artillery, was typical: "Recruits are wanted for duty with the Canadian Active Service Force. Applicants must be between the ages of eighteen and 45, physically fit and either married or single. Rates of pay for gunners are $1.30 per day. Enquire within."

After the first rush of volunteers died away, the Canadian Army turned to advertising for recruits.

By the end of September, 58,387 males and a few nursing sisters were accepted into the Active Service Force. Besides the $1.30 a day, they would get a dependents' allowance of $60 per month plus $12 for each child. Toss in three square meals a day, a warm greatcoat, a roof over their head, and the army looked pretty good for someone who perhaps was sleeping under a railway bridge a few weeks earlier, or standing in a soup kitchen queue.

Recruiting for the Royal Canadian Navy was almost non-existent because there were only a few ships to be manned. That would change within a year, when the vital importance of protecting Atlantic convoys became apparent, but at the end of August 1939, the RCN had only thirteen vessels. Included were six destroyers of varying age, some trawlers, and a training schooner. The schooner, HMCS *Venture*, was paid off on September 1 and became an accommodation vessel for naval staff.

The Royal Canadian Air Force had a tiny roster of both modern and elderly aircraft — until the Roosevelt-King blitz provided thirty-five modern planes rushed across the border in the week before the U.S. Neutrality Act kicked in. The RCAF's complement of just over 3,000 officers and men steadily increased and by October the number of active squadrons had doubled.

The prime minister had singled out the St. Lawrence as a defensive priority, but the newly formed Coast Defence Construction Committee

Library and Archives Canada, PA-168133

Soup-kitchen lineups, such as this one in Montreal, became rare after the onset of war.

in Ottawa had much more on its plate. Halifax, Sydney, Victoria, and Vancouver were considered prime targets, so they were put at the top of the list. An enemy cruiser standing offshore and lobbing eight-inch shells toward land could be answered by 9.2-inch coastal batteries, but inshore attacks from submarines, torpedo boats, or disguised armed merchantmen took different types of armament.

Property had to be found to store all this weaponry, not to mention the task of acquiring the guns themselves. Halifax, the major East Coast port and home to the RCN, was extensively fortified, although not completely until 1943. On the West Coast, the approaches to Vancouver and Victoria quickly had six-inch rifles in place, thanks to some interim planning. No attacks on the Dominion were made during the war (except for U-boat raids in the Gulf of St. Lawrence), but the political dictum that Canadians were fighting to defend Canada was well served.

* * *

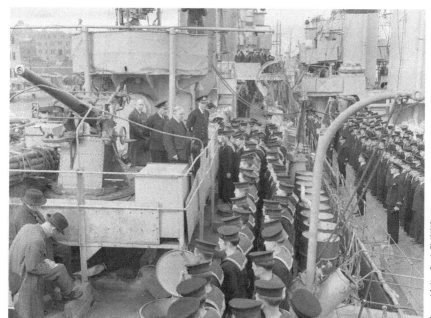

Crews of HMCS Restigouche *and HMCS* Assiniboine *listen to a speech by Prime Minister King.*

Just hours after His Majesty's Government had declared war, the British liner *Athenia* was torpedoed and sunk in the North Atlantic by a lurking German U-boat. Bound for Montreal from Glasgow and Liverpool, she was crammed with 1,418 passengers and crew, 217 of whom died, including eight Americans of the more than 300 who were aboard. The Nazis promptly denied one of their submarines had been responsible, and kept on denying it throughout the war. They remembered the sinking of the *Lusitania*, however, which had helped provoke the United States into entering the Great War; so, even when the naval high command confirmed that the U-30, commanded by an officer named Lemp, had sunk the *Athenia* believing it was an armed merchant ship, total secrecy was imposed.

Prime Minister Chamberlain expressed his outrage to the House of Commons. "No denial or invention on the part of Germany will convince the public of German innocence of this crime, which profoundly shocked and horrified the world." The Royal Navy, he added, had stepped up its protection of merchant shipping (a number of freighters had been sunk in addition to the *Athenia*) and a convoy system was being drawn up. The attack on a passenger ship only hours into the war had British and Canadian naval strategists nervous, because they fully expected troopships to be heading across the Atlantic within months. They didn't know, of course, that Hitler had immediately ordered that a signal be transmitted to all his submarines. It said, "By order of the Fuehrer, on no account are operations to be carried out against passenger steamers, even when under escort." The truth about the sinking of the *Athenia* did not surface until German naval papers were examined after the war.

Within days, Danzig fell to the Nazis. On September 19, Hitler made a speech in the former free city's Guild Hall before a crowd of cheering Germans, who sang "Deutschland Uber Alles" and the "Horst Wessel" song. In a voice dripping with scorn for the British and French, Hitler decried the propaganda against himself and the German peoples, as well as the Versailles Treaty, which separated a German populace from their homeland. He said that the battle against Poland was being fought well within the rules of war. This included German tanks mowing down gallant Polish cavalry charges and a non-stop bombardment of Warsaw that left the capital city in ruins before it capitulated on September 27.

Back in Canada, James Ralston's first budget was presented in absentia. Because he had yet to win a seat in the House of Commons, the budget speech was read on September 12 by James L. Ilsley, the revenue minister. It called for Canadians to help pay for the prosecution of the war. Taxes and duties were raised almost across the board. A war surtax of 20 percent was placed on income, while corporations had their income tax raised to 18 percent from 15. The surtax meant a single person earning $4,000 a year would pay approximately $200, and a couple with two children making the same amount, would pay approximately $56.

Excise duty on domestic and imported spirits was raised by $3 a gallon, and those on wine were doubled. Smokers could expect to pay an extra $1 per 1,000 cigarettes, and five cents more per pound on tobacco. Businesses faced an excess profits tax of up to 60 percent. According to Ilsley, revenues for the fiscal year ending March 31, 1940, were estimated at $495 million, with expenses expected to be $651 million, leaving a deficit of $156 million. Every citizen had to be ready to share the cost of the war, with the government adhering to the principle of equality of sacrifice based on ability to pay.

Then, on September 24, Premier Duplessis dissolved the Quebec Legislative Assembly and called an election for October 25. His rationale, he said the next day, was to give Quebecers the chance to reject the federal government's attempt to encroach upon provincial freedoms by proclaiming the War Measures Act. "The government of the province, conscious of the rights of the people, has decided to submit to the electorate questions of the greatest importance, some of which, the most vital ones, have arisen recently," he said. His Union nationale government, he added, considered provincial autonomy to be guaranteed by Confederation, which gave Quebec traditional rights and indispensable prerogatives.

"Let each and every one who has forgotten, or who may forget, understand that Quebec intends to preserve its full autonomy and to demand from the federal authority, such as it may be, the integral respect of rights which are guaranteed her by the constitution," he said. "For several years a campaign has been conducted and direct and indirect attempts have been made with a view to lessening considerably, and even to abolishing provincial autonomy for the purpose of forming but one government directed by Ottawa."

Duplessis's electoral antics distressed Prime Minister King deeply. He considered the provincial vote a serious crisis and a threat to Canadian unity. If Duplessis won a solid victory on the issue of provincial versus federal rights, then Mitchell Hepburn's Ontario could try the same tactic. "It is as diabolical act," King wrote in his diary. "Duplessis has betrayed his instincts just a little too soon. He is a thorough gangster which I think like Hitler has perhaps attempted something a little beyond his capacity."

The cabinet's Quebec ministers, led by Justice Minister Ernest Lapointe, and including Pierre Cardin (public works) and Charles Powers (postmaster-general), reacted strongly. Despite the prime minister's misgivings, they vowed to intervene in the campaign — something federal politicians usually avoided. They would campaign in support of the provincial Liberals, who held only a few seats in the Assembly, using the threat to resign their cabinet posts if Duplessis won a comfortable margin as their main weapon. "Under such circumstances we cannot remain indifferent and our duty is to take up the unprovoked challenge," Lapointe said. A precipitate election designed to criticize the federal government, "at a time when national unity is a sacred trust," meant Duplessis was openly trying to sow discord. Lapointe said that he and his cabinet colleagues would ask Quebec to "give us a testimony of confidence."

The Way Things Were

THE MOONLIGHT

On the Labour Day weekend — the last one of the peace, as many thoughtful Canadians realized — those who could afford it headed for the ocean beaches, the lakefronts, the riverbank fishing spots, the mountain vistas, or picnic grounds.

In Manitoba, many Winnipeggers took the train to Winnipeg Beach, thirty-five miles to the north on the western shore of Lake Winnipeg. Winnipeg Beach was a resort town, with a boardwalk, amusement park, concessions, and long stretches of sandy beach. A huge dance hall catered to the Friday and Saturday night crowds. There were several daily departures from the Canadian Pacific Railway station for the beach communities, but the most popular train was the "Moonlight." With several wooden coaches in tow, a Pacific-type locomotive would leave Winnipeg at 7:00 p.m. in the summer months and reach Winnipeg Beach in less than an hour. The return trip would depart at midnight, leaving plenty of time for a swim, some fun and games, or a little bit of dancing. Fare was fifty cents return. Canadian National Railways provided similar excursion trips from its station to Grand Beach, on the eastern shore. Although not offering as many attractions as its rival across the lake, Grand Beach also boasted a capacious dance pavilion.

Sawdust Trail. One of the inescapable by-products of British Columbia's forest industry is sawdust. Looking like unattractive, overgrown beehives, sawdust burners are a dead giveaway that a sawmill is close by, even in the twenty-first century. All that waste matter spewed out by whirring saws had to be disposed of somehow, and the sawdust burner, usually perched on a riverbank, was one solution. In 1939, another was commercially marketing the sawdust for business and home ranges. Vancouver newspapers even devoted separate listings in their classified advertising pages. A typical ad might read, "Double-screened No. 1 fresh fir sawdust. Kitchen range burner sawdust our specialty." Another selling point was "freshwater" sawdust. Prices ranged upward from $3.50 per unit (bagged).

Crop Numbers. An analysis of the western grain crop came to the conclusion that value of the 1939 harvest would be approximately $467.332 million. This figure was $217 million higher than the 1938 value, an increase of almost 50 percent. Western Canada's wheat crop was estimated at 451.672 million bushels, the largest since the bumper harvest of 1928. The value of the 1939 crop included freight and handling charges for delivery at Fort William, Ontario.

October

The outcome of the Quebec provincial election was not as significant as Parliament's decision to go to war, but it was in the same ballpark. On October 26, Maurice Duplessis, after one of the grossest miscalculations of his career, woke up as a man without a job. His Union nationale government had been thrashed in the election the day before by Adelard Godbout's Liberals as the voters soundly rejected his rallying cry that Ottawa's War Measures Act usurped the province's autonomy.

If Duplessis had won, havoc would have overtaken federal-provincial relations, severely impairing the Dominion's war effort. However, Prime Minister King's Quebec cabinet ministers' proactive stance was a major factor in amassing support for Godbout. Justice Minister Lapointe led the charge. In a broadcast from Ottawa early in the month, he publicly announced that he and two of his cabinet colleagues would resign if Duplessis won the election. The threat of dismembering the federal cabinet over a provincial election was, as author Conrad Black wrote in his book *Duplessis*, "perhaps Canadian history's greatest turning of the political tables."

"It would be cowardice for me to remain in the cabinet in spite of Quebec's wishes," Lapointe said on the radio. "I repeat it. If the people of the province prove by their votes that they believe the atrocious calumnies and the shameful lies which are the basis of Mr. Duplessis's campaign, how could we expect to continue to represent them and to speak for them at the council of the nation?" He charged that Duplessis called the election "in the hope of using the anxiety and the distress of the country to cover the abyss in which he has cast the province."

Pierre Cardin emphasized his opposition to conscription. "You mothers of families need not become alarmed or spill the necessary tears," he said. "Your children can stay home as long as they like. Those who do not want to go, won't." Later, when hecklers tried to sing the national anthem to forestall police action at a rowdy Montreal rally, Cardin criticized them for singing for Canada when "they are trying to destroy it." He said that such people singing the anthem was blasphemy. "A house divided against itself must perish."

Throughout the month-long campaign leading up to the October 25 election, Duplessis seldom strayed far from his theme of provincial autonomy, while accusing the federal government of having a secret agenda to centralize all power. At one point he claimed that the War Measures Act could be used to control all economy and finance in the country. "Ottawa takes all the money for destruction," he charged. "Ottawa centralizes credit and we get nothing for works of peace and construction." In a speech on the eve of the election, he said that it was time Ottawa and England should know "that we are not strangers on

Quebec Premier Maurice Duplessis lost a provincial election over his opposition to the War Measures Act.

Library and Archives Canada, C-031052

Quebec soil, that we have rights. We intend to be masters of our own destiny."

Unfortunately for Duplessis, his destiny was failure. When all the votes were counted, Godbout's Liberals had won seventy seats to fifteen for the Union nationale. It was a complete reversal from the 1936 election, when the UN had won seventy-six seats. The prime minister was pleased. After taking a shot at Mitchell Hepburn, who had advised Duplessis to be as antagonistic as possible toward the federal government, King became almost lyrical. "It is a great victory for the allied cause," he wrote in his diary. "Had results gone the other way, Germany would have felt dismemberment of the British Empire had already commenced. As it is, Canada has given another marvellous lead to other parts of the Empire, to the U.S. and indeed to all the democracies. It shows that the liberty guaranteed by British institutions stood the British Isles in their hour of greatest need."

King praised the three Quebec ministers who went to bat for Canada. "The issue was squarely faced and ably presented by all three," he wrote. "It has given them all, especially Lapointe, an exceedingly high place in public regard. I venture to say that Lapointe's place today is as far in esteem as Sir Wilfrid in the best of his days. He will have a place second to none in Canadian history, and well merited as a patriot."

The *Toronto Daily Star* was no less effusive. "It was a victory not so much for a political party as for Canadian unity in the face of the enemy," an editorial read. "It will hearten the Allied peoples everywhere. Germany will hear of it with disappointment. It is the best news for Britain that has gone out of Canada for many a day."

Maurice Duplessis did not speak to the press for several days, and when he did he complained of having had a heavy cold during the campaign. "I was threatened with bronchial pneumonia," he said. "I might have lost my voice but that would not have done because it would have suited too many people. Now that there is a real opposition, we will have — as we intend — to make ourselves heard."

He was more forthright in his home town of Trois Rivières. "You know me, my neighbours," he told a group of constituents. "Whatever I may be, I am not a coward. I have stood tall in the past and I will remain on my feet now. I predict that those who have successfully juggled the popular vote tonight will not have long to wait before tasting the disapprobation of the public of Quebec."

The Union nationale had only been in existence for a few years. A loose coalition of minor conservative parties, it had been cobbled together by Duplessis in time to win an unexpected, sweeping victory in the 1936 election. Born in 1890, Duplessis was a big "C" Conservative who was still only in his forties when his political manoeuvring spun him into the leadership of the Union nationale which, as its name implies, stood for an independent Quebec. Mercurial and high-stepping, Duplessis presided over a regime that was unlike any seen before in staid, Church-dominated Quebec. As a *Saturday Night* writer pointed out, "The first Duplessis term was something of a period piece, a grotesquely parochial, wildly hilarious 'government,' largely carried on in hotel suites amid numerous scandals, martinis, attendant ladies, and bright red herrings." After his defeat, Duplessis went through a period of humiliation and despondency, but told his sister, "I will be back." He did indeed return, regaining the premiership in the 1944 election.

In early October, Major-General A.G.L. McNaughton was chosen to command the 1st Canadian Infantry Division. Because of some questions about McNaughton's leadership style, the prime minister interviewed him personally before approving the appointment. King was impressed. "The interview was as deeply moving as any I have witnessed in my public life," he wrote in his diary.

> One felt the enormous responsibilities that were being placed on the individual. There could be no question about McNaughton being the best equipped man for the purpose. I have done my best with my colleagues to remove prejudice which I know there has been against him on account of his tendency to organize matters to the maximum with respect to possible conflict. However, the facts have vindicated the wisdom of his actions in this regard.

Arthur George Latta McNaughton was born in 1887 in the North West Territories settlement of Moosomin. "A tall, dark, slight, human dynamo of a man," as one Toronto reporter wrote, McNaughton was a career soldier, rising to become chief of staff of the army before accepting the presidency of the National Research Council in the mid-1930s. One of Canada's premier soldiers in the twentieth century, McNaughton had his flaws: He over-worked. His judgment was not the equal of his intellect in some circumstances. He was a nationalist, and made enemies among military bureaucrats and politicians. He found it difficult to compromise. McNaughton looked the part of a military leader, though. McNaughton "was the answer to a propagandist's prayer — iron-grey head, miraculously photogenic," one journalist wrote.*

The 1st Canadian Division that McNaughton led overseas during the Second World War was composed of nine regiments organized into three brigades, with seven regiments as supporting units. The order of battle was: 1st Canadian Infantry Brigade — The Royal Canadian Regiment, The Hastings and Prince Edward Regiment, 48th Highlanders of Canada; 2nd Canadian Infantry Brigade — Princess Patricia's Canadian Light Infantry, The Seaforth Highlanders of Canada, The Loyal Edmonton Regiment; 3rd Canadian Infantry Brigade — The Royal 22nd Regiment (The Van Doos), The Carleton and York Regiment, The West Nova Scotia Regiment. Divisional units were the 4th Reconnaissance Regiment (4th Princess Louise Dragoon Guards); The Saskatoon Light Infantry (Machine Gun); 1st Regiment, RCHA; 22nd Field Artillery Regiment, RCA; 3rd Field Artillery Regiment, RCA; 1st Anti-Tank Regiment, RCA; 2nd Light Anti-Aircraft Regiment, RCA.

For most of the regiments, there were lots of volunteers, but a shortage of experienced military personnel and, of course, few modern weapons and little equipment. One positive note was the new battle-dress uniforms, which were slowly becoming available as the month wore on. They were quite attractive, with the blouse-type jackets giving the men a neater appearance when on parade. Intensive training was a priority, both in Canada and after the division arrived in England. The

---

* Andrew McNaughton Biography, *http://www.answers.com/topic/andrew-mcnaughton*.

glamorous Princess Pats, at least, would be ready when the time came to fight, according to their commanding officer. "My boys are going to be absolutely equal to the Princess Pats of the last war," Lieutenant-Colonel W.G. Colquhourn told reporters early in the month. "They are young men, perhaps not as experienced as the boys who joined the regiment in 1914, but they are showing more stamina and enthusiasm." His sentiments were echoed by Sergeant-Major C. Leighton, a veteran of several campaigns, including service with the Grenadier Guards. "Soldiers in Canada are better than those in any unit I've been in," he said.

Halifax was well on its way to becoming a very busy, crowded city. During the war, it would be immortalized in press dispatches as "An East Coast Port," but behind that bland description lay the hub of Canada's connection with the European war. The port's biggest moment of 1939 had been the glittering ceremony attending the departure of King George VI and Queen Elizabeth in June. Four months later, the atmosphere was deadly serious as the convoy system took over. Royal Navy ships, including such no-nonsense heavy cruisers as HMS *York*, crowded the harbour as they augmented the tiny RCN roster. Commander Philip Oland, RCN, was the man who made the convoy system happen. An ex-officer turned businessman, he was brought back from retirement to head the Naval Control Service. His job was to organize the convoy system. Oland was so good at his job that he was decorated with the Order of the British Empire in 1941. (He also dropped dead of a heart attack at the age of forty-four that year, brought on by stress.)

The first convoy, HX-4, left on October 18, with ten merchant ships and three escorts. The freighters carried maize, paper, pig iron, lubricating oil, iron ore, and general cargo. They were escorted by the *York* and two Canadian destroyers, HMCS *Fraser* and HMCS *St. Laurent*. The convoy reached Liverpool, England, on October 22 without incident. It was the first of three conveys that crossed the Atlantic that month, gradually increasing in size to the fifty-six merchantmen in HX-6. Oland's first convoy, HX-1, had sailed on September 16. By the end of 1939, twenty-five convoys had crossed, with 523 of 527 vessels making it safely. Some convoys were designated HXF (*f* for fast), but these were intermittent since there weren't that many fast freighters around capable of fifteen knots or more. By the end of the European war, there would be 364 HX convoys sailing from Halifax, that is until September 17, 1942, when the terminus was switched to New York City.

On October 10, Canada had been at war for one month. Big news came from Prime Minister King, who announced a major training scheme for Empire airmen in Canada. Britain, Australia, and New Zealand, as well as Canada, would supply personnel to train pilots and other aircrew at Dominion facilities. Missions from the other countries involved were on their way to Ottawa, he said, to "discuss with Canadian authorities all future steps that are to be taken for the rapid execution of the plan, including provision of the necessary aircraft, instructors, ground personnel, and airdromes." Large-scale restructuring in Canada's aviation sectors was expected. This would include such training accommodations as flying schools, plus additional aircraft and technical equipment.

"The young men so trained will join either the air force squadrons maintained by their respective governments in the theatre of operations or the United Kingdom Royal Air Force units," King said. The governments of the countries involved had signed an agreement in principle, King added. "It has thus been assured that the many facilities and the great natural advantages for the training of the pilots and the other personnel and the production of aircraft which these countries offer in areas comparatively free from any risk of enemy interference will be utilized to the fullest and to the best advantage."

A report from Regina said, "Saskatchewan business lies under a golden flood of fall buying." Businesses and financial institutions were receiving a record number of cash and orders, the report said, with $15 million worth of business reported in one week. In Ottawa, it was estimated that the revenue from the war surtax on incomes added an extra $5 million to the Dominion's coffers in September, while a dispatch from the Ontario Motor Truck Owners' Association said there would be no shortage of trucks or tractors because of the war.

A shipment of clothes from the Imperial Order of Daughters of the Empire for evacuated children in England was gratefully received. A message from Lady Tweedsmuir praised the IODE for their "work during the present world crisis." The shipment included blankets as well as clothing. The Canadian Electronics Institute was offering home study courses for wireless operators. "The Dominion government is urgently calling for trained wireless operators to fill important, good-paying positions in the various communications systems on land, sea and air," a newspaper advertisement said. "If you are a British subject 17 years of age, mail this coupon now!"

Meanwhile, Charles Lindbergh stuck his nose into Canada's business. In a national radio broadcast from Washington on October 13, he criticized the Dominion for getting mixed up in a war. Although Lindbergh's theme was the maintenance of American neutrality and the threats posed by foreign involvement, he insisted that other countries in North America should be neutral, too. This included Canada.

Calling the Western Hemisphere "our domain," with Canada as one of the "outposts," he said the United States should not be forced to defend a sister country that has become enmeshed in European affairs. "Can we rightfully permit any country in America to give bases to foreign warships or to send its army abroad to fight while it remains secure in our protection at home?" Lindbergh asked.

> We desire the utmost friendship with the people of Canada. If their country is ever attacked, our navy will be defending their seas, our soldiers will fight on their battlefields, our fliers will die in their skies. But have they the right to draw this hemisphere into a European war simply because they prefer the Crown of England to American independence? Sooner or later we must demand the freedom of this continent and its surrounding islands from the dictates of European power. American history clearly indicates this need.

Lindbergh's broadcast came as the United States Congress was debating America's Neutrality Act. He was opposed to any changes. "Let us not dissipate our strength or help Europe to dissipate hers in these wars of politics and possession," he said. "For the benefit of Western civilization we should continue our embargo on offensive armaments."

The European war that so distressed the famous American aviator wasn't actually much of a war during October. After Germany smashed Poland into submission, a period of calm settled in. French and German troops massed on the Maginot and Siegfried Lines and sparred with little result. Great Britain saturated the Third Reich with airborne propaganda leaflets. Hitler offered an insincere peace plan that the Allies rejected. The German Navy did score a shocking victory by sinking the Royal Navy battleship *Royal Oak* in Scapa Flow by a U-boat, but there was no Jutland-like confrontation on the high seas. The Allies, believing the German economy was weak, expected that a war of attrition, brought about by strong defensive positions and a naval blockade, would result in a bloodless victory. All they had to do was wait. That this strategy was badly flawed would soon become apparent, but the period beginning in October 1939 came to be known as "The Phoney War." The term was derived from a caustic remark by William Borah, an isolationist United States Senator from Idaho, "There's something phoney about this war." Winston Churchill called it "The Twilight War," while the German term was "Sitzkrieg," sit-down war.

Adolf Hitler wasn't sitting down, though. In a *Top Secret* memorandum to his generals on October 9, Der Führer asked them to draw up plans to attack the West through Belgium, Holland, and Luxembourg. "The German war aim is the final military dispatch of the West, that is, the destruction of the power and ability of the Western Powers ever again to be able to oppose the state consolidation and further development of the German people in Europe," Hitler wrote. He wanted an autumn offensive, believing that time definitely was not on Germany's side. However, stalling by his generals (a few of whom wanted to get rid of this madman) and other distractions delayed the German breakout until the spring of 1940.

The Germany-Russia embrace from September was countered in mid-October by a three-way agreement between Great Britain, France, and Turkey. The treaty, signed in Ankara, bound each country to come to the assistance of the others in certain circumstances. Britain and France would come to Turkey's aid if she were attacked by a European power, and in the event of "an act of aggression by a European power leading to war in the Mediterranean area in which Britain and France might be involved," Turkey would become involved. However, the Turks were not obligated to fight against Russia.

The deal brought general approval from the British press. "Give your admiration to a people that staunchly keep their word and honour their signature," commented the *Daily Telegraph*. "Rejoice that we have the good-will of men who are stout foes and true friends. This is a triumph for Britain." Hitler considered Turkey to be "ruled by small minds, unsteady, weak men,"* but the agreement with the Allies cut the Nazis off from the Black Sea region's wheat and oil. Turkey's Mediterranean coast also gave it strategic dominance over the Italy-occupied Dodecanese Islands, and it was an important addition to Britain's control of the Suez Canal.

The treaty was signed after the abrupt, unexpected end of negotiations between Turkey and Russia. These events led the excitable Fleet Street press to exclaim that it was all Ribbentrop's fault. "Von Ribbentrop's diplomacy has become as erratic as it has always been mischievous, and his latest effort has only resulted in what is regarded even in Italian political circles as a diplomatic victory for the Allies," the *Times of London* said.

The German foreign minister had known about the failure of the talks in advance. His ambassador in Moscow had wired Berlin about Molotov's assurance that "in all likelihood a mutual assistance pact with Turkey would not be concluded." Shortly afterward, Ribbentrop prepared a speech on German-Soviet relations, which he submitted to Joseph Stalin in advance. The speech discussed a British "lie" claiming that Moscow turned down a Berlin request for military assistance: "I believe that this brief account is sufficient to sink once and for all the whole raft of lies of the British Ministry of Lies and the other blundering

---

* William L. Shirer, *The Rise and Faull of the Third Reich* (New York: Ballantine Books, 1960), 667

propaganda centres of our enemies, about the present German-Russian negotiations and the future pattern of relations between the two greatest countries of Europe."

Stalin's gaze was focused on the Baltic Sea rather than the southern rim of the Black Sea. As Germany gobbled up Poland (Russia eventually got its slice), the Soviet dictator demanded the Baltic states of Estonia, Latvia, and Lithuania cede military bases to the Red Army. They complied. Stalin made the same demand of Finland but was met with a resounding, "No." The flexing of Communist muscles alarmed the Finns, who had long been within the German orbit, even when fascism took over (as opposed to Helsinki's democratic institutions). So Finland asked Germany what its position was regarding the Baltic states and Berlin smugly replied that it would stand by its "well-known non-aggression pacts." Berlin also said it expected Russia's demands on Finland "would not be far-reaching." As part of their deal, Germany had actually assigned Finland to Moscow's sphere of influence, reversing a German policy that had been in place since the Great War.

On October 30, after its negotiators had returned from a three-day conference in Moscow, the Finnish Parliament endorsed the government's decision to flatly refuse permission for any Soviet military bases to be established on Finnish soil. It also started making defensive preparations. Finland would need them, because a winter war was in the offing north of the sixtieth parallel — the prospect of which made temperature-savvy Canadians shiver.

As October drew to a close, Mackenzie King took to the airwaves to address the nation. Although it came shortly after the Quebec election, the two were not connected. King's CBC radio broadcast had been planned for some time and was the first of two he would make about Canada's position in the present conflict.

Entitled "Canada's War Aims," the address first traced the development of Nazi power in Europe. It was the prospect of unchecked German expansion, King said, that had prompted Great Britain and France to act. "It is Nazism and Hitlerism, as thus understood, which has produced the present war, and which threatens — if not overthrown — to extend its tyrannical power to all nations," he said. It was this threat of triumphant Nazism engulfing the whole globe that brought Canada into the war at Britain's side:

> If today I am prepared to continue to lead a government charged with the awful responsibility of prosecuting a war, it is because, contrary to every hope and wish I have ever entertained, I have been compelled to believe that only by the destruction of Nazism and the resistance of ruthless aggression, can the nations of the British Commonwealth hope to continue to enjoy the liberties which are theirs under the British Crown and the world itself be spared a descent into a new and terrible age of barbarism.

The Nazi doctrine of force, the prime minister added, is the "very antithesis" of that which is taught by the Christian gospel. "That is why the present war is for the Allied forces a crusade," he said. "The time has come when to save our Christian civilization, we must be prepared to lay down our lives for its preservation…. It is the preservation not alone of national and of personal freedom, but of freedom also of the mind and of the soul."

The Way Things Were

DRIVE TIME

Motorists in pre-war Canada had a different vocabulary than their counterparts in the twenty-first century. Instead of sport utility vehicles, hybrids, and on-board navigation systems, early motorists talked of saloons, coupes, rumble seats, and running boards.

A saloon was a heavy, four-door sedan, sometimes with a twelve-cylinder engine. The Packard was a good example. In gangster movies of the 1930s, the bad guys — more often than not — could be seen careering around in Packards. A coupe was at the opposite end of the scale. It was a tiny little thing. Chevrolet and Ford were the leading suppliers of coupes. The roadster, with its rumble seat, was a variation of the coupe and was especially favoured by college kids. Suburban families often went for station wagons, which had lots of room for kids and had a substantial percentage of wood in the framework. As for the sedan, which was your basic, four-door, family-type car, there were several brands to choose from besides the top two: Hudson, Nash, Plymouth, Buick, to name a few.

How much did a car cost in 1939? A Nash sedan — "The car everybody likes" — was on the market for $1,298. For this, you got four-doors, ninety-nine horsepower, and a 117-inch wheelbase. A Ford V-8 coupe was available for $856. Hudson sedans were going for a special sale price of $899. The fine print, however, said this bargain was for delivery in Tilburg, Ontario, only. On the used-car market, a 1937 Ford Fordor was going for $575, a 1937 Chevrolet coach for $$595, a 1936 Packard sedan for $625, and a 1936 Buick sedan for $685. Those a little short of cash could pick up a 1931 Durant for $125 or a 1929 Chevrolet sedan for $60.

Fill 'Er Up. Gasoline prices in the United States in 1939 were as low as ten cents a gallon in some places, but approached the thirty-cent level in Canada. Oil companies catering to the Canadian driving public in the 1930s included Shell, Imperial, Esso, British-American, White Rose, and Texaco. In Toronto, the Joy Oil Company built sixteen unique, chateau-style filling stations, and sold gasoline for a few cents cheaper than the national chains.

Classical Act. Lily Pons, the word-famous premier soprano at the Metropolitan Opera in New York City for thirty years, sang before an audience of 6,000 at the Forum (a hockey arena) in Vancouver.

November

In the second instalment of his two-piece appreciation of the war, Prime Minister King assured his listeners that the final victory would be shaped on Canadian soil. This victory, he said in the coast-to-coast broadcast, would be more important to Canadian unity than anything else. To achieve this, he said, required cool judgment and balanced strategy. "We are not concerned to make it spectacular but we are vitally concerned to make it effective," he declared. "It must be a balanced and concerted national effort." He stressed that all segments of society must co-operate, from provincial and municipal authorities to business, labour, primary producers, and voluntary organizations.

"The government is determined that the difficulties experienced in the last war, in securing munitions and supplies rapidly, and in adequate volume, shall not arise from any failure to provide an adequate organization in Canada, to meet the demands of the present war," he said. "We therefore, as I have already indicated, obtained authority from Parliament to set up a separate department of munitions and supply, whenever it may be felt by the government that the progress of the war demands a more elaborate organization." Working from the foundation prepared by the government, he said, Canada could now concentrate on effective action:

> In its determination to sustain and further Canada's war effort, the government has found it necessary to be active on the political, as well as on the military and economic fronts. It is doubtful if Canada could have

made, within the first two months of war, a more helpful contribution to the cause of the Allies than that
signified by the decisive political pronouncement of a
week ago. Certainly nothing which has happened in
our country since Confederation has contributed more
to Canadian unity. Upon the maintenance of national
unity, more than upon all else, will depend the measure
of the success of Canada's effort in the present war.

The day after his speech, King met with various diplomats in his
office. The representative from the Netherlands, "a typical Hollander
in appearance and manner," expressed his support for the British, but
told Mackenzie King that his tiny home country must be careful not
antagonize Hitler. The new consul-general from Poland discussed his
escape from Warsaw. His description of conditions in the Polish capital,
and the plight of its residents, drew the prime minister's deepest sympathy. "The poor fellow's hand was hot and perspiring when I took it
in mine as we said goodbye," King recalled later. A diplomat from Italy,
which had yet to declare war on anybody (except defenceless nations
like Albania and Abyssinia), complained that it was difficult to get anyone in Canada to accept his view of events in Europe. Two Australians,
who were attached to the air-training mission, were King's last visitors.
They intimated that costs were a factor limiting the scope of their participation in the scheme. King replied that he considered the plan to be
a British one, not Canada's, and they should talk to London about it.

The prime minister, however, was rudely jolted by the discovery
that Great Britain viewed the air-training scheme as strictly a Canadian
one — and that Ottawa should foot the bill. In a meeting with one of
the British team's members, Skelton had learned that Lord Riverdale,
the head of the mission, had not been exactly forthright in earlier discussions with Canadian negotiators. Lord Riverdale expected Canada
to pay in the neighbourhood of $370 million, with Great Britain along
for the ride in a strictly advisory capacity. He had the attitude, King
wrote in his diary, that "we were a lot of children doing what we were
doing because the Mother Country was over and above us all."

In discussing the British frame of mind with Lord Tweedsmuir, King was told that Lord Riverdale's background was in industrial disputes, accompanied by an overbearing attitude. This vestige of the Colonial Office mentality led to protracted, and sometimes bitter, negotiations over the next several weeks. In mid-November, Lord Riverdale put on his happy face for the press. Negotiations were going well, he said, and he expected everyone to be home for Christmas. He claimed that there was no difference of opinion existing over the division of costs. "Great Britain will pay her share and there is no question and no difficulty over costs."

War to the last ounce. That was the pledge of five members of the British Empire as the Imperial Conference ended in London on November 17. Canada, Australia, New Zealand, South Africa, and India had committed the full strength of their war effort to help Great Britain defeat Nazi Germany.

"Canada has chosen to throw her full effort into the present struggle on the side of the Western democracies by the practically unanimous decision of the Canadian Parliament, which met almost immediately following the outbreak of war," T.A. Crerar, the Canadian representative, said in a statement. "No constraint from any source whatever was placed upon us. Our action was entirely voluntary, and our effort in support of the Allied cause will be exerted to the maximum of the power of the Canadian people."

During his stay in London, Crerar said, he was impressed by the "magnificent effort" of the English people, but realized that they needed help to carry the war to a successful conclusion. "To both France and Britain there is a determined will to victory, which assures one that it must in the end triumph," he said. Similar sentiments by the other Empire countries moved Anthony Eden, the secretary for the Dominions, to observe that the discussions were "many, many times worthwhile." He also praised the air-training plan being negotiated in Ottawa. "The scheme is unique," he said. "It is probably the greatest example of Empire co-ordination to be created and carried out in a part of the Empire other than Britain."

* * *

R.J. Manion, leader of Canada's loyal Opposition, wasn't feeling all that co-operative as November got under way. Ending the honeymoon that existed when Parliament met in special sessions, Manion said in Ottawa that the Liberal government was doing a lousy job. It must take responsibility, he said in a prepared statement, "for the very regrettable lack of military preparations which has been apparent to all observers since the declaration of war." For two years, Manion's Conservative Party had repeatedly warned everyone about the country's military unpreparedness, but the government had done nothing.

Much of the problem, Manion charged, was the "pernicious" system of patronage in the awarding of war contracts, and it must be eliminated if Canada was to enjoy a unified war effort. Although the prime minister had agreed with him during the special session that patronage wasn't acceptable, the practice was still around in many, if not all, parts of Canada. He said Canada needed a great national effort to co-ordinate its resources without resorting to favouritism and politics. The Conservative leader refused to give specifics, but his charges eventually brought a response from King. Several days later, the prime minister decreed that "no patronage of any kind" would be allowed in the awarding of contracts or in granting promotions.

The rush to get Canada on a war footing had resulted in a flood of appointments by the civil service commission, which maintained that "no political or other influence" was involved in filling federal government posts. "The trouble is, whenever a Liberal is appointed or gets any contract, the 'patronage' cry goes up," a government spokesman said. "Government suppliers, on the other hand, complain that it is like going through the proverbial needle's eye for a Liberal to get a contract or a position."

A study undertaken after the Manion charges showed that firms with no political affiliation were as likely to get approval as those with party connections. It said the number of Liberal and Conservative supporters involved was roughly equal.

* * *

President Franklin Delano Roosevelt, smiling and ebullient in his Oval Office at the White House, used two pens to sign a new United States Neutrality Act into law on November 4. It had been a long fight for the president in his campaign to keep Great Britain from being overwhelmed by Nazi Germany, against bitter opposition from isolationists in the United States Congress. What Roosevelt signed was an act allowing shipments of war materiel and other goods to belligerent countries in a repeal of the provisions of the previous act. This immediately benefited Britain, France, and Canada, along with other members of the Empire. The ink from those two pens was scarcely dry when long lines of trucks, stuffed with loads to be shipped across the Atlantic, began clogging the New York City waterfront.

There were some strict provisions in the new legislation. All deals were "cash and carry," with no credit and no loans. No belligerent vessels could be used to transport goods. American ships were banned from war zones designated by the president. Armed merchantmen were also banned. One provision was aimed directly at Canada. It said, in part, that "transportation by American vessels on or over lakes, rivers, and inland waters bordering on the United States, or ... transportation by aircraft on or over lands bordering on the United States" would be allowed. According to a newspaper report, however, one quirky link in the neutrality fence was a thirteen-year-old law forbidding "armed expeditions" flying across the United States border into a belligerent country. Apparently, the Harvard trainers that were being built at a California aircraft plant for Britain qualified, so they had to be flown to a Canadian border point and pulled or pushed across the line on the ground before taking to the air again. Berlin's response to this creative solution: "It's a shabby trick."

With a flood of foreign orders expected to reach $500 million in the immediate future, a government priority committee was established to make sure America's own defence requirements weren't overwhelmed. When the previous Neutrality Act's embargo went into effect on September 3, more than $75 million in orders were frozen. These included

$319,631 from Canada, $5,078,700 from Australia, $14,877,000 from Britain, $58,416,113 from France, and $49 from Germany.

The Munich beer hall explosion of November 8 was one of those bizarre events that helped liven up the early months of the Phoney War. According to Nazi propaganda, their beloved Führer, Adolf Hitler, narrowly escaped being assassinated while attending a reunion with some old Party comrades. An official Nazi paper blamed the bomb blast, which killed seven people and injured dozens more, on the British Secret Intelligence Service. Two British agents were then kidnapped in Holland, dragged across the border to Germany, and found guilty of the assassination attempt. They spent the rest of the war in a concentration camp for a dirty deed that they almost certainly had nothing to do with.

Almost from the beginning, questions were raised about the incident. Why did Hitler, who usually lingered for hours with his Old Guard, reminiscing about the 1923 *putsch* in that very beer hall (a failed attempt by the Nazis against the Weimar Republic), leave so hurriedly after only a short speech? And why did other important Nazi leaders leave along with him, so they were safely outside when the bomb went off behind the speaker's platform?

"It smells like another Reichstag fire," American journalist William L. Shirer wrote in his diary. (The Reichstag fire in 1933 was blamed on the Communists, but many observers felt it was set by the Nazis themselves to discredit a rival political party.) If the object of the exercise was to inflame public opinion against the perfidious British and enhance Hitler's stature, it apparently succeeded — no matter who blew up the beer hall.

"For two minutes today, one of Toronto's busiest and noisiest intersections was one of its most peaceful and reverent. For two minutes, the clang of streetcars, the squealing of brakes and the chattering of pedestrians ceased as thousands jammed about the city hall cenotaph, heads bowed, to pay tribute to the dead of the war of 1914–18." So wrote a *Toronto Daily Star* reporter about the Armistice Day service as a record crowd assembled in the city's core.

All across the Dominion, from Vancouver to Halifax, which was frantically preparing Canada's lifeline to Britain, a hush fell at the eleventh hour of the eleventh day of November as Canadians, two months into another European conflict, remembered those who fell in an earlier one.

On Parliament Hill in Ottawa, it was a cold and bright Saturday, with a bitter wind blowing, as Prime Minister King took the salute on the steps of the Peace Tower. "I found it difficult to conceal my feelings as the fine young men went by, many of whom are facing certain death," he wrote later. "I shall never forget the sight of the columns moving past."

The quiet Sunday night following the Armistice Day observances was rudely interrupted shortly before midnight on the West Coast. An earthquake under Puget Sound, twelve miles northwest of the Washington State capital of Olympia, struck at 11:47 p.m., shaking a wide portion of the Pacific Northwest. Residents in Seattle and Vancouver tumbled into the streets in their nightclothes. Masonry and plaster cracked. Some houses in Vancouver were rocked on their foundations. Pictures swung crazily on the walls. Furniture shifted and items slid off the shelves. Nervous callers swamped the telephone exchanges. Fire broke out at a lumber mill in Tacoma, Washington, and swaying hydro poles cut electrical power. There was no major damage, however, and no deaths or injuries were reported. The seismograph at the University of Washington in Seattle recorded vibrations for twenty-five minutes. The Richter Scale was not in wide use at the time, so no accurate record of the intensity is available. A geology professor at the university said he reckoned the quake was "a three."

The British Columbia Electric Railway Company's abbreviated interurban schedule that Sunday night was only briefly hampered by the tremor. On Monday morning, all its lines in the Lower Mainland were operating normally. Streetcars were a familiar sight in Canadian communities, from tiny Nelson, British Columba, to the big city landscapes of Toronto, Montreal, and Vancouver, but less common were the heavy, more powerful interurban coaches. British Columbia Electric had the most extensive interurban network of any province, stretching over 120 miles on the urban Lower Mainland and the Fraser Valley. A separate twenty-four-mile route operated on Vancouver Island out of Victoria. On the mainland, there were five routes, with the longest a sixty-four-mile rocking and rolling jaunt from Vancouver to Chilliwack at the head of the valley. The second longest was the connection with Steveston on Lulu Island, at the mouth of the Fraser River. Steveston was almost twenty-six miles from the BCER's terminus on Hastings Street in Vancouver.

There were also systems in southern Ontario, and a small segment of Quebec. Pilgrims visiting the shrine of Sainte-Anne-de-Beaupre could catch a Quebec Railway, Light & Power Company coach in Quebec City for the twenty-two-mile journey along the north shore of the St. Lawrence River. There was also a connection to Montmorency Falls on the slopes of the Laurentians. Travellers intent on visiting the Eastern Townships could take a Montreal and Southern Counties coach across the Victoria Bridge from the interurban terminal on McGill Street in Montreal. If they wanted, they could ride all the way to Granby, forty-seven miles away. The Hull Electric Company offered a service to nearby Aylmer. In Ontario, such entities as the Niagara, St. Catharines & Toronto Railway Company and the London & Port Stanley Railway Company whisked the paying customers to such destinations as Thorold, Niagara Falls, St. Thomas, Port Colborne, and Port Dalhousie.

On the East Coast, the voters did a little shaking of their own that November. In the New Brunswick general election, the Liberal government's overwhelming majority was cut down to a shaky, ten-seat cushion. Premier Alison Dysart's party hung on to power with twenty-nine seats to nineteen for the Conservatives, nothing compared with the 43–5 margin it had four years earlier. Dysart, a lawyer by trade, once had to relinquish his leadership post because of widespread grumbling in the ranks, but won it back just in time to lead the Liberals to the 1935 sweep. The party's campaign that year urged voters to "Give Dysart the chance to provide work and wages instead of dole and despair." Dysart was a hands-off premier, giving his ministers the widest possible latitude. This led to a certain amount of friction in the cabinet and the internal rifts were still there when Dysart called the 1939 election. This time, the Liberals' corny slogan, "Dysart Stays — Still Better Days," didn't work nearly as well. Running a lazy, overconfident campaign, the Liberals underestimated F.C. Squires, the Conservative leader. His fiery performances on the hustings won over many voters.

After all the ballots were counted, Dysart called the outcome "a vote of confidence in the government," adding that the reduced majority "will not hamper the government from going forward with its progressive policies." Squires said the election showed "conclusively that the people at least appreciated our efforts, even if we did not catch their full support. Let us make another start from such a strong vantage point and it will not be long before ultimate victory will be ours."

The bitter underground struggle against Nazi occupation in Czechoslovakia broke into the open mid-month when press dispatches reported that student protestors had been executed by the Gestapo. According to confidential reports by Czech police, thirty bodies of the elite Nazi guards had been pulled from the river in Prague during the previous few weeks. In the week following the bombing in Munich against Adolf Hitler, 6,000 Czechs were arrested and 600 sent to concentration camps. Other reports said German artillery shelled Prague in an attempt to subdue the dissidents. Police also warned that any strikes protesting the students' executions "would be suppressed sternly."

A commercial traveller returning from Prague told a London newspaper that the students barricaded themselves in university buildings and showered the secret police and storm troopers with desks, busts of Hitler, and other missiles. "It took the steel-helmeted Nazis two hours to take the building," the informant said.

Students fought from floor to floor before they were overpowered and their flag torn down. Elsewhere, armoured cars had to break up angry crowds, who had dragged down a Nazi motorcyclist and killed him. Senior Nazi officers were dispatched to Prague to take charge of "restoring order in the protectorate," according to reliable reports. The Germans claimed the Czech protests had been "completely" curbed and that the executions of twelve students and others should discourage further demonstrations. The uprising was not reported in the Czech press. A Nazi spokesman didn't release the number of Czechs arrested, but said "astronomical figures such as 50,000 are nonsense."

By land, by sea and by air, the Soviet Union attacked the Republic of Finland on the last day of November. Red Air Force warplanes roared out of a cloudy sky setting the capital city, Helsinki, ablaze. While warships bombarded the Karelian Isthmus connecting Finland to Russia along the Baltic Sea, twenty-one divisions and 450,000 men of the Red Army attacked at several points on the long northern border between the two countries. The invasion came suddenly, without a formality of a declaration of war. The Finnish Parliament, undaunted, proclaimed that a state of war existed, "with a view to maintaining the country's defence and the constitution."

Sweden, which bordered Finland on the west, dusted off plans for mobilization. Great Britain and France tried to figure out a way to send help, although they had no obligation to do so. President Roosevelt, in a statement read at a press conference in the White House, declared that the invasion came as "a profound shock to the government and the people of the United States.... All peace-loving peoples in those nations that are still hoping for the continuance of relations throughout the world on the basis of law and order will unanimously condemn this new resort to military force as the arbiter of international differences."

Hitler was not pleased with the Russian initiative. He had been chafing for some time about ceding control of the Baltic to the Soviets as part of their agreement, so this Red Army muscle flexing was a major irritant. In fact, the Moscow-Berlin marriage had already begun to grate, only months after they had vowed undying affection for each other.

As part of the non-aggression pact, the two partners agreed to increase trade. Germany needed oil and food from Russia, but the Communists were hard, shrewd bargainers. Hitler had planned to double-cross Stalin as far back as August, so this Russian obduracy was viewed at the highest level as temporary. In 1940, Hermann Goering, chief of the Luftwaffe, revealed that Germany reneged on its obligations when he told the command staff's financial section that "the Fuehrer desired punctual delivery to the Russians only until the spring of 1941." He added later, "We would have no further interest in completely satisfying the Russian demands." Until then, the marriage bed would become increasingly lumpy.

The Russian military behemoth would soon encounter problems. Filled with admiration at the Nazi blitzkrieg that conquered Poland in eighteen days, Red Army headquarters had planned a similar offensive on Finland. However, while Central Europe is extensively served by a network of paved roads and highways, there were virtually none in Finland. Even gravel and dirt roads were rare in a landscape of dense forests and marshes. The Red Army also had a command problem: Stalin had purged the officer corps earlier in the decade and sent more than 35,000 officers of all ranks into limbo. Their replacements were exceedingly loyal to Stalin, but much less competent as soldiers and commanders. All this contributed to dragging the war out through a cruel northern winter.

Two significant Canadians passed away in November: Dr. Norman Bethune, humanist, Communist, and medical innovator, died of septicemia on November 12. James Naismith, who invented basketball, died of a cerebral hemorrhage on November 28.

Henry Norman Bethune was born in Gravenhurst, Ontario, on March 3, 1890. A physician, he worked extensively with the poor in Montreal. Bethune was inspired by a visit to the Soviet Union in 1933 and became a Communist. He was a top thoracic surgeon in Canada, and went overseas in 1936 during the Spanish Civil War under the auspices of the Committee to Aid Spanish Democracy (a Communist front organization). On the battlefield, he pioneered the use of mobile medical units and developed the first practical method for transporting blood. Bethune switched battlefields in 1938, performing surgery in China for

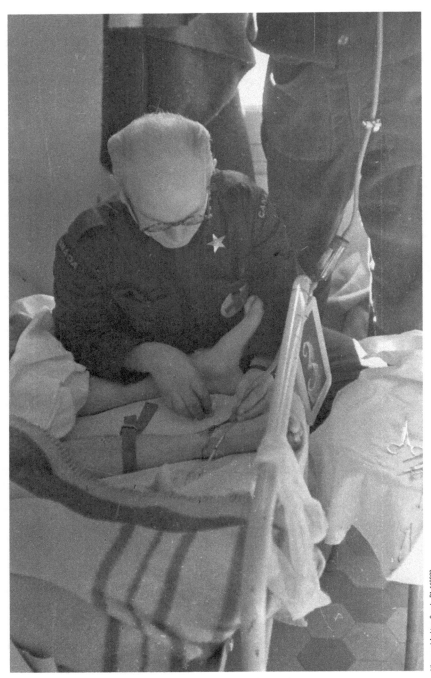

Dr. Norman Bethune operates on a wounded patient during the Spanish Civil War.

the Eighth Route Army during the Second Sino-Japanese War. When he accidently cut himself with a scalpel during an operation, he succumbed to septicemia.

Bethune's achievements were largely unknown in his homeland, but he was a hero in the Republic of China. A book by Mao Zedong titled *In Memory of Norman Bethune* brought him world-wide attention. According to one biographer, Bethune was a cranky, egotistical alcoholic and a womanizer. He married the same woman twice (and was divorced from her twice). He was also convinced that the rich — "a small class of men" — instigated wars so they could become richer still. "Threaten a reduction on the profit of their money, and the beast in them awakens with a snarl," he said in 1939. "They become as ruthless as savages, brutish as madmen, remorseless as executioners."

James Naismith's life and career, on the other hand, was more placid. He was born November 6, 1861, in Almonte, Canada West. His academic studies covered philosophy, theology, and medicine, with a degree from a YMCA training school in physical education thrown in for good measure. On December 15, 1891, in Springfield, Massachusetts, he devised a game to alleviate the boredom of students stuck inside a gymnasium during the winter months. Nailing two empty peach baskets to the wall at either end of the gym, he then selected two teams of nine players each. The following January, Naismith published the rules for basketball. Eventually, he moved to the University of Kansas, where he was the school's first basketball coach. Naismith became a naturalized American citizen in 1925 and died in Lawrence, Kansas.

The Way Things Were

NOT SO FAST FOOD

Convenience eating was not a widespread lifestyle choice for Canadians at the tail-end of the Great Depression. There were no McDonald's, Tim Hortons, Pizza Hut, or KFC. No (*gasp*) Starbucks, either. Drugstores had soda fountains (giving rise to the pejorative job description, "soda jerk"), with marble counters and little round stools. Apart from beverages, they didn't offer much of a menu. Plenty of small eating joints were available, along with sidewalk vendors and roadside stands. The big deal in many cities, however, was the fish and chip shop. Deep-fired fish chunks and french fries, sprinkled with salt and vinegar — now that was a Saturday night treat!

There was a cola war going on. Pepsi-Cola, a distant second in the soft-drink market, introduced a radio jingle in 1939 that took dead aim at rival Coca-Cola. Here's how it went: "Pepsi-Cola hits the spot, twelve full ounces, that's a lot. Twice as much for your nickel, too, Pepsi-Cola is the drink for you." The bottle contained twelve ounces of cola, compared with Coke's six ounces. The Coke folks stuck with their traditional product, a fancy, fluted, heavy bottle, with much more glass than contents. The company's marketing strategy, apparently, was to flood the urban and rural landscapes with thousands of red metal signs bearing the Coca-Cola logo. It worked. Kik Cola was a fringe player in Canada, which also offered a large bottle and was inexpensive.

Margaret Atwood. She was born in Ottawa on November 18 to Carl Atwood, an entomologist, and Margaret Killam Atwood, a former dietician and naturalist. She began writing at the age of sixteen and won the Governor General's Award for fiction (*The Handmaid's Tale*) in 1986.

Show Time. A war movie hit Canadian screens in November. Alexander Korda's *The Lion Has Wings* told of "The Royal Air Force's Death-dealing Answer to Planes Over Britain."

On The Hour. On November 5, CBC Radio began broadcasting the Dominion Observatory's official time signal, the long dash.

December

The regiments assigned to the 1st Canadian Infantry Division began assembling across the Dominion in December. This was not an expeditionary force, mind you, because Prime Minister King had said back in August before any declaration of war that Canada was not contemplating one. Nonetheless, final adjustments were being made at the armouries and army camps; Canadian Pacific and Canadian National were juggling their rolling stock in anticipation of a flood of khaki-clad passengers; ocean liners were being requisitioned and escorts assigned. The 1st Canadian Division was indeed going overseas. Sometime in the future, it would almost certainly be called upon to fight. That prospect made it an expeditionary force.

That a Dominion would declare war in support of Great Britain and the Empire, then keep its armed forces at home was classic Mackenzie King avoidance of real life. He knew an expeditionary force would be required, even though the declaration of war passed by Parliament never spelled out the nature or extent of Canada's commitment. His cabinet knew it and the country knew it, but let us not say it out loud.

By the end of the first week, the vanguard of the expeditionary force was being mustered aboard the waiting troopships. It was led by the Royal 22nd Regiment, the French-speaking Van Doos from Valcartier, Quebec, in an emphatic demonstration of Canadian unity. Troop convoy TC-1 sailed on December 10, with 7,450 men in five large ocean liners. The ships were the *Empress of Britain*, *Empress of Australia*, *Aquitania*, *Duchess of Bedford*, and *Monarch of Bermuda*. Aboard these posh vessels, along with the Van Doos and other infantry and artillery regiments, were General McNaughton and his staff. Both officers and enlisted men received first class service, table linen, gourmet meals, and soft bunks, because the liners had not yet been refitted to carry more men and fewer frills. The escorts were first class, too. Along with RCN and RN destroyers, TC-1 was kept under the big guns of the battle cruiser HMS *Repulse*, the battleship HMS *Resolute*, and the aircraft carrier HMS *Furious*. By year's end, almost 16,000 men would be ferried from all across Canada to Britain, after being brought to Halifax by twenty-five special passenger trains.

The censors tried to keep a lid on the troop movements, with mixed results. The Princess Patricias left Winnipeg without a murmur from the local press, as did any detachments departing Toronto. (A Toronto alderman's suggestion that a big farewell be staged at the Cenotaph had been quietly shelved.) In Moncton, a column of artillerymen marched toward the railway station with no fanfare, because the newspaper and radio were forbidden to tell anybody. By the time the troops reached the station, however, word had leaked out and scores of well-wishers were on hand to say goodbye.

Library and Archives Canada, PA-137186

Soldiers of the 1st Canadian Division boarding the liner that would take them to Great Britain.

In Vancouver, the city's beloved Seaforth Highlanders marched from their armoury on the south shore of False Creek all the way through downtown to Burrard Inlet on December 15. They were heading for the CPR station, but the three daily newspapers couldn't mention that fact. So the two larger papers did the next best thing. They printed detailed stories of the "parade." The *Vancouver Daily Province* also printed an eight-page supplement on the Seaforths ("unique in newspaper history") that week, so that anyone not clued in on the departure date knew that something was going on. The *Vancouver Sun* made do with running pictures of each serviceman. All this "hush-hush" drew the Front Page ire of the *News-Herald*, which ridiculed censorship laws that attempted to keep the movement of 900 soldiers secret. "These men might have been marching to a prison camp instead of beginning the most glorious adventure that their enthusiasm could conceive, and their young hearts imagine," The *News-Herald* wrote in an editorial, calling the secrecy childish and the censorship board "amateurs."

Perhaps they were.

On December 19, New York columnist and broadcasting icon Walter Winchell ("Good evening Mr. and Mrs. America and all the ships at sea") knew twenty minutes after the Canadian troops had sailed. Winchell wrote in his *Daily Mirror* column:

> Now that all concerned have arrived safely on the other side, it may be told.... The general staff and a boatload of Canadian troops sailed with the greatest secrecy from Montreal to Great Britain.... The troop-ships were convoyed by several of Britain's greatest battleships.... The censorship was greater than ever.... Twenty minutes after the sailing, a German radio announcer (speaking in English from Berlin) was heard to nonchalantly say, 'About twenty minutes ago the general staff and many Canadian soldiers sailed under convoy from Canada.' Naturally, there are spies in Canada who have powerful shortwave sending

> apparatus.... And the Berlin flash was obviously to
> terrify all concerned.... The maddening thing, we hear,
> is that Berlin added 'all the details.'

The troops actually sailed from Halifax, not Montreal, so neither Winchell nor the Germans were perfect. However, in Halifax the same day, four men and a woman were charged with attempting to communicate military information to persons in the United States.

On the morning of December 17, the stately components of TC-1 had slipped past the rocky islet of Ailsa Craig and anchored to a noisy welcome in the River Clyde. "As famous ocean liners — huge camouflaged shapes black against the sky — came slowly to anchor with guardian airplanes circling overhead and a flotilla of destroyers around them on the misty sea, the cheering could be heard from thousands of throats," wrote a newspaper correspondent.

As the young soldiers in the expeditionary force moved from Scotland into England, the welcome was equally warm. They were described in a Press Association dispatch as "Bronco Bills who have

Marching smartly, the vanguard of the 1st Canadian Division arrives in the United Kingdom.

Library and Archives Canada, PA-034185

crossed the wide prairies, lumbermen from the backwoods of Canada, fishermen from the Newfoundland banks and men from the lonely little post of Aklavik on the Arctic Ocean." As any Canadian knows, there was a bit of hyperbole in there, but the leading contingent of the 1st Canadian Division weren't exactly meek clerks or shop assistants. They erupted into lusty cheers and yells themselves when they arrived in the Old Country.

The seventeenth day of December was significant in other ways. Not only was it Prime Minister William Lyon Mackenzie King's sixty-fifth birthday, but half an hour after midnight, he and Lord Riverdale, representing the United Kingdom, signed the agreement launching the British Commonwealth Air Training Plan. The plan would generate 40,000 jobs at sixty-seven facilities across Canada, Prime Minister King said in a statement. "Many thousands" of pilots, air observers, and gunners would be trained every year. In addition, he said, the light aircraft needed for elementary training would be built in Canada. "In every page of it, I have safeguarded Canada's position as a nation," King wrote later about the agreement, "thereby making securer than ever the foundation of the British Commonwealth itself."

When the scheme was suspended in 1945, it had trained 131,553 airmen for the Royal Air Force, the Royal Canadian Air Force, the Royal Australian Air Force, and the Royal New Zealand Air Force. More than 5,000 Poles, Czechs, Norwegians, Belgians, Dutch, and Free French would also be trained for the RAF.

Great Britain and Canada concluded another deal in December. The British government agreed to buy all the bacon and ham that Canada could produce for the duration of the war. An estimated 500,000 pounds a week, most of it from hogs in Western Canada, were expected to be delivered to the United Kingdom. Producers had never attempted to reach this figure before, but Canadian negotiators assured the British that it could be attained. Britain's normal source for bacon was Denmark, but conditions on the Continent were so volatile that a service disruption was expected. By an order-in-council, the Canadian cabinet established the Bacon Marketing Board to facilitate shipments of bacon and ham, and to control the spread between what the producer received and the price of the finished product. It was expected that the price for the first shipments would be nine cents a pound.

One of the more famous battles in modern naval history has a Canadian connection. The Battle of the River Plate was fought in the South Atlantic in mid-December, ending with a decisive victory for the Royal Navy. The combatants were the *Admiral Graf Spee*, a German pocket battleship, and three British cruisers. The *Graf Spee* was a *Deutschland*-class heavy cruiser of a unique design. Along with the *Deutschland* and *Admiral Scheer*, she displaced only 10,000 tons, but carried eleven-inch guns. (The *Deutschland*'s name was later changed to *Lutzow* by Hitler because he didn't want a warship bearing Germany's name to be lost at sea.) Because of their distinct profile, with a lofty forward superstructure, they were labelled pocket battleships, although the Kriegsmarine simply called them "*Panzershieffe*" (armoured ships).

The German ships carried only light armour plating so that they could achieve speeds of twenty-eight knots. This lack of protection would cost the *Graf Spee* dearly when she met the British ships, HMS *Ajax*, HMS *Achilles*, and HMS *Exeter*, off the River Plate estuary on the coast of South America. The *Exeter* was a *York*-class heavy cruiser, with a displacement of 8,390 tons and eight-inch guns. The *Ajax* and *Achilles* were *Leander*-class light cruisers of 7,200 tons and six-inch guns. (On the Admiralty books as an RN ship, the *Achilles* was attached to New Zealand and would become part of that Dominion's navy.) Although badly outgunned, the British cruisers managed to get close enough to the *Graf Spee* to inflict significant damage. There has been some debate about how badly the German ship was hurt, but to Captain Hans Langsdorff, it was enough to force him to break off the action and retire to Montevideo. He sent this telegram to the German high command:

> Inspection of direct hits reveals that galleys except for the Admiral's galley have been badly damaged. Water entering flour store endangers bread supply, while a direct hit on the forecastle makes the ship unseaworthy

for the North Atlantic in the winter ... as the ship cannot be made seaworthy for the breakthrough to the homeland with means on board, decided to go into the River Plate at risk of being shut in there.

Then, the second phase of the Battle of the River Plate began.

Langsdorff knew that, because of the Hague convention rules about belligerents in neutral harbours, he couldn't linger in Uruguayan waters long enough to make meaningful repairs. Meanwhile, a British bluff about an overwhelming battle group closing in on the scene persuaded Langsdorff that the *Graf Spee* would be sailing to her doom if she left immediately. Actually, only the *Ajax* and *Achilles* were waiting offshore, along with HMS *Cumberland*, an elderly eight-inch cruiser. The *Exeter*, badly mauled by the *Graf Spee* in the first phase of battle, had been forced to retire to the Falkland Islands for emergency repairs.

According to a diplomatic source in Montevideo, who talked to a *Toronto Daily Star* reporter by telephone, the British had secret information that two-thirds of her crew had left the German ship, leaving Langsdorff with only two options: internment or scuttling. "With *Graf Spee* in the hands of a skeleton crew, we could see no possibility of a fight," the source said. Langsdorff chose to scuttle the proud vessel. He had her moved to an anchorage further out in the River Plate roadstead, where scuttling charges were detonated. "The first of the many explosions aboard her came as no surprise, although they did come as a bit of a shock," the source said. The *Graf Spee*'s crew were then interned in Buenos Aires, across the river from Montevideo, and Langsdorff committed suicide in a hotel room. His actions infuriated Hitler, who had preferred that the ship go down fighting.

Ajax, Ontario, which is not far from Toronto, was established in 1941 when a munitions factory was constructed on the townsite. The name of the war-born community was chosen to honour HMS *Ajax*. By 1945, 40 million shells had reportedly been produced at the plant and 9,000 people employed.

* * *

"Once again, a great disaster has visited a country, caused this time not by man's inhumanity to man, but by a gigantic force of nature," a *New York Times* reporter said of the earthquake that devastated the Erzincan province of eastern Turkey. "It is not likely that the new upheavals will teach the geologists anything new. They are evidence that nature has not yet finished with the earth."

The first of several shocks struck at GMT 11:57 p.m. on December 27, with the worst measuring 8.2 on the Richter Scale. Preliminary reports said 120,000 people had been killed, but the official death toll was set at 32,962, with 100,000 injured and thousands made homeless. Bit by bit, over disrupted communication lines, the scope of the disaster began to emerge. Scores of thousands of homeless people camped in fields as a raging blizzard swept the stricken area. Whole villages were set ablaze, and the army was called in to help dig out the dead.

Nature also wasn't fooling around on the Russian-Finnish border. When Soviet troops invaded Finland, they were marching into an exceptionally cold winter (the temperature in the Karelian Isthmus sank to -45 Fahrenheit in early January 1940). Many of the Soviets weren't prepared for the conditions, nor was their equipment. Some troops attacked over snow-covered fields wearing khaki-coloured uniforms. To make matters worse — as one dispatch from Europe put it — the soldiers were only puzzled peasants trying to comprehend Stalin's war machine. Many tanks in that war machine were still painted in standard olive drab. There were problems with lubrication for engines and gun barrels. Furthermore, the Red Army lacked proper winter tents and frostbite took its toll.

By the end of December, 400,000 Russian troops were reported dead, wounded, captured, or trapped. Stalin, who had already purged his top commanders, replaced the generals in the field, and sent in more men along with massed artillery. Meanwhile, the Soviets created a puppet regime and the Finns appealed to the League of Nations for aid. The League responded by expelling the Soviets. Its resolution said, in part, "that, by this act, the Union of Soviet Socialist Republics has placed itself outside the League of Nations. It follows that the Union of Soviet Socialist Republics is no longer a Member of the League."

Russia's *Tass* news agency responded with some classic invective. As part of a long statement, it charged that

> The Imperialists, who conceived the intention of trans-
> forming the League of Nations into an instrument of
> their interest, decides to seize upon the first pretext to
> get rid of the USSR as the sole force capable of oppos-
> ing their Imperialist machinations and exposing their
> aggressive policy. Well, all the worst for the League of
> Nations and its undermined prestige.

* * *

On a snowy winter's day, CPR locomotive 2321 prepares to depart Windsor station in Montreal.

Library and Archives Canada. PA-149057

The holiday season in Canada was cheerful enough. The Santa Claus parades had been held, the decorations were up, and an uncounted multitude of children were almost overcome with excitement and suspense. Every major department store had its Santa Claus perched in regal splendour on his throne, waiting to hear what the good little girls and boys wanted for Christmas. (As a wee lad in Winnipeg, I couldn't figure out how Santa could be in two places at once. We would get in line at Santa's display at Eaton's, then walk a few blocks up Portage Avenue to the Hudson's Bay store — and there was Santa again! How did he do that? Mother suggested one of them was an assistant, but I preferred to think of it as magic.)

Troop Convoy TC-2 sailed for the Clyde on December 22. Once again, it was heavily escorted by capital ships and several destroyers. The British battleship HMS *Revenge* was relieved by the French battleship *Dunquerque* and the French light cruiser, *Gloire*. Among the 8,125 passengers were the Princess Patricias and the Seaforth Highlanders.

King George VI's Christmas broadcast resonated more than usual that year. In his message of peace and goodwill, he quoted a short poem:

> *I said to the man who stood at the Gate of the Year*
> *"Give me a light that I may tread safely into the unknown."*
> *And he replied,*
> *"Go out into the darkness, and put your hand into the*
> *Hand of God.*
> *"That shall be better than light, and safer than a known*
> *way."*

Although a Quebec cleric claimed the poem was very similar to one of his, it was actually written in 1915 by a retired economics tutor from London named Miss Minnie L. Haskins.

In Germany, Joseph Goebbels, the Nazi propaganda chief, also invoked a higher power in a New Year's Eve speech. "The goddess of history looked down to earth," he said at one point. "German troops entered Bohemia and Moravia, and with breathless excitement the German people and the whole world saw the Fuehrer take up residence in the castle of Prague." Then, after fulminating about the "London warmongering clique" and its support of Poland, he concluded by quoting an old Prussian general: "Lord, if you cannot help us or choose not to, we ask at least that you do not help our damned enemies."

On New Year's Eve in New York, Guy Lombardo and his Royal Canadians were playing their usual gig at the Roosevelt Hotel (Lombardo was no longer a Canadian then, having taken American citizenship in 1938). Back in Canada, there were the usual celebrations, gay streamers, corks popping, dancing to big-band music, and lips colliding at the stroke of midnight, but there was a subdued air to it all. A certain solemnity. Many husbands, sons, and fathers were not there at the end of 1939, and those left behind wondered whether they would ever come home.

As was his custom, the prime minister spent New Year's Eve in seclusion. He prayed. He read his Bible. He talked to his dog. He feared for the future, writing in his diary that "it will be a miracle if London is saved from being destroyed — Westminster, St. Paul's, Buckingham Palace." And he reflected on the year which was drawing to a close. The Royal Visit, of course, was the biggest success of 1939. Because of the king and queen, Canada's roots were sunk much deeper

King George and Queen Elizabeth bid adieu to another Canadian community in a familiar scene repeated countless times during the Royal Visit.

Library and Archives Canada. PA-203283

into the soil of the British Empire by December than they had been in January. The air-training agreement was another success, and a clear demonstration of Canadian sovereignty. King had faced down the isolationists and the neutralists, and his loyal Quebec cabinet had gutted Maurice Duplessis. Even the Bren gun uproar had subsided (the Inglis company would go on to manufacture 63 percent of the light machine-guns produced during the war).

The prime minister's thoughts were "of the Unseen Power that Has led me on 'o'er moor and fen, o'er crag and torrent' that has enabled me in the strife of public life to play such part as I have and to come out stronger, I believe, in health and mind and spirit than I have been at any time." Mackenzie King may have believed all that, but he was also a different leader. In January, with R.B. Bennett hectoring in the background about the glories of Empire, Canada had been on the doorstep of a year that the old Conservative could barely imagine. King, the peacetime compromiser, the political contortionist, and the master of the quiet "maybe" was now a wartime prime minister. Charismatic was not his middle name; a Winston Churchill he would never become.

Canada was a country at war. It was still a little querulous, still a little schizo, but it was a stronger, more confident Dominion, ready to follow its dumpy little leader across that doorstep into the forties.

The Way Things Were

GREY CUP GAME

"A bruising, battering Winnipeg football machine," as the *Toronto Daily Star* put it, won the 1939 Grey Cup on December 9 with an 8–7 victory over the Ottawa Rough Riders. The Blue Bombers scored a last-minute rouge (single point) on a treacherous, snow-covered gridiron at Lansdowne Park in Ottawa to claim the Canadian football championship. Each team had scored a touchdown (worth five points in those days) earlier, but couldn't manage any other offence except kicks into the end zone. A crowd of 11,738 watched the game in temperatures hovering below the freezing mark.

Winnipeg had reached the championship game by defeating the Calgary Bronks, 33–20, in a two-game, total-points Western Interprovincial Football Union (WIFU) final, while the Rough Riders took a slightly longer route. They eliminated the Toronto Argonauts, 39–6, in the two-game Interprovincial Rugby Football Union final, then defeated the Sarnia Imperials of the Ontario Rugby Football Union, 23–1. (The ORFU was an amateur league that was privileged to challenge for the Grey Cup, and did so until 1954.) The Imperials, Hamilton Alerts, and Toronto Balmy Beach Beachers had won the cup in the past.

The Blue Bombers played out of Osborne Stadium, situated a few blocks south of Winnipeg's downtown core, next to the Amphitheatre, which boasted for several years the only artificial ice surface between Ontario and Vancouver. Looming over the north end zone of the stadium was Shea's Brewery. Other teams in the WIFU were the Edmonton Eskimos and Regina Roughriders. The Ottawa Rough Riders played in Lansdowne Park, so the Grey Cup final was essentially a home game for them. Other teams in the IRFU were Hamilton Tigers and Montreal Royals.

Holiday Treats. Christmas trees in the Guelph, Ontario, area cost anywhere from twenty-five cents up to one dollar. Fresh, large, grade A eggs were a bargain at thirty to thirty-five cents a dozen. Top-quality butter was twenty-nine and thirty cents a pound. Ducks, geese, and chickens were plentiful. Prices ranged from eighteen to twenty-two cents a pound for chickens, to twenty to twenty-five cents for geese and ducks. Apples were sold for twenty to thirty cents a basket and seventy-five cents to $1.50 per bushel.

Before and After

1938

The international crisis over the future of a slice of Czechoslovakia in September was the most pivotal event of 1938 — for Canada and the rest of the world. By making the ill-considered decision to back down, rather than stand firm against Adolf Hitler, the European powers only postponed war instead of averting it.

While Prime Minister King strove to shore up what shaky unity Canada had in this penultimate year of the Great Depression, Hitler sought to establish a unified Germany. His first bold step toward this unity was to send troops into the Rhineland in 1936. The Treaty of Versailles, which ended the Great War, had imposed several onerous penalties on the losers. Germany, for instance, could not have a military presence in the Rhineland, which bordered France. Hitler sent in the German Army anyway, bringing little more than an exasperated flutter from France and Great Britain.

Another treaty provision expressly forbade the joining of Germany and Austria. Nevertheless, Austrians woke up on March 13, 1938, to discover that they were now citizens of the Third Reich, despite the existence of another treaty guaranteeing their independence under the protection of the League of Nations. A *coup d'état* the day before had abruptly ended Chancellor Kurt Schuschmigg's attempt to hold a referendum on Hitler's plans for *Anschluss* (union).

Hitler was reported to have shed tears of joy when he heard Austria officially proclaimed as a province of the German Reich. Power was quickly transferred to Germany, and Nazi troops moved in to enforce

German law. Crossing the border at Linz, where he had spent his schoolboy days, Der Führer declared:

> When years ago I went forth from this town I bore within me precisely the same profession of faith which today fills my heart. Judge the depth of my emotion when after so many years I have been able to bring the profession of faith to its fulfilment. If Providence once called me forth from this town, to be the leader of the Reich, it must in so doing have charged me with a mission, and that mission could only be to restore my dear homeland to the German Reich. I have believed in this mission, I have lived and fought for it, and I believe I have now fulfilled it.*

Vienna, where Hitler had endured a miserable existence for so long, was next. He made his triumphant entry into the storied capital of Austria on March 14. In other European capitals, consternation prevailed. The Western powers, which were committed to uphold Austria's independence, could do little more than protest, which they did. "A protest in the strongest terms has been made in Berlin," a British communiqué said. "Previously the prime minister and foreign secretary made similar representations to Herr von Ribbentrop (Germany's foreign minister)." Paris, which was undergoing a political upheaval of its own at the time, vowed to keep in close contact with London. Across the Atlantic, Washington emphasized a "hands off" policy. Not a shot was fired during the whole episode.

The absorption of Austria was perhaps a "profession of faith" on Hitler's part, but the next step in his long-desired creation of a German empire was an undisguised grab for more territory. He threatened Czechoslovakia with war if it did not immediately cede the Sudetenland to Germany. The Sudetenland, along Czechoslovakia's northwest border, was mostly populated by ethnic Germans, so Hitler's ultimatum was,

---

* William L. Shirer, *The Rise and Faull of the Third Reich* (New York: Ballantine Books, 1960), 347

on the face of it, not unreasonable. The German chancellor had bigger plans, however, dreaming of a single Germany from the Baltic to the Adriatic. The Czechs, who had military treaties with France and the Soviet Union, demurred. Britain's Neville Chamberlain then got into the act. All the British prime minister had to do, as an ally of France, was threaten to intervene on the side of Czechoslovakia. London, however, did not want another war (and Chamberlain didn't realize how weak the Wehrmacht was in 1938), so he decided to negotiate.

Accompanied by a silent prayer from Canada's Prime Minister King, who wrote in his diary September 15 that he "spent the time quietly in contemplation and prayer and sending thoughts to Berchtesgaden," Chamberlain met the Nazi leader at his mountain retreat. Hitler stalled his British visitor and the tension remained high for several days. On September 26, Hitler spoke in Berlin's Sportpalast about the Sudetenland, vowing that "it is the final territorial demand which I shall make of Europe." It was a full-throated lie before a stadium overflowing with rapt worshippers. Four days later, Europe's four major leaders — Hitler, Chamberlain, Benito Mussolini, and France's Edouard Daladier — met in Munich. They talked and negotiated and lied until the German chancellor got what he wanted: the Sudetenland. Although the Munich Agreement is dated on September 30, it was not signed until the early hours of the following day. William Shirer, in his book *The Rise and Fall of The Third Reich*, recorded that Hitler looked pale and worried during the evening, and that Chamberlain yawned constantly.

Chamberlain returned to London and got off the plane waving a piece of paper. Dated September 30, it was the agreement personally signed by himself and Adolf Hitler. It read:

> We, the German Fuehrer and Chancellor, and the British Prime Minister, have had a further meeting today and are agreed in recognizing that the question of Anglo-German relations is of the first importance for two countries and for Europe. We regard the agreement signed last night and the Anglo-German Naval Agreement as symbols of the desire of our two peoples

never to go to war with one another again. We are
resolved that the method of consultation shall be the
method adopted to deal with any other questions that
may concern our two countries, and we are determined
to continue our efforts to remove possible sources of
the difference, and thus to contribute to assure the
peace of Europe.

The front pages of Canada's newspapers exploded with relief and
hope. Typical was a huge, black headline on the front page of the *Toronto
Daily Star*: BRITAIN, GERMANY SIGN PACT NEVER TO GO TO WAR AGAIN.
Positioned underneath was a reproduction of the agreement between
Chamberlain and Hitler. Later, Chamberlain made a short speech from
the steps of 10 Downing Street, home of Britain's prime ministers. "My
good friends, for the second time in our history, a British prime minister
has returned from Germany, bringing peace and honour," he said. "I
believe it is peace for our time. Go home and get a good night's sleep."
From Ottawa, Mackenzie King sent his own message to Adolf Hitler,
describing how "relieved and delighted I was that the all-power agreement has been reached, with all that its signatures mean to mankind."

So, the West clasped the phoney peace to its bosom while Hitler
resumed plotting the expansion of a Greater Germany — one that
didn't include Jews. The Nazis staged violent pogroms on November
9–10 against the country's Jews. During *Kristallnacht*, which is usually
translated as "The Night of the Broken Glass," rioting mobs burned or
destroyed 287 synagogues, vandalized or looted 7,000 businesses, and
killed at least ninety-one Jews. The supposed trigger for this violence was
the assassination of German diplomat Ernst von Rath on November 8,
1938, in Paris. Herschel Grynszpan, distraught over the expulsion of
his family from their Hanover home, marched into Rath's office with a
revolver and a box of bullets, and shot him in the abdomen three times.
Kristallnacht was the first step toward the Holocaust, the systematic,
state-sanctioned extermination of the Jewish people.

The depth of the Jewish tragedy hadn't yet become apparent in
Ottawa (although it really wouldn't matter) when the Liberal cabinet

discussed the problem of Jewish refugees. Prime Minister King pointed out that the conscience of the nation should prevail, not political considerations. The cabinet was unmoved, however, fearing the consequences of any help to the Jews. Such political upheaval was also on the prime minister's mind, despite his lofty sentiments about charity. Already that year, he had confided to his diary that "I fear we would have riots" if the immigration policy was too lenient. He had likened the "intermixture of foreign strains of blood" to the "Oriental problem."

King had a more pleasant duty to perform in the waning months of 1938. It was the signing of the Canada–Great Britain–United States trade agreement (which would be ratified by the House of Commons in early 1939). The prime minister's visit to Washington for the ceremony was also a chance to renew his friendship with President Theodore Roosevelt. After the functionaries had departed, the pair relaxed in the presidential library at the White House and discussed what to wear to their private dinners later that November evening. They decided not

Good friends, Prime Minister King and President Roosevelt pause for a photo opportunity during the American leader's visit to Kingston, Ontario, in 1938.

Library and Archives Canada, PA-052499

to wear dinner jackets, then FDR excused himself to have a nap. The strain of the president's battle with Congress over the New Deal was draining him, King thought, and he did not look well. Although he was only eight years older than Roosevelt, King's fatherly advice to his friend (and to Mrs. Eleanor Roosevelt) was to get plenty of rest.

President Roosevelt made a cross-border jaunt of his own in August 1938. Accepting an honorary degree at a special convocation of Queen's University in Kingston, he noted that "this hemisphere at least shall remain a strong citadel wherein civilization can flourish unimpaired," and promised that the United States would remain a strong ally of Canada. "The Dominion of Canada is part of the sisterhood of the British Empire," he said. "I give to you assurance that the people of the United States will not stand idly by if domination of Canadian soil is threatened by any other empire." It was a pledge he would make more than once over the next several months.

Meanwhile, the American president was also indulging his fascination with British royalty. In an extraordinary personal letter to King George VI, he had invited the monarch and Queen Elizabeth to visit his estate at Hyde Park during their visit to the United States. It was the first correspondence ever between an American president and a British sovereign. The stopover would be an "excellent thing for Anglo-American relations," as well as a chance for the royal visitors to relax among friends, Roosevelt wrote. Prime Minister King thought it was a good idea, too. The visit would be "a healing of the great schism of the Anglo-American race," King wrote in a letter to FDR.

In London, there was considerable discussion about the American portion of the 1939 trip. "I only know three Americans — you, Fred Astaire and J.P. Morgan," Queen Elizabeth told Joseph Kennedy, the United States Ambassador to the Court of St. James's.* Prime Minister King had been pressing to be Canada's representative during the American segment, using his friendship with Roosevelt as a selling point. King George was amenable, feeling that the prime minister would be less threatening to the Americans than Lord Halifax, the United Kingdom's formidable foreign minister.

---

* Will Swift, *The Roosevelts and The Royals* (New York: John Wiley & Sons, 2004), 77

* * *

The Vancouver jobless riot of June 1938 was the last, violent spasm of the Great Depression. One month earlier, the city's normal complement of unemployed single men was swelled by workers released from British Columbia's forest camps. When the provincial government remained firm about holding the line on benefits, 1,500 desperate men occupied the downtown post office, the Hotel Georgia, and the art gallery. They were quickly persuaded to leave the hotel, but hunkered down at the art gallery and the post office.

Because the postal service is a federal responsibility, the Dominion government in Ottawa finally got around to doing something. On June 19, the RCMP attacked the 600 squatters in the post office using tear gas and clubs as their main weapons. The building was emptied in ten minutes of violent confrontation, and the squatters started roaming through downtown streets. "The fleeing jobless, maddened by gas and galvanized by blows from police truncheons, stormed east along Hastings and Cordova streets, smashing windows in business houses as they ran," the *Vancouver Daily Province* reported the next day. Damage was estimated at $30,000. At the art gallery several blocks away, the squatters noted the heavy police presence in the area, not to mention a few stray tendrils of tear gas in the air, and dispersed quietly.

A false peace among those suffering in Europe, euphoria and firm handshakes in Washington, anticipation in London, and hungry men in Vancouver: this was the tale of 1938. But it had nothing on the dramatic year which was to follow.

1940

When 1940 dawned, Mitchell Frederick Hepburn had been premier of Ontario for more than five years. He had been Prime Minister William Lyon Mackenzie King's bitter enemy since 1937. The two Liberal politicians had starkly disparate philosophies and lifestyles, with the cocky, fast-moving, hard-drinking, womanizing Hepburn scorning the prime minister's plodding, Christian sensibilities. This disdain turned into active enmity in 1937, when King refused to help the Ontario premier break up a bitter auto workers' strike by sending in the RCMP.

Hepburn's sniping at King's policies intensified after war was declared in September 1939. Calling Ottawa's war effort inefficient and inadequate, he rammed through a resolution in the Ontario legislature early in the new year that condemned the federal government for making "so little effort to prosecute Canada's duty in the war in the vigorous manner the people of Canada wish to see."

King reacted with uncharacteristic swiftness. He had, in fact, been stewing about the expiration of his government's five-year mandate later in 1940. An election would have to be called sooner or later, and King realized that the conduct of the war so far had not been dramatic or sexy enough to catch the voters' attention. He needed a campaign issue, and Hepburn provided it only days before Parliament was to be recalled for its first session of the year. Calling a federal election in response to some provincial grumbling was unprecedented and a huge

Why are these men smiling? Although they were bitter political opponents, Prime Minister King (left) and Ontario Premier Mitchell Hepburn share a lighter moment in Hepburn's office.

Library and Archives Canada C-087863

risk. King took it, though. By January 20, he had made up his mind to appeal to the country, and alerted his staff to prepare for dissolution of Parliament the very day it convened. Besides, the prime minister was prescient enough to realize that the war news could only get worse "in April or May at the latest." As for Hepburn, his motion was an "almost shocking betrayal of Liberalism and of Liberal principles and of the party of which he is the leader," King wrote in his diary.

On January 25, the prime minister told the startled House of Commons that the Members all had to go back home to fight an election campaign. "There is only one authority higher than Parliament and that is the people, whose decisions we can trust," King said in a statement. "We propose to leave it to the people of Canada to say whom they wish to carry on the government of Canada in this period of war." The election was set for March 26. Opposition Leader R.J. Manion, who had challenged King to call an election on the Liberal record all through 1939, finally got his wish. However, he could not offer the voters a compelling alternative vision, and his Conservatives were swept away once again. The Liberals won 179 of 245 seats, a slight increase from the 1935 total.

The sudden death of Governor General Lord Tweedsmuir in early February cast a pall over the campaign. Lord Tweedsmuir suffered a stroke and fell in his bathroom. On February 11, he succumbed to brain damage caused by striking his head in the fall. Prime Minister King reflected the loss felt by all Canadians when he said in a radio broadcast, "In the passing of His Excellency, the people of Canada have lost one of the greatest and most revered of their Governors General, and a friend who, from the day of his arrival in this country, dedicated his life to their service."

The Canadian election campaign was entering the home stretch when the Winter War between Russia and Finland ended. The Moscow Peace Treaty on March 12 gave the Soviet Union some vital chunks of Finnish territory, including the entire Karelian Isthmus and a large strip of land north of Lake Ladoga. The area was home to much of Finland's industrial output, as well as its second largest city, Viipuri. The territory's 422,000 residents were forced out of their homes. Finland also ceded some northern territory. The 105-day war had a profound impact on the Finns, who waited in vain for international support. In fact, the chaotic attempts of both Great Britain and France to help led to the resignation of French Premier Édouard Daladier in May, over that country's weak response to the Soviet attack.

Moscow's victory came at some cost. A reported 126,875 Russians were killed, with 264,908 wounded, and 5,600 captured. Some 2,268 tanks and armoured cars were lost. The Finns reported 26,662 killed and 39,886 wounded. The Supreme Military Soviet reviewed the short-comings of both men and machines, as well as the role of the political commissar on the front lines. Clothing, equipment, and tactics for win-ter warfare were improved, which would eventually pay dividends after Germany attacked in 1941.

On April 9, Adolf Hitler's Wehrmacht invaded Denmark and Norway. Just as Prime Minister King foresaw back in January, the war between Germany and the Allies was about to get ugly. The strategic importance of Norway to the Third Reich was twofold. Firstly, Germany relied heavily on iron ore from northern Sweden, which was loaded at the Norwegian port of Narvik. This link had to be protected. Secondly, Norway's coastline dominated the upper entrance to the North Sea and German warships stationed in its numerous southernmost fjords could theoretically stare right down the throat of the Royal Navy's northern base in Scapa Flow. The British War Office attempted to deny Narvik to the Germans, but the operation was so botched that the ill-fated expedition led to Neville Chamberlain's resignation as prime minister on May 10. The Princess Patricia's Canadian Light Infantry and the Loyal Edmonton Regiment had been slated to sail to Narvik, but were told to stand down at the last moment.

After flexing the Wehrmacht's muscles against the Scandinavian countries, Hitler then unleashed his *blitzkrieg* against Belgium and the Netherlands. On May 10, German armoured divisions (the Panzers) swept into the Low Countries, executing a classic end-run around France's Maginot Line. They rolled into France, punching a wedge between the British and French forces. As the overmatched British Expeditionary Force began falling back on the Channel port of Dunkirk, the French Army disintegrated. The War Office, realizing that the French needed support if they were to hold the BEF's flank, dispatched the 1st Canadian Brigade to Brest to help out. The Royal Canadian Regiment, the Hastings and Prince Edward Island Regiment, and the 48th Highlanders of Canada were to link up with the French about 200 miles inland and provide some backbone. Ignorance was almost fatal for the Canadians. Unbeknownst to them, France had capitulated while they were heading for their target area, and Paris, which didn't want to suffer the same fate as Warsaw, was awaiting the Wehrmacht with limbs outspread. Informed by excited locals that the French Army had given up and that a powerful Panzer force was bearing down on them, only forty miles away, the brigade reversed course and returned to Brest, where it was safely evacuated.

A 25-pounder gun crew of the 17th Field Regiment, Royal Canadian Artillery, in action in Italy. The author's father fought with the 17th Field in Italy and the Low Countries during the Second World War.

Library and Archives Canada. PA-193901

The 2nd Canadian Infantry Division shipped overseas in 1940. Six of the regiments aboard the fleet of troopships — Royal Regiment of Canada, South Saskatchewan Regiment, Royal Hamilton Light Infantry, Cameron Highlanders of Canada, Essex Scottish Regiment, and Les Fusiliers Mont-Royal — saw action in the ill-considered Dieppe raid of 1941. Another regiment in the Division, the Winnipeg Grenadiers, didn't get to England. Instead, in a meaningless gesture of Empire solidarity, it was sent to Hong Kong to bolster the British garrison there. The Grenadiers arrived in December 1941, only days before the colony was overwhelmed by the Japanese. Those Canadians who survived the assault were to spend almost four ghastly years in Japanese prison camps.

The collapse of France and the narrow escape of the British Expeditionary Force from Dunkirk had the Canadian government entertaining thoughts about the imminent defeat of Great Britain. An invasion of England seemed inevitable, followed by the collapse of the Empire. Already, hundreds of British schoolchildren were being ferried to safe haven in Canada, and Prime Minister King knew that plans had been laid to bring the Royal Family and other members of the British meritocracy here also. But would they be safe? A ravenous Adolf Hitler might very well target Canada next.

It was time, then, for President Roosevelt to put his pledges about being the Dominion's ally into a formal liaison. He and King met in the border town of Ogdensburg, New York, on the weekend of August 17, 1940, to draft a joint defence framework. The Ogdensburg Agreement, as it came to be known, established a permanent joint board of defence between Canada and the United States. Members from both countries "will consider in the broad sense the defence of the north half of the Western Hemisphere," the two leaders said in a joint statement. Speaking to the press a few days later, Prime Minister King refused to divulge any details. "Everything I have to say at present in this regard was said in Saturday's statement," he told reporters. "The board speaks for itself and all that is done under it will speak for it." One of the more visible fruits of the board's labours was the building of the Alaska Highway. Not so well known was the establishment of a string of American radar stations in the Canadian Arctic.

* * *

Life bordering on normalcy went on in Canada throughout 1940, despite regular sharp reminders that there was a war on. On April 21, the women of Quebec were given the right to vote and to stand for office. Quebec was the last province to extend voting rights to women, and Premier Adélard Godbout received much of the credit for pushing through the legislation.

In July, the Jehovah's Witnesses religious sect was declared illegal under the War Measures Act as a subversive organization. A new governor general arrived. He was the Earl of Athlone, uncle of King George VI. Many Canadians also got to see Gracie Fields live. The iconic singer of sentimental wartime ditties was forced to spend much of the war in North America because her husband was an Italian alien. She performed two concerts in August in Winnipeg's Amphitheatre, featuring such favourites as "There Will Always Be an England," "Wish Me Luck as You Wave Me Goodbye," "The Biggest Aspidistra in The World," and "When I Grow Too Old to Dream."

The Rowell-Sirois Commission on Dominion-Provincial Relations tabled its report during the year. Because of the report's emphasis on the centralization of power in Ottawa, it was strongly opposed — especially by the Western provinces — and was shelved. However, such recommendations as a federal unemployment insurance scheme and equalization of payments eventually did pass. In fact, the King government instituted the first unemployment insurance in August 1940. The plan was somewhat narrow in scope, excluding such types of employment as agriculture, forestry, fishing, hospital care, and teaching. Anyone making more than $2,000 a year was ineligible.

As 1940 came to a close, the dizzying events of 1939 seemed far in the past, as indeed was the Great Depression. The Dominion was on a war footing now. There was no more talk of neutrality or isolationism or becoming a republic. Canadian boys were overseas, preparing to fight and to die. There was a future to be endured, a future made possible by the pivotal events of 1939.

Selected Bibliography

Once upon a time, newspapers concentrated on reporting history as it happened. Therefore, a major portion of this book is drawn from news pages of the past. The author has also consulted magazines, journals, official reports, government sources, diaries, websites, and the memories of his own childhood.

Abella, Irving and Troper, Harold. *None Is Too Many*. Toronto: Lester Publishing Ltd., 1983.

Barr, John J. *The Dynasty: The Rise and Fall of Social Credit in Alberta*. Toronto: McClelland & Stewart, 1974.

Berg, A. Scott. *Lindbergh*. New York: C.P. Putnam & Sons, 1998.

Black, Conrad. *Duplessis*. Toronto: McClelland & Stewart, 1977.

Granatstein, J.L. and Morton, Desmond. *A Nation Forged in Fire*. Toronto: Lester & Orpen Dennys, 1989.

Hutchison, Bruce. *The Incredible Canadian*. London: Longmans Green, 1953.

Lindbergh, Charles A. *Autobiography of Values*. New York: Harcourt Brace Jovanovich, 1976.

Mackay, Donald. *The People's Railway: A History of Canadian National*. Vancouver: Douglas & McIntyre, 1992.

MacDonnell, Tom. *Daylight Upon Magic: The Royal Tour of Canada, 1939.* Toronto: Macmillan of Canada, 1989.

Massie, Robert K. *Dreadnought.* New York: Random House, 1991.

Neatby, H. Blair. *William Lyon Mackenzie King*, Vol. 3. Toronto: University of Toronto Press, 1976.

Nicholson, Col. G.W.L. *The Gunners of Canada*, Vol. 2. Toronto: McClelland & Stewart, 1972.

Pigott, Peter. *Royal Transport.* Toronto: Dundurn Press, 2005.

Rayner, William. *Images of History.* Victoria: Orca Book Publishers, 1997.

Reader's Digest. The Canadians at War, 1939–45, Vol. 1. Toronto: Reader's Digest Association (Canada) Ltd., 1969.

Shirer, William L. *The Rise and Fall of The Third Reich.* New York: Ballantine Books, 1960.

Swift, Will. *The Roosevelts and The Royals.* New York: John Wiley & Sons, 2004.

Zuelke, Mark. *The Gallant Cause: Canadians in The Spanish Civil War, 1936–1939.* Vancouver: Whitecap Books, 1996.

Index

Of Related Interest

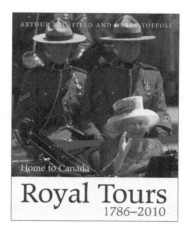

ROYAL TOURS 1786-2010
Home to Canada
by Arthur Bousfield and Garry Toffoli
978-1554888009
$24.99

Royal Tours 1786–2010 is a penetrating look at the tours of eleven royals who were or would be monarchs, viceroys, and commanders-in-chief of Canada. Leaving California in 1983 to tour British Columbia, Queen Elizabeth II said she was "going home to Canada." Since its pioneer days, the Royal Family has made the country home through tours of public service, naval and military duty, and residence. Beautifully illustrated, featuring photos from the June/July 2010 tour of the queen, *Royal Tours 1786–2010* is a captivating look at how these tours shaped Canada and the royals themselves, with an eye for the significant, interesting, and humorous. Included are the young naval captain who became King William IV, the long Canadian residences of Queen Victoria's father and daughter, those who would be kings and governors general, the triumph of the first reigning monarch's tour, and the current queen's six decades of regular presence.

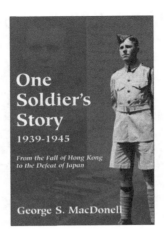